FOOTPRINTS IN CYPRUS

As a Tribute to Sir David Hunt

A friend of Cyprus

This edition was sponsored by:

Bank of Cyprus Group
Centenary Celebrations

Bank of Cyprus
(London) Ltd

The arms of Caterina Cornaro, last Queen of Cyprus

FOOTPRINTS IN CYPRUS

an illustrated history

edited by
SIR DAVID HUNT

CONTRIBUTORS
Prof. Nicolas Coldstream
Sir David Hunt
Prof. Vassos Karageorghis
Dr Demetrios Michaelides
Prof. Edgar Peltenburg
Sir Steven Runciman
Dr Veronica Tatton-Brown

TRIGRAPH – LONDON

in association with
The Bank of Cyprus (London) Limited

**This book is dedicated
to the memory of
A.G. Leventis
a distinguished Cypriot
whose devotion to his native
island was expressed in
many generous benefactions**

First published 1982
Paperback edition 1984
Revised edition 1990
Reprinted 1994, 1999
Trigraph Limited West Africa House
Hanger Lane
London W5 3QR

© Trigraph Limited 1990
© Contributors of the text 1990
© Photograph owners listed on page xiii 1990

British Cataloguing in Publication Data

Footprints in Cyprus
1. Cyprus — History
I. Hunt, *Sir* David
954.45 OOOO DS54.5

ISBN 0 9508026 0 3 hardback

Phototypesetting by Typestream Ltd, Bournemouth
Printed and bound by Ekdotike Hellados SA, Athens, Greece

CONTENTS

LIST OF ILLUSTRATIONS

Colour

194. A woman donor (detail) from the composition of the Virgin and Child; wall painting in the church of Panayia Phorbiotissa, Asinou. 14th century

195. The Nativity; wall painting in the church of St Nicholas of the Roof, Kakopetria; middle of the 14th century

198. Bowl of sgraffiato ware, a type of glazed pottery used in Cyprus in the 14th and 15th centuries AD
(London, British Museum)

200. The Presentation of Christ; wall painting in the church of St Nicholas of the Roof, Kakopetria; second half of the 14th century

201. Wall painting representing the Communion of the Apostles (detail); church of Panayia Podithou, Galata; 1502

204. Kantara Castle, originally built in the 9th century, strengthened and enlarged under the Lusignans

205. Kolossi Castle was the headquarters or Commandery of the Knights of St John. The three-storey keep was built in the 15th century

207. SS George and Theodore (detail); wall painting in the church of St Nicholas of the Roof, Kakopetria; 15th century

208. John II (wrongly named Philip), King of Cyprus (1432-1458); sketch from the *Diary of Georg von Ehingen* (Stuttgart, Württembergische Landesbibliothek)

209. The Royal Manor, Kouklia, stood in a Lusignan sugar plantation

210. Portrait of Caterina Cornaro, Queen of Cyprus (1473-1489), believed to be a copy of a lost original by Titian (Nicosia, Cyprus Museum)

211. Charlotte, Queen of Cyprus (1458-1485) entering her name in the registry of members of the confraternity of S Spirito; wall painting by Guidobaldo Abbatini (Rome, church of S Spirito)

213. The Miraculous Draught of Fishes; wall painting in the church of Panayia Chryseleousa, Emba; late 15th century

214. The Presentation of the Virgin; wall painting by Philip Goul in the church of the Holy Cross of Ayiasmati, Platanistasa; 1494

215. The Virgin Mary, *Orans*, Blachernitissa type; wall painting by Philip Goul, church of the Holy Cross of Ayiasmati, Platanistasa; 1494

216. The Adoration of the Magi (detail); wall painting in the Enkleistra, St Neophytus Monastery, near Paphos; early 16th century

217. The Virgin and Child; wall painting, church of Panayia Podithou, galata; 1502

218. Ayia Napa Monastery; although Greek Orthodox, it contains a Latin chapel

219. Kiti Tower, built in the early 16th century

243. Cypriot iconostasis of carved, painted and gilded pinewood; 1757-1762
(Berlin, Staatliche Museen)

Monochrome

3. Aerial photograph of the Neolithic settlement of Khirokitia; 7th millennium BC

4. Visible remains of a house of the Khirokitia settlement

5 (1). Stone and shell necklace; from Khirokitia; 7th millennium BC
(Nicosia, Cyprus Museum)

5 (2). Head of unfired clay; from Khirokitia; 7th millennium BC
(Nicosia, Cyprus Museum)

6. Pottery bowl with spout, Combed ware; from Khirokitia; 4500-4000 BC
(Nicosia, Cyprus Museum)

8. Conical seal; from Lemba-*Lakkous*; *c.* 2500 BC
(Nicosia, Cyprus Museum)

9 (1). Limestone female figurine; from Lemba-*Lakkous*; *c.* 3000 BC
(Nicosia, Cyprus Museum)

9 (2). Red-on-White painted pottery figurine; from the cult deposit at Kissonerga; *c.* 3000 BC
(Nicosia, Cyprus Museum)

12 (1). Jug, Red Polished ware; from Ayia Paraskevi; 2700-2300 BC
(Birmingham, City Museum and Art Gallery)

12 (2). Cult vessel, Red Polished ware; from Vounous; 2600-2300 BC
(Birmingham, City Museum and Art Gallery)

13. Bronze dagger; from Vounous; 2500-2000 BC
(Birmingham, City Museum and Art Gallery)

16. Necklace of faience beads; from Kalavassos; *c.* 1950-1850 BC
(Nicosia, Cyprus Museum)

17. Kamares ware cup, imported from Crete; Karmi; 1900-1800 BC
(Nicosia, Cyprus Museum)

CREDITS FOR ILLUSTRATIONS

*We are grateful to the following copyright owners for allowing their
photographs to be used in this edition. Objects belonging to museums
appear by kind permission of their directors and trustees; in the case
of Cyprus of the Director of the Department of Antiquities.*

Fratelli Alinari, Florence − 212
The Department of Antiquities, Cyprus − 4, 5 (1), 5 (2), 6,
8, 9 (1), 9 (2), 16, 17, 20, 25, 30, 33 (1),33 (2), 41, 50, 51, 52,
54, 55, 62, 68 (1), 72, 79, 82, 90, 99, 101, 104, 106, 108 (2),
111, 121, 123, 124, 126, 127, 131, 135, 150 (1), 150 (2), 151,
213, 245
The Bank of Cyprus (London) Ltd − 240, 249, 257, 260,
264, 265, 266, 267, 268, 269, 270, 272
The Bank of Cyprus Cultural Foundation − 143
The Birmingham City Museum and Art Gallery − 12 (1), 12
(2), 13
A and C Black (maps drawn by D. London) − 305, 308, 309
Osvaldo Böhm, Venice − 223 (1)
The British Museum − 24, 40, 48, 69, 70, 73, 76, 80, 83, 88,
89, 92, 96 (1), 96 (2 and 3), 96 (4), 100, 102 (1), 102 (2), 105,
107, 108, 115, 116, 134, 149, 152, 153 (1), 153 (2), 198, 223 (2)
Duckworth − 307
Ekdotike Athenon SA − 27, 29, 31, 34, 37 (1), 37 (2), 44, 56,
57, 58 (1 and 2), 61, 63, 74, 75, 85, 94, 117, 118 and 119, 130,
133, 144, 145, 204, 205
S. A. Georgiades − 224 (6)
Chr. Hadjiprodromou − 11
Lord Harding of Petherton − 278
The Hulton Picture Company − 114
Lady Hunt (drawings by Tessa Henderson) − 138 and 139,
140 and 141, 155, 156 and 157, 158, 159, 160, 161, 162 and
163, 164, 165, 166, 167, 168, 169, 171, 172, 173, 181, 182,
184, 192 and 193, 196, 202 and 203, 206, 220, 221, 222, 232
and 233, 234 and 235, 236, 237, 239, 244, 246 and 247, 250
and 251
Lady Hunt (drawings by John Hawes) − frontispiece, 197
The Illustrated London News − 258, 271, 273, 275 (1), 275
(2)
George Lanitis − 289
Musée du Louvre − 68 (2)
Medelhavsmuseet, Stockholm − 67, 93
The Metropolitan Museum of Art, Cesnola Collecion − 86,
87
Museo Storico Navale, Venice − 228, 230
The National Maritime Museum, London − 227
Nigel Press − 306
H. C. Perry − 231
The Pierides Foundation Museum − 10, 103
Andreas G. Pitsillides − 224 (2), 224 (2), 224 (3), 224 (4). 224
(5), 224 (7), 224 (8), 224 (9), 224 (10), 224 (11), 224 (12)
The Public Information Office, Nicosia − 281, 283, 284,
287, 288
Punch − 253, 257
The Royal Commonwealth Society Library − 263
Spectrum Colour Library − 183 (2), 188, 189
Staatliche Museen, Berlin − 243
Dr Andreas and Dr Judith Stylianou − 211, 229
Trigraph Ltd (photographs by Andreas Malecos) − 2, 7, 14,
15, 18, 19, 23, 26, 32, 33 (3),38, 42, 43, 45, 49, 66, 71, 77, 78,
91, 95, 103, 113, 120, 128, 129, 132, 148, 176, 177, 178, 179,
180, 191, 194, 195, 200, 201, 207, 214, 215, 216, 217
UNFICYP, Nicosia − 286
The Victoria and Albert Museum, London − 190
Reno Wideson − 3, 154, 183 (1),185, 186, 187, 199, 209, 210,
218, 219, 238, 276
Württembergische Landesbibliothek, Stuttgart − 208

ACKNOWLEDGEMENTS

My first acknowledgement must be to the publishers Trigraph Ltd and its original directors Iro Hunt, Demetra David and Fofi Myrianthousis, three public-spirited Cypriots who specially commisioned this book in 1982. My wife Iro has continued with this work of love and is responsible for the whole artistic planning and supervision of the project. My second is to the distinguished authors who have contributed the first eight chapters: Prof. Edgar J. Peltenburg, Prof. Vassos Karageorghis, Prof. J.N. Coldstream, Dr Veronica Tatton-Brown, Dr D. Michaelides and Sir Steven Runciman.

On behalf of the publishers and myself I should like to acknowledge with gratitude the financial assistance given for previous editions by the A.G. Leventis Foundation; the late Mr C.P. Leventis; the Cultural Foundation of the Bank of Cyprus; Ekdotike Athenon SA for lending several photographs from *Istoria tou Ellenikou Ethnous;* Ekdotike Hellados SA for the production of this volume; all organisations and individuals who contributed photographs and whose names appear on page xiii. I should like to give special mention to Ms Tessa Henderson whose drawings of so many historic monuments add new interest to the book, Mr A. Malecos and Mr R. Wideson for a great number of coloured photographs and Mr A. G. Pitsillides for those of the Lusignan coins.

I should also like to thank the following: Mr P. Attwood; Mr D.M. Bailey; Mr J. Bastias; Mrs R. Bennett; Miss Susan Bird; Mme Annie Caubet; Mrs Celia Clear; Mr B.F. Cook; Mr A. Coudounaris; Mr G. Dicomites; Mr E.J. Finopoulos; Mr G.P. Gezerlis; Mr R. Gorgé; Dr H. Habibis; Dr Maria Iacovou; Mr C. Jordan; Mr N. Kofou; Mr C. Leventis; Mr D. London; Mr P. Loverdos; Mr A. Nicolas; HE Mr Tasos Panayides; Dr A. Papageorghiou; Mr A. Patsalides; Mr W.W. Percival-Prescott; Mr S. Pewsey; Mr M. Pick; Mrs Theodora Z. Pierides; Dr P.G. Polyviou; Dr M. Pricy; Mr K. Psyllides; Mr I. Robertson; Dr A. Stylianou; Dr Judith A. Stylianou; Dr C.G. Styrenius; Mr D. Symons; Dr Susan Walker; Mr. P. Williamson.

FOREWORD

When the first edition of this book was published in 1982 it claimed, with justice, to be the first attempt to give a comprehensive narrative of Cypriot history from prehistoric times to the present day since Sir George Hill's great work *A History of Cyprus,* whose four volumes came out between 1940 and 1952. In the intervening thirty years there had been many additions to knowledge. If the course of the island's history, covering nine millennia and more, can be compared to a long and stately corridor stretching back into the growing obscurity of the past there is always fresh light breaking in at many points thanks to the discoveries of archaeologists. There are also eight more years of the history of the present to be considered. Meanwhile the original printing, and a reprint in paperback, have been exhausted and demand for a second edition has increased. In consequence the book has been subjected to a fundamental revision: all the contributors have revised their articles, the chapter on the Roman period has been written by a new, expert contributor and a completely new selection of illustrations has been made. The articles represent the present state of archaeological and historical knowledge; opinions expressed are those of the individual writers.

One of the principles most clearly demonstrated by Cypriot history is that geography is destiny. Cyprus has always been more acted upon than active and a proper understanding of its history calls for a full appreciation of the changing international scene in the eastern Mediterranean. Throughout the ages the dominating power in that area, whether based in Europe, Africa or Asia, has found itself by some kind of inevitability in possession of Cyprus; the effect of these external influences is what is meant by the title *Footprints in Cyprus*. It would be quite wrong, however, to suppose that Cypriot civilisation has had no definite character of its own. At least from the end of the second millennium BC, which is the period when Greek settlers arrived in the island, the line of cultural tradition has run clear down to the present day. Whatever the vicissitudes, which, as explained more at large in the Epilogue, were shared by the inhabitants of other Greek lands, Cyprus has remained faithful to its roots in Homeric times and to the legacy of Athens and Constantinople.

Over the past sixteen years Cyprus has suffered invasion, and the occupation of a third of her territory by a foreign army. In spite of the best efforts of the Security Council and the weight of world opinion, this unlawful state of affairs has not been rectified. From these tragic circumstances has arisen another reason for the publication of the book. There has been a great increase in the number of emigrants who have left their native island, often with no expectation of returning. Many English-speaking countries, and especially Great Britain, now have large Cypriot communities, whose families are in danger of growing up estranged from their history and their civilisation. At the same time the British public, who have shown much affection for Cyprus, not least by choosing it so often for their holidays, will be able to understand from this book the monuments they see when they are in the island and to connect them with the past in which their country also had a share for eight centuries.

I

PALAEOLITHIC TO LATE BRONZE AGES

8500–1600 BC

Prof. E.J. Peltenburg

To imagine that the fertile island of Cyprus lay deserted while there was settled village life on the intervisible coasts of Syria and Anatolia and while boats criss-crossed the Aegean to exchange precious stone from Melos seems hardly credible, yet that is precisely the situation before *c.* 7000 BC as revealed by archaeology. Most nearby populations had progressed beyond what has been called the Agricultural Revolution and were engaged in farming activities which, amongst other things, encouraged population growth. Despite these increased numbers, Cyprus remained unoccupied. Or did it? Is our evidence simply deficient on this critical point and are there hidden under the alluvium mantle of the central plain or buried in the limestone caves of the Kyrenia Mountains the elusive traces of Palaeolithic man? A cave on Akrotiri Peninsula reveals the presence of man on Cyprus *c.* 8500 BC but in the manner of island colonisations in general this may be evidence for no more than passing hunting parties, a preliminary step in the process of colonisation. Such are the numbers of butchered pygmy hippopotami from the cave, however, that they may have been responsible for the extinction of this species on the island. Their tool kit and associated radiocarbon dates suggest that they are best regarded as epi-palaeolithic hunter-gatherer bands. The settlements established at the end of the 8th millennium are now also disclosing much earlier phases of occupation that need to be analysed.

By any standards, these communities are remarkable. In a relatively short period some developed into large, fortified centres with

Bowl of dark-grey
andesite; from Khirokitia;
H 10 cm, W 27.5 cm; 7th
millennium BC
(Nicosia, Cyprus Museum)

population estimates for the largest, Khirokitia near the south coast, of around 2,000 inhabitants. This precocious centre, however, lacked many of the characteristics that accompany early large-scale population densities elsewhere such as consistently produced pottery and even nearby fields for agriculture. So there are several contradictions to the expected pattern of developments in the Near East in general and since this distinctively Cypriot phenomenon is so exciting in any study of early man, we can leave the question of origins temporarily to one side. Suffice it to say that well before 6000 BC there emerged in Cyprus a remarkable series of related communities which disappear from our records in circumstances that are mysterious as are their origins.

Some fifteen communities are known at present and they are mainly strung out along the north coast or are located in the short river valleys that descend from the Troodos Mountains in the south. Despite the distances between them, they seem to possess standardised settlements in which round buildings huddle together on the tops and slopes of hills, in the latter case much as Cypriot mountain villages today. The lower parts of these buildings are often of stone and attain massive proportions by constant additions of further skins of stones or pisé. The small interiors have hearths, presumably used for cooking and also heating in winter, benches and windows, but in many cases the area is further restricted by

2

large, in one instance painted, piers to support an upper floor. In winter the heat would gather usefully at that higher level and smoke there would help to cure stored venison in the form of the now extinct fallow deer which seems to have been a staple part of the diet. A collapsed flat roof of one building at Khirokitia indicates that not all roofs were beehive shaped as was once thought to be the case.

Except for cornelian and obsidian, a volcanic glassy rock prized for its cutting properties, there are no hints of external contact and indeed these villages are of a type not found elsewhere. Artefacts found inside them are equally unique and many exhibit a path of

Aerial view of the Neolithic settlement of Khirokitia; 7th millennium BC

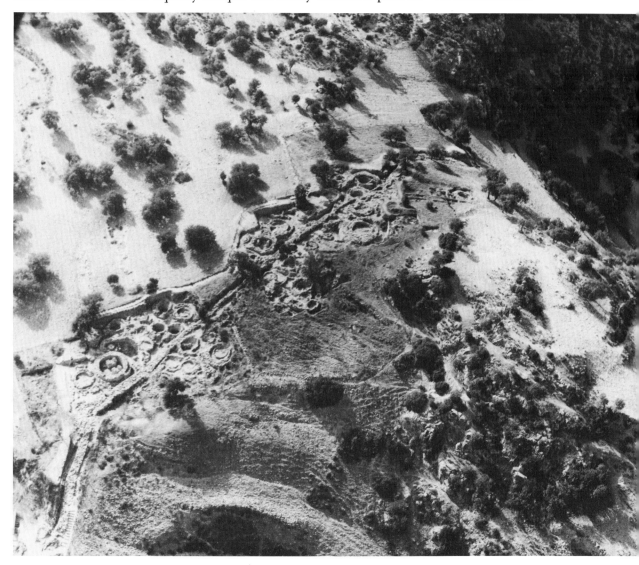

development that is radically separate from that of their neighbours. Thus, although Khirokitians were familiar with clay, they laboriously produced ground stone vessels in preference to pottery ones, many no doubt in imitation of now lost wooden containers. Archaeologists therefore conventionally call this the aceramic neolithic period.

We can but speculate on the organisation of this assertively independent society and why some centres, like Khirokitia, grew to such a large size and others, such as the islet Petra tou Limniti, remained small. A possible insight is provided by a settlement near Kalavassos which is dominated by an exceptionally-large courtyard building stained with red ochre. Surrounding it are some structures so small they may be for storage rather than for living and the whole is enclosed by a wall and ditch. The dominant edifice points to a distinct authority. The earliest known culture in Cyprus therefore consists of a well-organised, developed society primarily engaged in farming, hunting and perhaps herding. Its links with the earlier pygmy hippopotamus hunters of Akrotiri are unknown.

Tenta —

In all settlements the dead were buried just under floors in crouched positions but occasionally with their artificially-deformed skulls raised. In some instances provision was made for offerings so presumably a form of ancestor cult existed inside households. There is also the suggestion of a higher mortality rate before the desertion of Khirokitia and so it may be that natural causes, such as diseases, to which island populations are particularly susceptible, played a part in the disappearance of this group from our records.

Like the post-Darwinian story of evolution, the documentation of early man on Cyprus is episodic and comprises a series of fully-formed cultures with little evidence to show how and why they emerged or, for that matter, declined. The next recorded entity, the Sotira group, is a good case in point. Radiocarbon dates place it between 4500 and 4000 BC and there are only faint hints of prehistoric man on the island between its advent and the demise of the Khirokitia group some 1500 years earlier. Since it differs so much from the latter, scholars are divided on its origins, either native or intrusive, as in the case of the Khirokitian group. Once again, there are no close parallels elsewhere for this new Cypriot culture, so if people did cross to the island at its inception they underwent a radical sea-change when they pioneered their new settlements.

The Sotira group is known from some thirty settlements scattered in all areas save the high Troodos and the central plain. They are small villages on promontories, hilltops and slopes. One of the largest, Sotira, probably had no more than fifty, mainly single-roomed, buildings at any one time, each with its own circular platform hearth and bench, often with working installations and alcoves set against walls. The free-standing but tightly-clustered buildings are comparatively thin walled and tend to a square rather than circular plan. However, such planning was altered where

1
Stone and shell necklace; from Khirokitia; L 40 cm; 7th millennium BC (Nicosia, Cyprus Museum)

2
Head of unfired clay; from Khirokitia; H 10.5 cm; 7th millennium BC (Nicosia, Cyprus Museum)

1

2

5

Pottery bowl with spout;
Combed ware; from
Khirokitia; H 15 cm,
W 32.5 cm; 4500-4000 BC
(Nicosia, Cyprus Museum)

circumstances dictated, as at the north coast subterranean village of
Ayios Epiktitos-*Vrysi*. There spacious natural or man-made hollows were deeply indented into an otherwise flat coastal promontory and wedged inside them were irregularly-shaped buildings, six
or more per hollow. Their roofs were well below ground level so
that the whole village was concealed from the casual viewer except
for the smoke rising from the promontory. Since there was an
evident desire to remain below ground, the houses were not widely
dispersed but in the course of time they accumulated one above the
other in columnar fashion inside the hollows thus, ironically, yield-
ing some of the best-preserved prehistoric architecture on the island. This subterranean aspect of the Sotira group is also evident in
a network of shafts, tunnels and chambers below the similar houses
at the inland site of Philia. Its excavator has suggested that such a
complex may have been used for non-utilitarian purposes, but
storage cannot be precluded.

Despite slight differences in the plans of village buildings, their
overall size and interior appointments remain quite standardised, so
there should have been contact between these meagre and widespread communities. Evidence for this comes from the occurrence
of beads and pendants of blue-green picrolite (like steatite or
soapstone) in the north where it is not found naturally. It occurs in
and near the Troodos Mountains and was frequently used for
simple pendants at Sotira. Either the northern inhabitants obtained
it from the Troodos directly, which seems unlikely because there is
so little of it in their villages, or they obtained it by exchange.

Pottery tells a similar story of exchange and communications.
Vessels of fired and decorated clay now comprise the major artefact
type from Cyprus and regional styles can be identified. Thus in the
south a peculiar style known as combed, because of the use of
multi-toothed instruments to effect designs, was prevalent but it is
only found occasionally in the north. It too may have reached there

by exchange but the clays could well be local in which case the idea of the idiosyncratic combing technique was somehow passed on. This pottery is handmade and because its decoration is so varied it may have been a household craft suggesting that movement of people, perhaps through inter-village marriage, could also be a unifying agent of the Sotira group.

Only one material aspect of this culture shows clear signs of development and that is the pottery. At Philia it seems to develop out of an earlier monochrome variety. This is the only clue that we

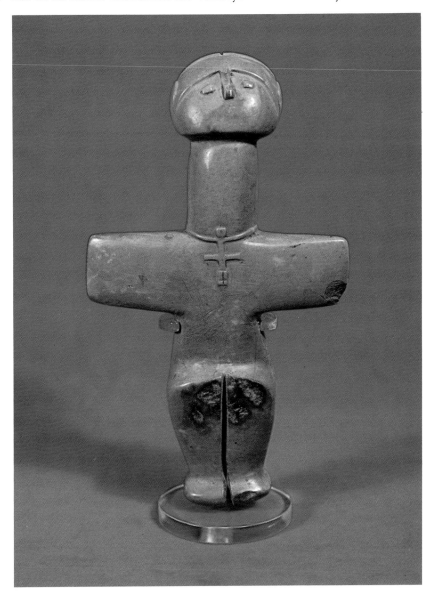

Cruciform figurine of blue-green picrolite; from Yialia; H 15.3 cm; *c.* 3000 BC (Nicosia, Cyprus Museum)

Conical seal; from Lemba-
Lakkous; L 3.1 cm, D 2.6
cm; *c.* 2500 BC
(Nicosia, Cyprus Museum)

have concerning the group's native emergence and so important ceramic changes are taking place in Cyprus about 4500 BC. It would, however, be misleading to think of the Sotira group, once it had become established, as unenterprising and fossilised. Population was on the increase as can be seen from the expansion of some settlements. Decoration on pottery shows rapid changes in a lively painted tradition in the north, where Red-on-White designs include regular lattices, bold circles and festoons, accurate chevrons, filling patterns executed with a sponge and, most typical of all, dazzling ripples. Traces of decoratively entwined reeds or grasses on stones remind us of the tremendous loss in perishable arts and crafts.

It is often assumed that because a group of people are later in time they must in some way be more advanced than their predecessors, but this is difficult to confirm in a comparison of the Khirokitia and Sotira groups. The latter may have realised the potential of pottery but their villages are defended in a similar manner as before, they lack the earlier large centres which may have fostered specialists, burials are still in simple pits though outside houses, and there is no evidence for external trade. Their diet shows no great increase in variety or emphasis except for a concentration on domestic sheep and goats in the north. Yet they did successfully adapt to their Mediterranean environment, population did increase and their traditions, unlike those of the Khirokitia group, did persist. These features would seem to be the lasting contribution to Cyprus of the Sotira group.

Radiocarbon dates and pottery studies are unanimous in revealing a general population shift *c.* 4000 BC. This in itself is not surprising, since early settlements generally in the Near East and Aegean were often abandoned for a variety of reasons. One difference between Cyprus and the adjacent mainland however is that there is little perceptible increase in the size of settlement centres. This may be due to the difficulty that island populations have in recovering from such adversities as famine, disease, earthquake and invasion, all amply documented later in Cyprus. The development of urbanisation and of a complex society therefore came late. Small-scale, shifting society remains typical of the island until well into the Bronze Age.

Symptomatic of these cycles of settled prosperity followed by apparent upheaval and a return again to a new form of settled existence is our lack of knowledge concerning the intervening eras of disruption. Recent discoveries of the period shortly after 4000 BC have now begun to penetrate this particular Dark Age. It would seem that no outsiders were involved in the transition from the Neolithic to the Chalcolithic period, but the islanders forsook established methods of building and adopted more perishable

8

1
Limestone female figurine;
from Lemba-*Lakkous;*
H 36 cm; *c.* 3000 BC
(Nicosia, Cyprus Museum)

2
Red-on-White painted
pottery figurine; from the
cult deposit at Kissonerga.
She is shown in the act of
giving birth; H 20 cm;
c. 3000 BC
(Nicosia, Cyprus Museum)

materials. They continued their underground activities as another site near Kalavassos with impressive tunnels demonstrates and the Paphos District now begins to flourish. There, at the site of Lemba, dwellings in small hollows evolved into the substantial circular stone buildings that are the hallmark of the succeeding Erimi group of sites. In this way we can see how recourse to more temporary accommodation such as wattled huts around circular shelter pits eventually gave rise to a radically new architecture.

No doubt other cultural changes accompanied this dislocation. For example, evidence is accumulating for a greater economic reliance on fallow deer, implying increased herding and hunting. In the transformed society that emerges in Cyprus perhaps as early as *c.* 3500 BC there are no overt signs of immigrants, but there are several of continuity. This transition therefore seems to be an internal affair and we may better treat it as a formative stage in the evolution of prehistoric Cypriot society than a true Dark Age.

The Erimi group takes its name from a south coast site which Porphyrios Dikaios, the pioneer of Cypriot prehistoric studies, examined briefly in the 1930s. As at Lemba, pottery associated with the early timbered buildings includes the last appearance of combed decoration and, with the later substantial buildings, a fine-line style of Red-on-White. This style has many affinities with the earlier Red-on-White but a greater range of elegant shapes and larger vessels point to different uses, especially for storage. It is one which is now found widely in Cyprus and, although useful for the relative dating of sites, the suspected regional variations and time scales remain to be worked out.

Askos, Red-on-White ware; from Souskiou; H 16.4 cm; 3900-2500 BC (Larnaca, Pierides Foundation Museum)

10

Red-on-White ware zoomorphic vase with a human face; from Souskiou; H 13.5 cm; L 22cm; *c.* 3000 BC (Famagusta, Hadjiprodromou Collection)

If continuity and only very gradual change are to be found in pottery and buildings, innovation marks other aspects of this group. Metalwork appears for the first time on an island whose fortunes were later so closely bound up with the exploitation of its copper resources. The copper chisels, hooks and jewellery of this period are relatively pure, but the inclusion of minute amounts of tin in one or two pieces has encouraged some scholars to look to a source in Anatolia where copper-working was long established. Very occasionally now obsidian, almost certainly from Anatolia, occurs in Cyprus so the possible opening of transmaritime exchange could account for this metalwork. On the other hand, some of the Cypriot copper objects are peculiar to the island and as their advent takes place exactly during the formative stage of the Erimi group, we can by no means rule out an indigenous role in this momentous breakthrough.

That enhanced exploitation of rocks — and native copper would be regarded as such — took place now is made clear by blue-green picrolite figurines in cruciform shape. They too were an innovation, but they are a facet, albeit the most distinctive one, of an exuberant display of representational art that is one of the chief distinguishing features of the Erimi group. Most picrolite examples were meant to be worn as pendants either singly or alternating with dentalium shell spacers on necklaces and the number of figures represented can multiply so that two are depicted one above the other or three in a Legs of Man formation. Where the sex is

11

indicated, the female is usually portrayed. Scarcity of wear marks and their recurrence in graves suggest that they were primarily intended for the dead.

An astonishingly rich hoard of painted pottery figurines ritually deposited at Kissonerga in the West also provides insights into religious customs. They were found inside a deliberately defaced building model with protomes over the entrance, swivel door, unusual hearth and platform presumably as a focus for the figures. The largest of these originally sat on a stool and is shown in the act of birth, so the continuity of life in an unstable world was vividly expressed. There are so many features of later sanctuaries in this hoard, including a triton shell, that a special cult building and perhaps goddesses are portrayed.

These discoveries are difficult to place in terms of Cypriot society as a whole since only a few sites of this long period, *c*. 4000-2500 BC, have been excavated. Developments of major significance are known to be taking place. Thus the recurrence of differently-sized buildings including the largest in prehistoric Cyprus at Kissonerga, the introduction of the stamp seal, evidence for cult buildings and imports are all new and they suggest the establishment of social hierarchies, administration of goods and property, specialisa-

1
Jug, Red Polished ware; from Ayia Paraskevi; H 44 cm, D 22.7 cm; 2700-2300 BC (Birmingham, City Museum and Art Gallery)

2
Cult vessel, Red Polished ware; from Vounous; H 26.9 cm, D 15.8 cm; 2600-2300 BC (Birmingham, City Museum and Art Gallery)

1

2

tion and transmaritime contacts respectively. Since most Erimi group burials are without grave goods and in simple pits the rich multiple burials in shaft graves at the Souskiou cemeteries near Palaepaphos demonstrate the existence of wealth-accumulating centres.

The paucity of information from the Kyrenia and west Nicosia Districts renders any reconstruction of ensuing events highly speculative since it is at least clear that it was especially in those districts that major changes took place, ones which ushered in the Bronze Age in Cyprus. The evidence to hand for this transition to what is known as the Early Cypriote, comes chiefly from very limited excavations and surveys. There are essentially two schools of thought, that which follows Gjerstad in believing in an immigration from Anatolia and Stewart's school which considers that developments now are a Cypriot affair. All are agreed that the changes were decisive and that they profoundly affected the island for centuries to come. New evidence from the west moreover shows how dramatic and complex were events surrounding these changes. All save one of the many Late Chalcolithic villages were abandoned and Lemba was destroyed by fire. Kissonerga on the other hand survived into the transition period. Even before that period however burial customs altered radically to include chamber tombs, usually regarded as the hallmark of the Bronze Age, and urn burials, a startlingly new departure but a tradition well known in Anatolia. Kissonerga itself was then abandoned and our task of monitoring subsequent developments is made extremely difficult by the absence of successive settlements for comparison.

The older fine-line style of Cypriot Red-on-White pottery is found on the adjacent mainland at Tarsus, so contacts certainly existed with an area that was soon to be in the throes of conflict surrounding the arrival of Indo-Europeans. It may be that some mainlanders found their way along known exchange routes to Cyprus and were instrumental in inaugurating widespread change. The history of many Indo-European groups is replete with examples of aristocratic minorities assuming political control of other ethnic units, so not many need be involved. At the other extreme end of a host of possible solutions is Stewart's school which discounts all direct foreign participation, suggesting instead that such wealth gathering as is exhibited earlier at Souskiou eventually generated enough momentum, particularly through the exploitation of and trade in the rich copper resources of Cyprus, to bring about change internally. Whatever the answer, the new managers swept aside the existing props of the stage and they created a transformed Cypriot scene in the north, to a lesser extent in the south and west.

The cemetery of Vasilia demonstrates the effects of new-found

Bronze dagger, from Vounous; L 17.8 cm, W 3.7 cm; 2500-2000 BC (Birmingham, City Museum and Art Gallery)

13

wealth. Most tombs of Cypriot necropoleis have rather simple rock-cut chambers with blocked approach passages, dromoi, but here there are prestigious plaster-lined complexes up to 16 m in length with niches in the walls and in at least one case a small hole connecting the burial chamber with the world above. Amongst the grave goods are impressively large stone vessels and a type of pottery known as Philia which may be the earliest Bronze Age fabric but one which carries on alongside other Red Polished styles. Their fragile and elaborate nature indicates that many were specifically intended as furnishings for single and multiple burials. Such burials at Vounous, one of the largest cemeteries of the period, also on the north coast but to the east of Kyrenia, were amply pro-

Ritual vessel, Red Polished ware, with miniature animals and cups on the rim; from Vounous; H 53 cm, D 35 cm; 2200–2000 BC
(Nicosia, Cyprus Museum)

14

visioned with slaughtered cattle, joints of meat in jars and basins, specialised cult and other drinking vessels, pottery replicas of daggers and sheaths, spindles and carding combs, decorated long copper pins to fasten robes at the shoulders and several kinds of metal tools and weapons.

Until the dating of the very localised styles of Red Polished pottery is put on a firmer basis it will be difficult to elaborate on the settlement patterns in different parts of the island and interaction between them. Nonetheless, it is likely that by the end of the period population had expanded and settlements are to be found in all areas previously occupied. Two aspects of their distribution may be noted. In the west the apparent scarcity contrasts with an earlier density so either depopulation took place here or we have still to recognise adequately human traces of the period. Elsewhere, on the

Clay model of an open air scene, Red Polished ware, representing a man kneeling before attached pillars, seated figures with folded arms, dancers and woman with child beholding penned bulls; from Vounous; H 12 cm, D 37 cm; *c.* 2600-2300 BC (Nicosia, Cyprus Museum)

15

Necklace of faience
beads; from Kalavassos;
c. 1950-1850 BC
(Nicosia, Cyprus Museum)

'copper belt' of Cyprus stretching along the north-eastern foothills of the Troodos Mountains from the Bay of Morphou to Kalavassos in the south there is a new concentration of sites that may well reflect increased interest in copper resources. Indeed, if that is their principal *raison d'être*, then considerable demand must have existed, more so than would be needed to satisfy insular requirements, and with it unprecedented technological and organisational expertise.

Red Polished pottery found deep in copper mines at Ambelikou proves the determined nature of copper exploitation now. A 'copper belt' settlement, Alambra, has crucibles containing traces of copper and radically new aligned rectangular buildings and streets. Previously, villages possessed isolated and dispersed buildings, henceforth they have contiguous buildings that can expand or subdivide more readily in a pattern long familiar on the Asiatic mainland.

Other architectural evidence in the form of a terracotta model from Vounous demonstrates the concurrent persistence of the Erimi circular building traditions, perhaps for cult places only given the nature of the activities so vividly displayed in the model. The inclusion of penned bulls here and of bulls' heads as terminals for engaged pillars on other models suggests that a bull cult is an important element in Early Cypriote religious beliefs. That it is a new religious force is rendered likely by the complete absence of cattle bones in Cyprus before this period, but it would be over-simplification to identify this bull cult as the dominant component of the religion. Other figures, perhaps of religious significance, include highly stylised plank-shaped females executed in the ubiquitous Red Polished pottery.

During this period infrequent imports and what may be copies of foreign goods are found in cemeteries. To the former group may be attributed Asiatic and Minoan pottery, Minoan metalwork, Egyptian stonework and perhaps Asiatic beads of shiny blue faience, to the latter Asiatic spindle-whorls and metalwork and Cycladic pottery. Contacts therefore now existed with all those areas which were to be the island's major contact partners during the remainder of the Bronze Age, and, if the actual numbers of objects are few, the quantity must be weighed in the balances of a most defective record. Much hinges on the interpretation we wish to give to these objects. They could be nothing more than random but increasing numbers of imports of little significance to social and political developments in Cyprus itself. The nature of trade in adjoining lands, however, follows another, largely non-random, pattern in which large merchant colonies are established and royal expeditions, such as that of the Egyptian King Sahure (*c.* 2480 BC) to Asia, cross the seas to cities with which there are political ties. Cyprus may have remained on the periphery of such formal and formative contacts between city states and empires, but there is tantalising evidence to indicate that such an isolated role was no longer possible by *c.* 2000 BC, if not before.

Part of this evidence relates to the enterprising kings of Middle-Kingdom Egypt (*c.* 2134-1786 BC). Inscribed objects of the royal family and other high officials of the XIIIth and especially the XIIth Dynasties have been found in the cities of Syria, especially at Ugarit, a most important port-of-call and one close to eastern Cyprus. In a colourful and convincingly accurate story of the beginning of the XIIth Dynasty a high-ranking Egyptian fugitive in Syria or Palestine speaks of a flurry of Egyptian messengers suggestive of diplomatic and trading contacts. We have already seen that long distances were no barrier to direct trade links in Asia and so the appearance of Cypriot Red Polished pottery at Ugarit, although poorly dated, and North Syrian painted pottery in Cyprus indicate some kind of Cypriot integration into this complex network. The Egyptian evidence at once lends a literate dimension and chronological precision to these relations.

The second major body of evidence concerns the identification of the place names *Alasia* and *Asy* which first occur *c.* 1750 BC in such a manner that the writers would seem to be quite familiar with the place, though for how long is not possible to say. Assuming that the name *Alasia* has not experienced geographical displacement in the course of time, a known phenomenon affecting remote places and movement of people carrying with them a place name, then it is

Kamares ware cup, imported from Crete; from Karmi; H 9 cm, D 8.5 cm; 1900-1800 BC (Nicosia, Cyprus Museum)

17

to be located by the sea with close connections to Ugarit and north Syria, Egypt and the Hittites, and it is most widely known for mining and disseminating copper. These characteristics suit Cyprus admirably, but clear corroboration from the island itself is still lacking and hence there is often reluctance to apply this historical evidence fully to an interpretation of insular developments. Here it is regarded as positive circumstantial evidence which demonstrates that Cypriot copper was reaching Mesopotamia by *c.* 1750 BC and that Cypriots were living abroad, in north Syria by *c.* 1650 BC. It remains to be seen what, if any, the impact of this involvement was on the island. Factors that impinge on this major issue are population size, political integration and remoteness since distant regions

Terracotta sanctuary model, Red Polished ware; from Kotchati; H 19 cm; *c.* 1900 BC (Nicosia, Cyprus Museum)

with desirable raw materials lacking numbers and political cohesiveness such as the copper-bearing areas of Timna in Palestine and Sinai are frequently exploited and seldom turn such commodities to their own advantage.

Apparently lacking urban centres contemporary with Middle-Kingdom Egypt, it is unlikely that Cyprus could have participated in the inter-state exchanges just mentioned, or at least not in the same manner. At the beginning of this period the Cypriot population was still located in the older centres, especially in the north, but it is becoming clearer that the south-west was also well populated if not as rich in material goods. As it progressed settlements appear on the southern slopes of the Kyrenia Mountains overlooking the potentially rich, but perhaps well-wooded, central plain. By *c.* 1650 BC there are new foundations on the south and east coasts, ones which were to become international urban emporia. There is little reason to doubt that they owe their origin to the realisation of the potentials of trade with the east and so it is striking that their

Terracotta model of a ploughing scene; from Vounous; L 41 cm; *c.* 1900 BC
(Nicosia, Cyprus Museum)

19

Bronze axe; L 19 cm; 1900-
1625 BC
(Nicosia, Cyprus Museum)

inception takes place after the Middle Kingdom when Egypt lacked traditional central authority and when the largely Asiatic cities in the Nile Delta prospered. We are still woefully ignorant of the size and complexity of the new cities, but at some stage during these centuries a diversified response to the situation makes its appearance, the fort.

There is unlikely to be a single all-embracing cause for fort construction since the twenty or so known examples vary considerably in type. They occur primarily along the edges of the central plain and in the Karpass. The best-known, Nitovikla, consists of a square fortress at the edge of an enclosed plateau. Two square towers flank its gateway, which was built of massive ashlar blocks. Leading off its central court, a range of chambers may have acted as the base for a parapet walk behind the very thick walls. Nitovikla, which is placed at the base of the Karpass overlooking the Bay of Famagusta, contrasts with Dhali-*Kafkallia*, an inland fort not far from classical Idalion. There a low straggling wall encloses 12 hectares (30 acres), much of it occupied by rectangular buildings. It lacks a fortress and much of it would be difficult to defend against a determined aggressor. So novel is the concept of these enclosed sites that intruders, as in the case of renewed fort-building at the end of the Bronze Age, have been adduced to explain Nitovikla, though more inland forts are frequently interpreted as a result of localised hostilities. Yet Nitovikla has produced no foreign goods, whereas a tomb at Dhali-*Kafkallia* has yielded a rare bronze belt of a type known only from the Nile Delta in Egypt and from Palestine. Clearly, the patchy nature of our information from these forts can only permit the most speculative of explanations. Their distribution, at least, confirms the decline of the importance of the north though not of the area around the Bay of Morphou which was soon to become seriously involved with Minoan Crete. Their distance from the sea indicates that they are not a response to sea raiders known from slightly later historical records. It is also the case that at least one, Nitovikla, was violently destroyed and so, far from mere symbols of prestige, they do reflect a period of unrest. Mass burials under immense tumuli may also hint at such a state of affairs.

Two conflicting tendencies can thus be observed in Cyprus in the earlier part of the 2nd millennium BC. Developments in ceramics and metallurgy are essentially variations on themes established previously. These expressions of continuity also exist in settlement size and in burial practices which, apart from the eastern tumuli just mentioned, only become more elaborate in cultic matters. Subsistence economy too shows little change from that known in the Erimi group, but we could be better informed about the intervening period when the introduction of ox-drawn ploughs probably

20

permitted heavier soils to be cultivated. Against this picture of innate conservatism must be placed the early hints of innovation, mainly in the form of imitations and imports, for example of a type of Syro-Cilician painted pottery which at the Syrian city of Ebla was deemed important enough to include amongst the funerary gifts of a dignitary. Closer to 1650 BC, Cypriot pottery in turn began to penetrate Levantine markets in increasing quantities where previously Cypriot copper had been dispatched to Mesopotamia. Even within the fairly uniform metalwork in Cyprus, there are anomalies such as a series of shaft-hole axes which are sophisticated display objects indicative of the adoption of Asiatic status symbols. Whether or not foreigners at any level of society are involved, and there is no question of mass invasion, it seems likely that these opposed tendencies led to stresses which precipitated the creation of forts and presumably a kind of military aristocracy that usually accompanies such works. At the moment the simplest but by no means only explanation would seem to be that the observed changes and copper exports are inter-dependent. The new cities that were generated by this trading have yielded developed, but thoroughly Cypriot, materials and hence the ultimate impact was not foreign exploitation but a positive Cypriot response.

II

THE LATE BRONZE AGE
(LATE CYPRIOTE)
c. 1600 - *c.* 1050 BC

Prof. Vassos Karageorghis

Cyprus entered the Late Bronze Age experiencing the same atmosphere of unrest which prevailed towards the end of the Middle Bronze Age. It is difficult to determine whether this was the result of raids from external enemies such as the Hyksos or of friction between East and West, the two traditionally antagonistic parts of the island, for the control of the island's resources of copper and fertile arable land. Forts and refuges were built in various areas and mass burials are observed in tombs, mainly in the north; the latter, however, may also be explained by an epidemic.

When the Hyksos were expelled from Egypt *c.* 1555 BC and peaceful conditions were established in the eastern Mediterranean, many causes of the unrest of the earlier half of the 16th century BC were removed. Peace encouraged trade which in turn aided growth of the major urban centres, both those inland which had an agricultural economy as well as the main harbour towns. Thus the acute problems which the growth of population had created could not be solved satisfactorily. This is the time when Morphou-*Toumba tou Skourou* flourished on the north-west coast, and Enkomi on the east coast emerged as a major harbour town. Several other harbour towns such as Hala Sultan Tekké and Maroni developed along the south coast. There was free communication throughout the island, which facilitated the expansion of trade, especially the transport of copper ore from the mines to the 'industrial' centres and harbours, and brought about the development of a homogeneous culture.

Artistic achievements, notably the pottery industry, are wide-spread. Two major wares make their appearance: the White Slip and Base Ring wares which were to dominate Cypriot ceramics for over three centuries and to gain great popularity in the Near East and even in the Aegean.

Pottery production was particularly lively in the Morphou region. A potter's quarter was excavated there which illustrates the extent of the industry and, judging from the vases found in the adjacent tombs, the quality of the products.

The area of Palaepaphos, whose role in the Late Bronze Age was hitherto confined mainly within the 12th century BC proves now, thanks to discoveries in tombs at site *Teratsoudhia* excavated in 1984 and 1985 (Department of Antiquities), to have been a prosperous region already during the 16th century BC. Some of the finest White Slip I and Base Ring I ware vases ever to have been found have been produced in these tombs, as well as an extraordinary — but unfortunately fragmentary — large pithoid jar of Bichrome Wheelmade ware bearing a most unusual decoration: a human figure and a bull (taken for sacrifice) as well as geometric motifs and spirals. Whether this fabric was made in Cyprus or was produced in

Necklace consisting of seven pomegranate-shaped beads and eight in the form of dates. There is a pendant in the form of a Babylonian cylinder seal. The beads are of Aegean type; the pendant is oriental, characteristic of the mixed style in Cypriot art of the Late Cypriote II period; from Ayios Iakovos; 14th century BC (Nicosia, Cyprus Museum)

Faience vessel in the form of a conical lotus flower decorated with the Egyptian god of infinity Heh; probably made in Egypt; from Enkomi; H 22.3 cm; *c.* 1350-1150 BC (London, British Museum)

the Levant is still a matter of considerable controversy. The same necropolis produced also a fragment of a stone vase of imported serpentine, obviously Egyptian, with the cartouche of Ahmoses, the first Pharaoh of the XVIIIth Dynasty (1552-1527 BC), engraved on it. This is the earliest cartouche of an Egyptian Pharaoh ever to have been found in Cyprus. We know that contacts with Egypt started already in the 16th century BC, not only with the introduction of Tell el-Yahudiya pottery from Egypt but also with their imitation in north-western Cyprus, as *Toumba tou Skourou* Tomb V has demonstrated. The discoveries at Palaepaphos show that the western part of Cyprus can claim relations with both Egypt and the Levant, as much as the eastern part of the island. Relations continued between the region of Palaepaphos and Egypt during the 16th and 15th centuries BC, if we consider a large commemorative scarab from an 11th-century tomb at Palaepaphos-*Skales* as an heirloom.

Traditional trade-links with the Syro-Palestinian coast continue, but a new element is now introduced: trade with the Aegean. Though only very few Cypriot objects dating to the 16th century BC have been found in the Aegean region and Aegean objects uncovered in Cyprus are rare, trade is nonetheless apparent in the 16th century BC. This is about the time when the Cypriots borrowed a linear script from the Cretans which is known as the Cypro-Minoan script. Cyprus could export raw copper and foodstuffs to the Aegean, but there is no conclusive evidence for the nature of this trade.

Several major sites dating to the Late Bronze Age have already been excavated and have revealed architectural remains of a military, religious and domestic character, mainly of the Late Bronze Age II period (*c.* 1450-1200 BC).

Despite these peaceful conditions during the Late Bronze Age cities in Cyprus were fortified. A mudbrick city wall was built around the town of Kition on the south coast at the beginning of the 13th century BC. It has rectangular bastions at intervals built of blocks of stone (ashlars) against its mudbrick façade. At Enkomi a fortress was constructed in the northern part of the town.

Religion was based on fertility, which formed the nucleus of the religious beliefs of the Cypriots from the 4th millennium BC onwards. Sanctuaries exist in rural centres like Kition and Myrtou-*Pigadhes*. The sanctuaries of Kition, of which two have already been excavated, follow a Near Eastern plan, with courtyard and a Holy-of-Holies associated with a 'sacred garden'.

Domestic architecture is known mainly from Enkomi. Dwellings consist of a rectangular open courtyard with rooms on three sides. The courtyard was also used for burials in chamber tombs. There were no separate cemeteries.

24

Workshops have been found at Kition, Enkomi and Apliki for the smelting of copper. Near the workshops at Kition there was a bathroom with a cemented floor. At Enkomi there were also lavatories and bathrooms and a well-organised drainage system. Bathtubs of clay or limestone point to the high standard of living of the inhabitants of the urban centres.

The site of Kalavassos-*Ayios Dhimitrios* was an important centre from the 14th down to the very end of the 13th century BC. Its proximity to the copper mines no doubt may account for its prosperity and importance. Recent excavations have brought to light a major public or administrative building, known as Building X. It is almost square, covering an area of about 1000 sq m ; it is symmetrically arranged and massively constructed with ashlar wall facings on exterior and other important areas, using blocks up to 2.5 m long. A wide entrance leads into a central courtyard about 10 m square, flanked by corridors and rooms, including a columned hall, 7.5 by at least 20 m long, filled with huge storage jars (*pithoi*) standing on and set into the floor. Five Cypro-Minoan inscriptions on small clay cylinders have been found in this building, reinforcing its interpretation as administrative. There is no evidence of a religious function for it. The size and well-organised plan of the

A cylindrical box for cosmetics; from Kalavassos-*Ayios Dhimitrios*. It is made of glass, silver and gold; H 3.5 cm; early 14th century BC (Nicosia, Cyprus Museum)

25

Mycenaean amphoroid krater decorated on both sides with an octopus with stylised tentacles spreading over the greater part of the surface; H 34 cm; early 14th century BC (Nicosia, Cyprus Museum)

building make it one of the most important so far discovered in Late Bronze Age Cyprus.

Another building uncovered recently at Kalavassos consists of at least fourteen rooms. The finds seem to indicate working and storage as its main functions. The discovery here was a collection of bronze weights which were found in a small hole cut through a floor. They are in the form of cylindrical types (with relief decoration), animal heads, a duck, and a very unusual and finely-made negroid human head; most of them are hollow and were filled with lead.

The site of Kalavassos-*Ayios Dhimitrios* flourished mainly during the second half of the 13th century BC and seems to have been abandoned before the turn of the century.

Another site, which will no doubt soon be in the limelight of Late Bronze Age discoveries in Cyprus, is that of Maroni-*Vournes*,

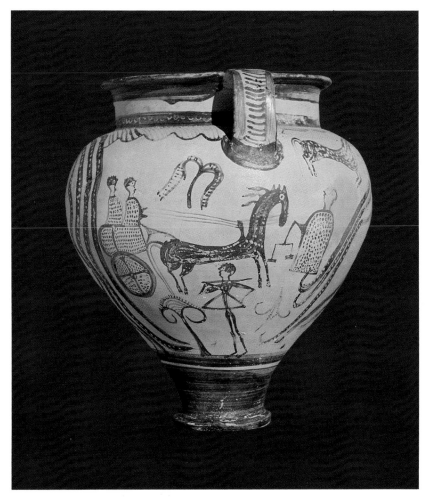

Mycenaean amphoroid krater, known as the 'Zeus Krater', from the principal scene which apparently depicts Zeus holding the 'scales of destiny' before warriors departing for war; from Enkomi; H 37.5 cm; early 14th century BC (Nicosia, Cyprus Museum)

at a short distance east of Kalavassos, where an American–British mission is is now excavating a large building comparable to the administrative building of Kalavassos mentioned above. This building measures 30 by 20 m and was partly built with fine ashlar blocks, of the same quality as those of Kalavassos Building X. It was connected with copper smelting and other industrial activities (an olive-press was discovered within its boundaries) and some of its rooms were used for storage in large *pithoi*. As far as the present evidence goes the building was abandoned at the very end of the 13th century BC, not unlike Kalavassos Building X. The character of this building may have been 'administrative', as Kalavassos Building X, and the proximity of the Kalavassos mine may suggest a co-operation between the two settlements for the export of copper.

A third site which has recently been investigated is that of Alassa-

Pano Mantilaris, (Department of Antiquities) which will soon be
covered by the waters of a dam on the river Kouris. The site lies in
the valley of the river which runs down to Kourion (seven miles to
the south), which also flourished during the Late Bronze Age. The
area excavated so far produced a settlement which was abandoned
soon after 1200 BC. Very close to the excavated area there are large
ashlar blocks lying on the surface, of the kind found at Kalavassos-
Ayios Dhimitrios and elsewhere. They obviously belonged to a
public building and were extracted several years ago when the
owner of the land planted vines. At the site of *Pano Mantilaris*
several tombs have so far been excavated. They are chamber tombs,
of the type which is known also in Palaepaphos, with benches on
either side of a depression which runs from the *stomion* to the rear
end of the chamber.

The site produced ample evidence for metallurgical activity (pot
bellows and copper slag, as well as a votive bronze ingot). No
doubt this must have been one of several Late Bronze Age settlements along the valley of the river Kouris which served as a route
for the transport of copper ore from the mines of Troodos.

The tombs are usually chambers with a passage (dromos). The
burial was accompanied by gifts: vases, jewellery, other luxury
goods such as alabaster and faience vases, cylinder seals, etc.
Occasionally built tombs are found, the chambers of which are
either rectangular with a flat or corbelled roof and with a stepped

dromos, or 'tholoi' with a domed roof, following Near Eastern prototypes.

A chamber tomb excavated at Kalavassos-*Ayios Dhimitrios* in 1984 (KAD T. 11) provides ample evidence for the wealth and importance of this site during the 14th century BC. If we accept the theory that soon after the destruction of Knossos the Mycenaeans needed more copper for weapons and that Cyprus provided this copper, then the wealth of the contents of Tomb 11 could easily be interpreted. Kalavassos, a copper-producing area, must have been a commercial centre where the Mycenaeans would exchange luxury goods for copper, hence the extraordinary wealth of Tomb 11 in Mycenaean pottery, gold (432 g in weight), ivory and glass objects, which surpass in quality and quantity even the contents of the richest 14th-century tombs of Enkomi. By the beginning of the

Silver bowl, inlaid with gold and *niello;* from Enkomi; H 6 cm, D 15.7 cm; early 14th century BC (Nicosia, Cyprus Museum)

Clay tablet inscribed in the
Cypro-Minoan script; from
Enkomi; H 10 cm,
W 9 cm; 13th century BC

14th century the Mycenaean ships must have ploughed the eastern
Mediterranean, trading not only in Mycenaean goods but in other
peoples' goods as well, a role which was taken over several centuries later by the Phoenicians. When the 14th-century BC levels of
Kalavassos-*Ayios Dhimitrios* will have been excavated the picture
will no doubt be further elucidated.

Trade in copper resulted in the influx of considerable wealth as is
apparent from the quality and quantity of gifts which were deposited in the tombs of rich merchants also at other sites such as
Enkomi, Kition, Hala Sultan Tekké.

In addition to the numerous types and fabrics of Cypriot vases
from tombs and settlements of the Late Bronze Age II period there
is also a profusion of Mycenaean pottery. Though pottery from the
Greek mainland and Crete made its appearance in Cyprus during
the 16th and 15th centuries BC, it was after *c.* 1400 BC that such
pottery was brought to the island in quantity. There has long been
controversy among scholars as to the place of manufacture of these
Mycenaean vases: whether all were imported from such centres as
the Argolid in the Peloponnese, or whether some at least were

Faience rhyton; from
Kition; H 26.8 cm; 13th
century BC
(Nicosia, Cyprus Museum)

made in Cyprus by Mycenaean artists who established themselves on the island together with merchants after 1400 BC when the Mycenaeans expanded *en masse* eastwards. Whatever the solution of this problem may be, the fact remains that extraordinarily large numbers of Mycenaean vases of the 14th and 13th centuries BC have been found in Cyprus, particularly of the so-called 'pictorial' style which must have been favoured by the local population. Such vases are decorated with purely Aegean motifs and compositions and constitute a fine expression of Mycenaean art, with occasional influences from the Near East, especially in the repertory of shapes.

Other artistic accomplishments of the 14th and 13th centuries BC illustrate not only the taste of the Cypriots but also the cosmopolitan character of the urban centres in which this art flourished. There is a preference for a combined style which betrays both Near Eastern and Aegean elements as is evidenced in glyptics and jewellery. The gold diadems with embossed decoration of sphinxes, flowers etc., are cases in point. Worthy of special mention are two exceptional pieces which were found in Cyprus and date to the 14th and 13th centuries respectively. Whether they were made locally or were imported is not certain, but they indicate the

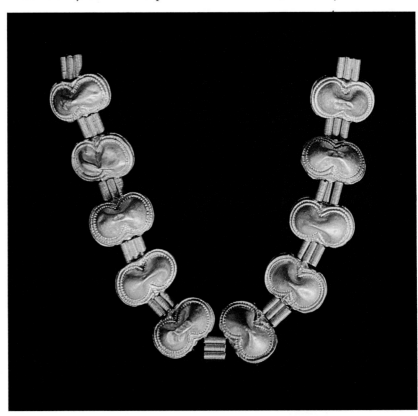

Necklace with gold beads in
the form of figure-of-eight
shields and tubular spacers
of gold wire; from Enkomi;
L 31.7 cm; 13th
century BC
(Nicosia, Cyprus Museum)

32

artistic taste which prevailed among the island's inhabitants. The first is a hemispherical silver bowl with a wishbone handle from a 14th-century BC tomb at Enkomi. It is decorated with ox-heads and flowers in an inlaid technique with gold and a black substance known as *niello*. Only one other vase, found at Dendra in the Peloponnese, is comparable. The second is a conical rhyton (ritual vase) of faience from a tomb at Kition, dating to the second half of the 13th century BC. Its surface is covered with blue enamel and it is decorated in three registers with galloping animals, a hunting scene and running spirals. The decoration is painted in yellow and black or inlaid in red enamel. The style of the motifs is characteristic of the mixed Aegeo-Oriental style mentioned above.

Writing would have been a necessity in this developed and sophisticated Cypriot society during the Late Bronze Age, and even more so in a country whose economy depended largely on trade

An altar built of ashlar blocks, topped by 'horns of consecration'; in the courtyard of a rural sanctuary near Myrtou; early 12th century BC

34

with neighbouring countries. The Cypro-Minoan script developed and became current throughout the island. Though long written documents in the form of baked clay tablets of a cushion-shaped variety like those of the Near East have been found only at Enkomi, there is evidence of the script in all parts of the island. Signs from it are engraved or painted on vases or engraved on bronzes, cylinder seals, clay balls, ivory objects, clay loomweights, etc. There are about eighty signs in the Cypro-Minoan script. Several attempts have been made to decipher the Enkomi tablets but no satisfactory results have yet been reached and the language of the documents remains unknown. Several theories have been advanced, the latest being that it is Hurrian. What is certain is that these tablets are not lists of objects or inventories, like the tablets of the Mycenaean and Minoan palaces, but continuous texts; it has been suggested that they may be poems. Some texts in the Cypro-Minoan script have also been found at Ugarit, the cosmopolitan town on the Syrian coast opposite Cyprus, with which the island maintained close commercial relations. The suggestion has been put forward that there was a commercial colony of Cypriots at Ugarit.

At this time of lively interrelations in the eastern Mediterranean, in which Cyprus played such an active role, it is not surprising that the island should be mentioned in Near Eastern texts. In the correspondence found in the palace of Akhenaten at Tell el-Amarna in Upper Egypt dating *c.* 1375-1350 BC between the Pharaoh and the King of Cyprus, which is called Alashiya, it is recorded that the King of Alashiya used to send copper ingots to the Pharaoh as tribute for Egypt's peace-keeping role in the eastern Mediterranean. (Some scholars, however, still do not accept the equation of Alashiya with Cyprus.) The island was known even earlier as a copper-producing country, since it is also mentioned in the tablets from Alalakh in Syria and Mari in Mesopotamia in the 18th and 17th centuries BC respectively. There is valuable information concerning the internal problems of the King of Alashiya in his correspondence with the Egyptian Pharaoh. In one letter the King explains that for three years he had not been able to send the amount of copper promised to the Pharaoh because most men in his country had been killed and there was nobody to smelt it. This may have been because of the invasions of the Lukki from western Anatolia who are mentioned in the same correspondence.

Reference to Cyprus (Alashiya) is also made in the Hittite tablets. The Hittites claimed that Cyprus formed part of their empire, but archaeological evidence is lacking and therefore this may simply be a boastful assertion.

The end of the 13th century BC witnessed the disruption of Mycenaean society on the Greek mainland and the destruction and abandonment of the main Mycenaean centres in the Peloponnese

35

such as Mycenae, Tiryns and Pylos. The inhabitants of these towns left their homes and sought their fortunes by sailing eastwards. On their way to the eastern Mediterranean, a route which they knew already from their trading ancestors, they may have passed by Anatolia where they were joined by other bands of adventurers with whom they raided coastal towns until they finally reached the eastern Mediterranean. We propose that these were the 'Peoples of the Sea' who are mentioned in oriental documents.

Their appearance coincides with major events in Cyprus: there is a catastrophe at Enkomi and Sinda, changes at Kition, Myrtou-*Pighades*, Apliki and Hala Sultan Tekké, abandonment of Kalavassos-*Ayios Dhimitrios*, Maroni-*Vournes* and Pyla-*Kokkinokremos*; Maa-*Palaeokastro* and Episkopi-*Bamboula* lasted a little longer. It should be emphasised that all these events in Cyprus do not happen at exactly the same moment but form episodes of the same phenomenon extending over a period of several decades (see below).

Some of the 'Sea Peoples' may have settled in Cyprus and rebuilt the destroyed cities, while others may have continued eastwards to the Syro-Palestinian coast, where they seized and occupied towns belonging to their Canaanite predecessors. There must have been several groups of such adventurers and soldiers of fortune roaming around the eastern Mediterranean. Egyptian records graphically tell how *c.* 1186 BC one of these groups invading Egypt was defeated by Rameses III. There is an echo of these troubled times in the correspondence between the King of Alashiya and King Hammurabi of Ugarit with whom Cyprus had an alliance. They exchanged information on the appearance of foreign ships near their coasts and advised each other on what measures should be taken to avert the dangers which menaced their lands.

The period which followed the destruction of the main cities of Cyprus is known as Late Cypriote III and begins soon after 1200 BC. Though it is not easy to define with certainty the chronological limits of the various phases of this period and the events which brought about the destruction and rebuilding of the coastal towns, recent archaeological discoveries have thrown light on the matter. On the promontory of Maa-*Palaeokastro*, on the west coast in the Paphos District, the latest excavations have revealed a well-fortified military outpost built at a time when Mycenaean IIIB pottery was in use, at the very end of the 13th century BC. This outpost was utilised for less than fifty years, and since there was no previous continuity at the site it is easy to define the beginning and end of the settlement. Two distinct building periods have been observed. The first is associated with the construction of a formidable 'cyclopean' wall, 3.5-4 m thick, to defend the settlement from the sea and from inland; there was also a building, constructed of ashlar blocks near

37

Bronze statuette of a male
figure wearing a conical
helmet with horns; known
as 'The Horned God'; from
Enkomi; H 54.2 cm; early
12th century BC
(Nicosia, Cyprus Museum)

the dog-leg city gate, which may be an administrative building. There were also other buildings, consisting of storerooms at the basement with residences on the first floor, which either belonged to prominent members of the settlement or were also administrative. These were violently destroyed by fire at a time when Mycenaean IIIC:1 pottery (locally made) had already been introduced, about the beginning of the 12th century BC. New houses were built on a smaller scale and much more modest in character above the debris of the destroyed houses. These were abandoned at a time when Mycenaean IIIC:1 pottery was still in use, in any case before the middle of the 12th century. The inhabitants may have shifted gradually to the nearest urban centre of Palaepaphos.

A second military outpost has recently been investigated on the plateau of a hill at Pyla-*Kokkinokremos* north-east of Kition. The duration of this settlement was even shorter than that of Maa-*Palaeokastro*. There is only one floor in the buildings along the ridge of the plateau which were used at the same time as storerooms and guardrooms. Mycenaean IIIB and local pottery of the very end of the 13th century BC was found but little or no Mycenaean IIIC:1 wares. The settlement was abandoned very abruptly, the inhabitants having left behind them their treasures, hoping to return and rescue them, but they never did.

The newcomers whom we find at Maa-*Palaeokastro* and Pyla-*Kokkinokremos* are sometimes referred to as Achaeans, a name which is given to the Mycenaean Greeks by Homer. Though it is too early yet to speak about a complete colonisation of Cyprus by these Achaeans at the beginning of the 12th century BC, no doubt we have the initial stages of it. The phenomenon of 'colonisation' is a long and complex one and may have lasted for about one century, with the continuous arrival of new waves of Greeks from the Aegean. It is only at the beginning of the 11th century BC that the process of colonisation is completed.

A site which was very prominent during the whole of the Late Bronze Age is that near the Larnaca Salt Lake, excavated by a Swedish mission. Remains of buildings (including some constructed with ashlars) and dating to the early 12th century BC have been uncovered, as well as some rich burials which produced bronze vessels and jewellery. We mention from this site the discovery of a silver bowl with an engraved inscription in the Ugaritic alphabet, illustrating the relations between Cyprus and the opposite Syrian coast.

The beginning of the 12th century BC heralds a new era for Cyprus. The newcomers inject a new vigour into the cultural and artistic life of the island, introducing new skills in metallurgy, building and art.

At Enkomi the city wall was reinforced and a new grid was

39

Ivory draughts box; from Enkomi; L 29 cm; early 12th century BC (London, British Museum)

established for the whole town, crossed by streets running from one end of the city wall to the other and intersecting at right angles, connecting the various city gates with one another. There was a paved 'public square' at about the middle of town. Public buildings were constructed of large hewn blocks of stone (ashlars). The sanctuary of the 'Horned God' is noteworthy, consisting of a hall and two inner cult rooms. In the hall was a sacrificial altar and a table of offerings around which were found large numbers of skulls of horned animals, mainly oxen. These were probably worn as masks during ritual ceremonies; there were also many bowls for libations. The god who was worshipped in this sanctuary was a fertility god, whose bronze cult statue was found in one of the inner cult rooms. He was a god who protected cattle and shepherds. He appears as a youth wearing a kilt and a horned helmet and has been identified with 'Apollo Keraeatas' (the horned Apollo) who was worshipped on the mountains of Arcadia and who may have been introduced to Cyprus by the Achaean settlers. On one inscription of the 4th century BC the name of a god called Apollo Keraeatas is mentioned and on another that of Apollo Alasiotas (Apollo of Alasia, the god of Cyprus). Both these names may have been attributed to the Horned God of Enkomi whose cult was to survive in the island for at least seven centuries.

A second sanctuary uncovered at Enkomi and constructed with ashlar blocks consists of a propylaeum and a cella (main hall). In the centre of the cella there was a stone pillar, perhaps an element incorporated from Mycenaean religion in which the pillar cult is well attested. Next to the pillar base there was a large stone capital of 'Mycenaean' type and a well. A third sanctuary was constructed at Enkomi around the middle of the 12th century BC. It comprises a rectangular east-west oriented hall or cella (16.4 x 9.6 m), with a small room (2 x 1.9 m) in the north-east corner and a second one (2.5 x 3.5 m) to the west of the principal hall. The entrance was through a porch from the south-west. There was a hearth in the cella and two stone blocks which were used as tethering blocks for sacrificial victims. In the small room in the north-east corner the bronze cult statue of a bearded god was found. He stands on a base in the form of a copper ingot and is fully armed with greaves of a Mycenaean type, shield and spear. He is known as the 'Ingot God' and has been identified with the god who protects the copper mines of Cyprus. A statuette of a female divinity of Cypriot manufacture and of the same date is now in the Ashmolean Museum at Oxford. She also stands on a base in the shape of a copper ingot and is identified with a goddess symbolising the fertility of copper mines. Dual divinities are common in the ancient world and these two, connected with metallurgy which was of primary importance to the island's economy, call to mind the Homeric association of Hephaestos, the smith-god of Greek mythology, with Aphrodite.

At Kition a 'sacred area' was uncovered at the northernmost part of the town near the city wall. I have already mentioned that a 'sacred area' with two sanctuaries and a 'sacred garden' existed there in Late Bronze Age II. During the Late Bronze Age III period one of the small sanctuaries (sanctuary 3) was replaced by a much larger one (sanctuary 1) and sanctuary 2 was remodelled. Two further sanctuaries (4 and 5) were constructed in the same area. Sanctuary 1 consists of a large rectangular roofed courtyard with two lateral entrances, and a narrow compartment at the west end of the hall which was the Holy-of-Holies and communicated with the court-yard through three openings. This is one of the largest sanctuaries known from the period, measuring 33.6 m in length and 22 m in width. It is built of large ashlar blocks, some of them measuring 3.5 m in width and 1.5 m in height. On the south façade of the temple there are graffiti of ships, very appropriate for a harbour town from where vessels loaded with copper ingots would set sail for the Near East and the Aegean. Votive stone anchors were also offered in the sanctuaries by sailors to the Baal of sea-farers. The other three sanctuaries were constructed on Near Eastern models, comprising courtyard and a Holy-of-Holies.

In the Holy-of-Holies of sanctuary 4 a hoard of ivories was found, among which was a pipe for the smoking of opium. Opium-smoking was known in antiquity for medicinal purposes and in sanctuaries was perhaps used for divine revelation through dreams. There are indications that Cyprus was exporting opium to

Ivory mirror handle; from Palaepaphos; L 21.5 cm; early 12th century BC (Nicosia, Cyprus Museum)

Bronze statuette of a male
figure with shield and spear
standing on an ingot; from
Enkomi; H 35 cm; middle
of the 12th century BC
(Nicosia, Cyprus Museum)

Egypt in specially-made flasks. A perforated cylindrical vase, probably also intended for the inhaling of smoke, was found in the adjacent sanctuary 5. Skulls of oxen and other horned animals were revealed on the floor of sanctuary 5, as at Enkomi; they would have been worn by the priests and worshippers during ritual performances. In addition to the main sanctuaries, two large open courtyards called *temene* were excavated adjoining the sanctuaries. In both there was a table of offerings and an altar for animal sacrifices. The table of offerings is associated with stone horns of consecration, a symbol of Creto-Mycenaean religion. A monumental altar crowned by similar stone horns of consecration was found in a sanctuary at Myrtou-*Pigadhes* near the north-west court.

The sanctuary of Aphrodite at Palaepaphos was a major religious centre during the whole of the 1st millennium BC. It was constructed during the Late Bronze Age III period with huge ashlar blocks, as at sanctuary 1 at Kition. Stone horns of consecration were found in the area of the sanctuary as well as 'Mycenaean' stone capitals.

The 'sacred area' of Kition is in the immediate vicinity of workshops for the smelting of copper. Moreover the workshops communicated directly with the sanctuaries, which would suggest a close relationship between metallurgy and religion. This phenomenon is encountered at other Late Bronze Age sanctuaries in Cyprus, for example at Athienou north of Kition, and is also known at Near Eastern sites. The idea was to place metallurgy, the basis of the economy of Cyprus, under the protection of the gods, while at the same time allowing the religious authorities to control the daily production of copper and thus its export. Storerooms for offerings and for the general use of the main sanctuary 1 were also revealed at Kition.

I have already referred to the military architecture of this period, namely two 'cyclopean' walls. They were built in their lower courses of two rows of large stone blocks, the outer row being of larger blocks, and a core of rubble. The superstructure was of sun-dried bricks. There were bastions against the walls, similar to those uncovered at Kition and Enkomi. Cyclopean walls have also been found at Maa-*Palaeokastro* (with dog-leg gate) and at Sinda. At Pyla-*Kokkinokremos* a 'casemate' wall was found, recalling Near Eastern prototypes.

The newcomers, with their advanced metallurgical techniques, made a major contribution to the artistic production of Cyprus during the 12th century BC. The two bronze statues of the divinities of Enkomi illustrate this, as do a series of remarkable bronze four-sided stands, resting on four wheels, which are decorated with pictorial compositions in the *ajouré* (cut-out) technique and which are fine examples of Cypriot craftsmanship. They were doubtless

Ivory plaque carved on both sides in the *ajouré* technique, representing the Egyptian god Bes. The lower tenon bears an inscription in Cypro-Minoan script; from Kition; H 22 cm; 12th century BC (Nicosia, Cyprus Museum)

43

Bronze four-sided stand
with bulls in relief;
H 10.8 cm; 13th century
BC
(Nicosia, Cyprus Museum)

influenced by ivory carving which also flourished on the island.
There is a profusion of bronze vases and weapons in tombs. Swords
of Aegean type are introduced to the island as well as a new light-
framed war-chariot which replaced the old-fashioned Mycenaean
chariot with a solid body. The draught box from Enkomi, now in
the British Museum, is carved with hunting scenes and animal
compositions on all four sides, and is truly a masterpiece betraying
Aegean and Near Eastern stylistic tendencies. A plaque representing the god Bes, carved in the *ajouré* technique, was found in
sanctuary 4 at Kition. Remarkable also are the ivory handles of
mirrors from Enkomi and Palaepaphos which are decorated with
human and animal figures in lively compositions.

We should also mention the appearance at several Late Bronze
Age sites in Cyprus (e.g. Enkomi, Kition, Sinda, Hala Sultan

44

Tekké, Maa) of a new fabric, known as Handmade Burnished ware or 'Barbarian' ware. It first appeared in the Aegean towards the very end of the 13th century BC and is associated with people who came down to the Greek peninsula and to Crete from the north (the Balkans) or the north-east. The appearance of this fabric in Cyprus soon after 1200 BC is of great historical significance and strengthens the evidence for the arrival in the island of foreign elements from the Aegean soon after 1200 BC.

The beginning of the 11th century BC witnessed a renewal of contacts with the Aegean. New ceramic styles were introduced, probably by people who fled from the Aegean after the 'Dorian' invasion and finally settled on Cyprus. Some of them may have been Cretans, judging from the Sub-Minoan influence not only in the ceramics but also in coroplastic art and even religious affairs. For the first time on the island the 'goddess with uplifted arms' appears who is predominant in Crete and who in Cyprus is identified with the goddess of fertility. We find her in the sanctuaries of Kition, Enkomi and elsewhere. The anthropomorphic 'centaur' or sphinx, in a form known from Crete, was also introduced. Large bicephalic 'centaurs' or sphinxes were found in the sanctuary of the Ingot God at Enkomi.

Other arts flourished at this period, particularly jewellery where the introduction of the new cloisonné technique is evidenced. There are some superb specimens of this technique which previously was thought to have been invented much later. A gold sceptre has a globular head topped by two falcons and is decorated in cloisonné, having inlaid enamel of different colours within small compartments separated from each other by thin walls of gold. The same technique was also applied to the bezel of gold rings from Palaepaphos dating to the 12th century BC.

In metalwork various objects such as the bronze fibula (safety-pin) are of Aegean origin. This indicates that women's dress fashions were influenced by newcomers from the Aegean. Hitherto Cypriot women had used ordinary pins to fasten their dresses.

Important changes are also attested in funerary architecture, a phenomenon which occurs for the first time since the arrival of the Achaean colonists. Tombs now have small rectangular chambers with long narrow dromoi. Such tombs existed in Rhodes and Crete and thus indicate the route taken by the colonists before they reached Cyprus. This last wave of Achaean colonists must be those who are referred to in mythical tradition concerning the foundation of cities in Cyprus after the end of the Trojan War, for example Teucer is the traditional founder of Salamis and Agapenor of Paphos. The 11th century BC witnesses the establishment of new cities in succession to those of the Late Bronze Age which had been destroyed by a major catastrophe, perhaps an earthquake or a flood,

Gold and enamel sceptre; from Kourion-*Kaloriziki;* L 16.5 cm; 11th century BC
(Nicosia, Cyprus Museum)

45

shortly before the middle of the 11th century BC. Thus Salamis succeeds Enkomi on the east coast. Enkomi was gradually abandoned after the silting up of its inner harbour but there was a period of about twenty-five years from *c*. 1075 to *c*. 1050 BC when both towns co-existed. Other towns, such as Palaepaphos and Kition, were not abandoned immediately. Kition was rebuilt and continued to be inhabited until *c*. 1000 BC, when the town finally shifted towards the sea following the silting up of its harbour.

The events of the first half of the 11th century BC laid the foundations for the future historical and cultural development of Cyprus. The cultural changes in the island which had started as a very slow process *c*. 1200 BC are now complete. Meanwhile the Mycenaean aristocracy dominated the local population both politically and culturally while at the same time accepting influences both from the local indigenous culture and also from the Syro-Palestinian coast, with which they kept up trade relations as their forefathers had done in the 14th and 13th centuries BC. It was during this time that the Greek language was introduced to the island, a fact which had recently been demonstrated by the discovery of the first Greek inscription in a tomb at Palaepaphos. We may now speak about the Hellenisation of Cyprus, an event of major importance.

The Late Bronze Age may thus be described as one of the most formative periods in the life of ancient Cyprus. It prescribed the island's evolution through the 1st millennium BC; indeed, in some ways, down to the present day.

III

EARLY IRON AGE

(CYPRO-GEOMETRIC)

The Rise of the Ancient Kingdoms

c. 1100 – 700 BC

Prof. J.N. Coldstream

The 11th century BC is one of the most decisive periods in the history of Cyprus. In archaeological language, the island now enters its Iron Age. Yet the substitution of iron tools and weapons for bronze is but a trivial change when compared to the massive immigration from the Aegean world which was now transforming Cyprus into a predominantly Greek-speaking land. Earlier, Mycenaean settlers had merged with the indigenous Cypriots at Enkomi and the other mercantile cities of the Late Bronze Age. Now, whole communities were fleeing from the final ruin of Mycenaean civilisation at home, and were to grow into the capital cities of the ancient Greek kingdoms: Kourion, Paphos, Marion, Soloi, Lapithos, and Salamis which now replaced Enkomi as the leading settlement in eastern Cyprus.

Various legends place their foundations at the close of the heroic age, in the aftermath of the Trojan War. Thus Pausanias tells us how King Agapenor of Tegea in Arcadia, sailing home from Troy, was blown off course and settled at Paphos, where he built the temple of Aphrodite. Tacitus, however, records an earlier and native Cypriot founder Kinyras; it is surely no coincidence that the site of Palaepaphos (Kouklia), alone of the ancient Greek kingdoms, has a history going back into the Bronze Age. Kourion, according to Herodotus, was founded by Argives; he receives some corroboration from the place-name of Asine, brought from the ancient port of the Argolid to an ancient village in the territory of Kourion.

Flask, White Painted ware. The bird-shape for flasks was introduced to Cyprus from Crete and appears in the Cypriot pottery repertoire from around 1125 BC; L 22 cm; *c.* 1050-1000 BC (London, British Museum)

Likewise Salamis was so named by its founder Teucer, half-brother of the great Ajax, after the island in the Saronic Gulf which had been his original home.

If the foundation legends preserve at least a kernel of historical truth, the arrival of Aegean immigrants *en masse* is amply confirmed by archaeological evidence. New to Cyprus at this time are the terracotta figures of a fertility goddess rendered in the Mycenaean manner, raising her arms in benediction; given the extreme conservatism of indigenous Cypriot worship, this sudden introduction of a new type of idol must imply a new Aegean strain in religious practice. Another novelty of 11th-century Cyprus is the first appearance of the typically-Mycenaean chamber tomb with a long dromos leading into a carefully-cut rectangular chamber, quite distinct from the traditional Cypriot form where the chamber opens out of a small vertical shaft. Tombs of the Mycenaean type, often richly furnished and suggestive of a newly-arrived Greek aristocracy, have come to light at Kourion-*Kaloriziki*, Lapithos-*Kastros*, Salamis, Gastria-*Alaas* north of Salamis and most recently in the Paphian cemetery of Palaepaphos-*Skales*.

The five inscribed objects from the Palaepaphos cemetery are of great historical importance. A bronze bowl, a stray find, bears a graffito in the indigenous Cypro-Minoan syllabic script, confirming its survival into the 11th century. The other four inscriptions all come from a single rich tomb of *c.* 1050-950 BC. There a few more syllabic signs, too few for their script to be identified, occur on a stone, and on two bronze obeloi or spits. On another obelos, however, a fifth inscription foreshadows the Cypro-Classical syllabary of later times and yields the genitive case of a Greek personal name in a form later shared by the Arcadian and Cypriot dialects: Opheltau, i.e. belonging to Opheltes. Here, then, we have the earliest known syllabic Greek inscription from Cyprus, contemporary with the latest in Cypro-Minoan, and establishing beyond doubt the origin of the new settlers; they had only to adapt the

Terracotta statuette of a goddess with uplifted arms; from Morphou-*Toumba tou Skourou;* H 16 cm; 1050-950 BC
(Nicosia, Cyprus Museum)

49

Deep bowl of White Painted ware, decorated in matt black with geometric patterns and a central panel with trees and birds; from Lapithos-*Ayia Anastasia;* H 14 cm; D 18.5 cm; 1050-950 BC (Nicosia, Cyprus Museum)

earlier script to the needs of their own language, thereby evolving the Greek syllabary which we know as Cypro-Classical. So these finds bring with them a long-awaited confirmation that the art of writing was never forgotten in Cyprus, at a time when it had certainly vanished from Greece. Nor is it surprising that this evidence of continuity in literacy should have come from the Paphos region, which at the end of the Bronze Age had mercifully escaped the devastation and turmoil suffered by Enkomi, Kition, and the other great cities of eastern Cyprus.

While their kinsmen in the Aegean had already been plunged into a Dark Age of poverty, isolation and illiteracy, the Greeks of Cyprus still enjoyed a modest prosperity in their new homes, and were still freely in touch with their eastern neighbours. Many tombs contain simple gold ornaments — finger rings, earrings and pendants — often of Levantine character. Lavish bronze cauldrons, representing both Aegean and eastern types, have recently come to light in the Palaepaphos-*Skales* cemetery. But the choicest work of this age is the gold sceptre from a rich tomb at Kourion-*Kaloriziki*, with an orb crowned by two hawks, elaborated with polychrome cloisonné enamelling: a tomb gift in every way worthy of a prince.

The fine painted pottery, as one might expect, acquires a strong Aegean flavour from 1100 BC onwards. After the disappearance of the native Bronze Age fabrics there arises a new tradition of painted ornament on a pale ground, destined to last all through the Cypriot Iron Age. The first phase, *c.* 1100-1050 BC, is called Proto-White Painted (because it foreshadows the White Painted pottery of the ensuing Cypro-Geometric period) or Proto-Bichrome if a second reddish colour is added to the usual black. This bichrome idea is of

50

Levantine origin, as are a few of the shapes, for instance, the lentoid 'pilgrim flask'. Otherwise the new style is purely Aegean, derived from the Sub-Mycenaean of the Greek mainland and the Sub-Minoan of Crete, and yet far superior to either in the quality of its fabric and in the variety of its ornament. For example there are specimens, some lavishly decorated, of the stirrup-jar, the large container of perfumed oil with deep roots in the Mycenaean past. The tall jar (or pyxis) is a shape of Cretan character; in one instance the painter has had the imagination to add to its austere rectilinear ornament an oriental lotus flower. Even figured subjects are sometimes attempted: birds, fish, agrimi (wild goats) with Cretan affinities; now and again, a crudely simplified human being.

Then follows the pottery of Cypro-Geometric I (c. 1050-950 BC), the first phase of the island's Iron Age. This style is largely contemporary with Greek Proto-Geometric, to which it is related through a common Aegean ancestry, even though direct communication with the Aegean was now rapidly declining. The leading wares are White Painted I and Bichrome I. The vase-forms — notably amphorae, jugs, plates, cups, and kylikes or drinking

Phoenician temple of Astarte, Kition, founded in c. 850 BC on the ruins of a Late Bronze Age temple, and in continuous use until the fall of the Phoenician kingdom in 312 BC

51

Gold plaque decorated in *repoussé;* from Kouklia-*Skales;* H 9.4 cm; 950-750 BC
(Nicosia, Cyprus Museum)

bowls — continue to be robust and well proportioned, carrying just enough decoration to define the shape. The ornament, however, is less varied than before, and more austerely abstract. A pleasant exception to this austerity is a kylix showing a charming picture of two little birds settled upon the shoots of a palm tree. Their miniature silhouette style recalls the pottery of Hama in north Syria, and this is one of many Cypriot renderings of the oriental Tree of Life flanked by a symmetrical pair of living creatures. The shape, however, is directly descended from the late Mycenaean deep bowl, with the addition of the high foot which is a common hallmark of this phase.

No fresh impulses came from foreign parts to enliven the pottery of Cypro-Geometric II (*c.* 950-850 BC), which was on the whole an uneventful, lethargic, and to us somewhat obscure period. The same wares and shapes continued, in debased form. As the descendants of the original Greek settlers merged with the indigenous Cypriots the vitality of their way of life was becoming increasingly diluted. Let us take stock of this gradual symbiosis, from the 11th century onwards.

As yet, we know very little of any town site in the Early Iron Age, owing to lack of excavation; but, as in several earlier periods of Cypriot antiquity, the tombs and their contents come to our rescue. In some of the Greek kingdoms it seems that the native communities must have been absorbed into the new Greek towns. Thus, near Kourion, the indigenous site of Episkopi-*Bamboula* was deserted by the end of the 11th century, although without any sign of violence; Kourion, with its rich Greek cemetery at *Kaloriziki*, supplanted *Bamboula* in much the same way as Enkomi had been superseded by Greek Salamis. Again, far inland, the western acropolis of Idalion had been a stronghold and sanctuary of the indigenous Cypriots during the troubles at the end of the Bronze Age; but this site, too, was deserted in the 11th century, when the arrival of Greeks in the area is indicated by the fine Proto-White Painted pottery from tombs in the plain below.

At Lapithos the merging of the two peoples was more gradual, and possibly more peaceful. Each had its own cemetery of chamber tombs, the native form being usual in Lapithos-*Skales*, while the Mycenaean type with long dromos at first prevailed in Lapithos-*Kastros*. Extra bodies in several of the latter tombs have been interpreted as the sacrifices of slaves destined to attend their masters in the next world — evidence of a somewhat savage temperament in some of the incumbents. But by the 9th century this Mycenaean type of tomb is dying out, as even the *Kastros* tombs begin to follow the traditional form. In funerary matters, at least, the Greeks of Lapithos were themselves going native.

One indigenous community, on the south coast, was never taken over by the Greeks. This was Amathus, first settled in the 11th century, and destined to become one of the leading states of the Cypriot Iron Age, no less powerful and prosperous than the Greek kingdoms. From its early days, Amathus was an unusually outward-looking place, trading freely with both Greeks and Levantines, and freely accepting ideas from both directions. It is a curious paradox that during Cypro-Geometric II, when Cyprus had few links with the outside world, it was Amathus which received the first post-Mycenaean imports of pottery from the Greek homeland, three Proto-Geometric drinking vessels from the island of Euboea. The discovery of similar imports at Tyre, however, shows that Amathus was a convenient staging post for Greek shipping on its way to the Phoenician metropolis.

Some time well back in the 9th century, Cyprus was aroused from her lethargy by a new impetus from the East. Kition, whose sacred area of the Late Bronze Age had been derelict since 1000 BC, was now resettled by colonists from Tyre, the leading city of the Phoenician homeland and the metropolis of a flourishing commercial empire. The coming of the Phoenicians to Cyprus is but one stage of a steady westward expansion which was to take them as far afield as western Sicily, Sardinia, Carthage and Spain. A Phoenician inscription on an 8th-century bronze bowl gives the name of their Cypriot outpost as Qart Hadasht (New Town) — the same name as was given to Carthage and Cartagena — and reveals that it was then a colony in the imperial sense, ruled by a governor responsible to the King of Tyre. Its foundation may well have occurred during the reign of King Ethbaal of Tyre (887-856 BC), father of the ill-famed Jezebel who became Queen of Israel, for Ethbaal had been the High Priest of Astarte before he seized the throne as a usurper and it was to Astarte, goddess of fertility, love and death, that the first colonists of Kition dedicated the finest temple yet found anywhere in the Phoenician world.

The Phoenician masons built this temple upon the massive ashlar ruins of the Late Bronze Age Sanctuary 1 (see Chapter II). What had once been an open courtyard now became a columned hall, with colonnades on both sides and a narrow central aisle open to the sky. At the far end a tripartite Holy-of-Holies was roofed over and approached through three doors side by side. In front of the central door are two huge square bases for free-standing pillars; we are reminded of the famous pillars Jachin and Boaz which had stood in the temple built by earlier Phoenician masons for King Solomon in Jerusalem. After an accidental fire in around 800 BC the temple of Astarte was rebuilt with fewer and stouter columns in the hall, and entrance to the Holy-of-Holies was now confined to the central door.

Once settled at Kition the Phoenicians made no effort as yet to extend their political control elsewhere on the island, but their impact on Cypriot art was immediate. In earlier times Astarte had been no stranger to Cyprus, being easily assimilated with the island's goddess of fertility. But now she begins to appear in Phoenician guise on gold plaques which formed part of a lady's tiara, sometimes in full frontal nudity, and sometimes — as in one of the Lapithos-*Kastros* tombs — as a bust wearing a Phoenician wig. Another important art-form introduced by these Cypro-Phoenicians is the shallow metal bowl decorated inside with figured scenes. One of the earliest is a silver bowl from Idalion of *c.* 800 BC showing an oriental cult scene: a seated goddess is approached by a

Vase known as the 'Hubbard' Amphora, depicting a seated goddess drinking through a siphon; Bichrome ware; probably from Platani; H 68 cm, D (mouth)38 cm; 850–750 BC (Nicosia, Cyprus Museum)

54

Decorated rim of a krater; White Painted ware; from Chrysochou; H 59 cm, D (mouth) 36 cm; 870-750 BC (Nicosia, Cyprus Museum)

The coming of the Phoenicians also increased the repertoire of pottery wares in the Cypro-Geometric III period (*c.* 850-750 BC). To the traditional White Painted and Bichrome they added two important fabrics of their own; Red Slip and Black-on-Red: fabrics which are especially connected with Phoenician commerce and colonisation from Cyprus to Sardinia and Spain. Although samples of both fabrics had previously come to Cyprus as imports, it was only after the foundation of Kition that they were regularly manufactured on the island. A number of Black-on-Red juglets, probably intended for precious unguents, form part of a large deposit to consecrate the rebuilding of the Kition temple after the fire of *c.* 800 BC. To the shiny orange surface of the slip, lines and small circles are added in dull dark paint. Red Slip is similar, but without decoration.

In the traditional fabrics the Geometric ornament becomes much more varied, and regional styles within the island can now be distinguished. A conservative spirit prevails in the west, where small circles are especially popular. Meanwhile eastern Cyprus preferred the motifs to be organised in square panels, and on the whole rectilinear. Eastern potters were also more enterprising in trying out figured themes in which there is now a notable increase. Aesthetically the most successful theme is the isolated bird, easy to draw, and having an obvious appeal to the vase-painter's decorative sense. When more ambitious themes with humans were attempted, the painter's imagination often outran his technique, so that his intention is not always easy to fathom; but even if the scenes appear crude and maladroit to our eyes, they may nevertheless have a rare historical or religious importance. Best known is the Hubbard amphora, an eastern Bichrome III vase with a religious scene recalling that on the Idalion silver bowl. A libation is being offered to an

55

Restored bed of wood, covered with ivory plaques; from Salamis; H 88.6 cm, L 188.5 cm; c. 700 BC (Nicosia, Cyprus Museum)

enthroned lady. She is surely a goddess; behind her is a winged sphinx smelling a flower, and sphinxes do not usually attend mere mortals. In the Syrian manner she prepares to drink through a siphon from various vessels placed on a table for her by an attendant priestess. The bull's head on the extreme left is an age-old symbol of fertility in Cyprus, recalling the shrine models of the Early Bronze Age. The scene continues on the reverse with a chain of female dancers and a male lyre-player.

More baffling are the scenes on a Bichrome III krater. On one side, two palm-trees stand outside what looks like a tripartite building of symmetrical design into which two women have been somehow embodied. Was the painter perhaps thinking of a great oriental shrine, like the Holy-of-Holies at Kition, with its sacred trees outside the forecourt, and its 'women at the window' inside the temple — the sacred courtesans who attended Astarte's worshippers? On the other side of the krater, however, the 'shrine' has come apart, one woman holds a wreath, the other a comb. Possibly the central part of the supposed 'shrine' is also a comb, passed by one lady to the other, but we cannot be sure. Nevertheless, some reference to the Astarte cult is implied.

A good example of the White Painted III style is a krater with a chariot team and rider which comes from Chrysochou near Marion in the far west. This area had been least affected by the orientalising ideas following in the wake of the Phoenicians, and it may be no coincidence that both the shape and the theme have precedents in the Mycenaean chariot kraters. The details of the chariot group, however, are more Assyrian than Greek – especially the horse's elaborate crest, the standard behind the charioteer, the large wheel with many spokes, and the idea of lodging spears in the chariot box. This is the work of an unusually accomplished painter, who brought up to date a traditional theme with the gear of his own day.

These vase paintings take us well into the 8th century, an age of

Restored throne of wood covered with ivory and with cut-out plaques between the arms; from Salamis; H 72 cm; *c.* 700 BC (Nicosia, Cyprus Museum)

57

Two open-work cloisonné ivory plaques; from Salamis; probably originally on the arms of the throne found in the same royal tomb; H 16.4 cm; *c.* 700 BC (Nicosia, Cyprus Museum)

expanding horizons and rapidly increasing prosperity. Mainland Greece was at last recovering from the isolation of her Dark Age. Phoenician merchantmen often hawked their wares in the Aegean and Greek traders from Euboea were established at a new emporium at Al Mina on the north Syrian coast. From the Phoenicians the Greeks quickly learned the art of alphabetic writing, thereby putting an end to several centuries of illiteracy. A steep rise in population caused them to found colonies in Italy and Sicily, and to order their own affairs through the evolution of the *polis* system — the network of small autonomous city-states, each with its own clearly defined republican constitution, and its own centre of public life.

The coastal cities of Cyprus must have profited greatly as staging posts for visitors from East and West, and the lively interplay of Greek and oriental influences added much to the vitality of 8th-century Cypriot art. And yet, in two important respects, Greek and native Cypriots remained aloof from these new developments. Having never forgotten the art of writing since the Bronze Age, they saw no reason to abandon their syllabic signs, even with the more convenient Phoenician alphabet displayed before their eyes at Kition. To the very end of Classical times one syllabary was used for the Cypriot dialect of Greek, another for the Eteo-Cypriot (i.e. the true Cypriot) tongue spoken by the indigenous people of Amathus and elsewhere. In political matters, too, the Cypriots were rigidly conservative. No *polis* system ever took root among them, they were never to know any form of government other than absolute monarchy, inherited from Mycenaean tradition and in line with eastern despotism. So Cyprus remained a land of about ten petty kingdoms, at first wholly independent, and then still enjoying local autonomy even after their nominal submission to the Assyrian Empire in 709 BC (see Chapter IV).

One new development, however, made a profound impression upon the Cypriot Greeks. Memories of the heroic Mycenaean past, embodied in the saga of the Trojan War, had survived orally all through the Greek Dark Age, and were now finding monumental expression in the Homeric *Iliad* and *Odyssey*. Through recitation at public festivals, these and other epics quickly became known throughout the Greek world. Thus a recollection of bygone glories came to be shared by all Greeks whether they lived in the Aegean homeland, or in the western colonies, or in the Greek kingdoms of Cyprus. Indeed, the Cypriot Greeks could boast their own epic poet in Stasinos, whom they claimed to have been Homer's son-in-law; his lost poem, the *Cypria,* formed a long prelude to the *Iliad,* telling of how Aphrodite the Cyprian goddess had provoked the Trojan War through the fatal Judgment of Paris.

Against this historical background, let us now consider the royal tombs of Salamis: the tombs of a small but wealthy kingdom under a Greek monarch and ruling class. While advertising their prosperity with a fine display of oriental luxuries, the Salaminians had also become deeply interested in their Mycenaean roots, as we shall see from the manner in which they honoured their deceased princes.

These tombs, nine in all, occupy a plot of their own to the west of the settlement, but set apart from the cemetery for commoners known as the Cellarka (see Chapter IV). They form a series throughout the 8th and 7th centuries, and most of them were built and furnished on a scale lavish enough to be called royal. We shall concentrate our attention on tomb 79, the best-preserved, and one of the richest tombs ever to be excavated in Cyprus. It received two princely burials, the first shortly before 700 BC and the second shortly after.

Like others in the royal cemetery, this tomb is lined with fine ashlar blocks. The dromos, nearly 13 m wide, leads through an anteroom to a small burial chamber roofed with a huge monolith.

The great width of the dromos was dictated by the special honours paid to royalty. A dead prince would be conveyed to the tomb on his hearse or chariot, which had to be wheeled round so that its back faced the chamber doorway. The team of horses was then slaughtered as though to accompany the master to the next world, and buried with the chariot in the dromos. In this tomb, however, four vehicles and the skeletons of ten horses were found, a four-wheeled hearse and a two-wheeled chariot for each prince. From the chariot with the earlier burial all the metal parts survive, and the impressions left by its wooden parts were clear enough to allow a reasonably certain reconstruction. The whole team was decked out in bronze finery. Each of the four horses wore a breastplate, a pair of massive side pendants, a front band on the head, and a pair of blinkers, all adorned with oriental figured imagery. On the yoke were four standards in the form of an oriental palmette. A bronze warrior in Assyrian armour stood beside each wheel on the linch-pin, each end of which was covered by a hub cap in the form of a sphinx's head.

The other offerings, too, were of royal magnificence. Beside the dromos wall stood two bronze cauldrons. One is of north Syrian type, decorated with twelve protomes or foreparts of living creatures: eight griffins, and four bearded sirens with faces on both sides of their heads. This is by far the most elaborate example of a class which became widely known in the West, and helped to set off an orientalising movement in Greek and Etruscan art.

In the same deposit were the remains of the royal furniture. Like the cauldrons, they went with the first burial, and had been brushed aside in a heap to make way for the second incumbent. As with the vehicles, the perished wood had left clear impressions; thus, with the help of the ivory fittings, it was possible to reconstruct three thrones, a footstool and a bed. The main decoration of the bedstead consists of three ivory friezes carved in relief, portraying kneeling Egyptian gods, interlaced palmette and lotus blooms, and confronting sphinxes. Some details are picked out in blue glass inlays, and there are traces of a gold leaf covering. One of the thrones has a comfortably concave back inlaid with ivory guilloche patterns; to decorate its sides, two splendid pairs of ivory plaques have been set back to back, so that their openwork designs seem to be in the round. One design is a sacred 'Tree of Life' based on the lotus, with palmettes trailing along the ground. The other set presents a sphinx, the guardian of royalty, wearing the crowns of Upper and Lower Egypt, and a characteristically Egyptian headdress; in the field are more lotuses and palmettes. All these ivory panels are in the Phoenician style, a suave blend of Egyptian and Asiatic elements; typically Phoenician, too, is the soft, dreamy expression on the sphinx's face.

Bronze figurine of a soldier.
It was originally attached to
a linchpin of the chariot
found in tomb No 79; from
Salamis; H 26.5 cm;
c. 700 BC
(Nicosia, Cyprus Museum)

61

Furniture of this quality, richly adorned with figured ivory plaques, was an essential amenity in any royal palace of the eastern Mediterranean at this time. When we read in the First Book of Kings of the 'ivory house' built for Ahab, King of Israel, at his new capital of Samaria, this is what is meant. Indeed, the nearest parallels to the Salamis ivories are to be found at other royal seats, some at Samaria, others at the Assyrian capitals of Nimrud and Khorsabad. In each case the Phoenician style predominates in the furniture ivories; and the ruler buried in this tomb, like the kings of Assyria and Israel, must certainly have employed Phoenician craftsmen to decorate his household.

And yet, in spite of all this oriental luxury, these tombs cannot be fully understood without looking westwards, to the ancestral land of the Salaminian kings. In the next world as in this, they were expected to keep a convivial table and a hospitable hearth, so the first prince of tomb 79 was given twelve iron spits or skewers (oboloi) and a pair of iron firedogs in the form of a ship, for roasting meat over a charcoal fire. Similar sets have been found in contemporary aristocratic burials in Argos and east Crete, recalling the gear used by Achilles when he entertained visitors to his tent at Troy; in the *Iliad* even the most distinguished heroes did not disdain

Chariot burial in tomb 79,
Salamis; *c.* 700 BC

62

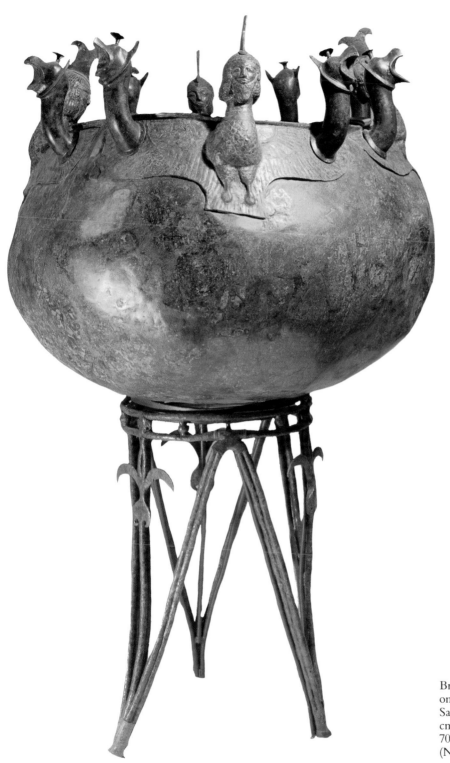

Bronze cauldron supported
on an iron tripod; from
Salamis; H (of cauldron) 55
cm, H (of tripod) 70 cm; *c.*
700 BC
(Nicosia, Cyprus Museum)

the role of chef. Furthermore, almost every stage of a Homeric funeral is mirrored among the burial practices of Salamis. We have already observed how the chariot horses were sacrificed in the dromos, just as Patroclus' team was slaughtered at his burial by his friend Achilles. Sheep and cattle were also sacrificed in Patroclus' honour, and his other offerings included amphorae containing honey and oil; a large bone came to light in tomb 2, while an amphora from tomb 3 is inscribed *elaion*, olive oil, in the Cypriot syllabary. When Patroclus' body had been burnt, his pyre was quenched with wine; a pyre deposit in tomb 1 was covered with a thin muddy layer, above which were six unburnt unbroken vessels for putting out the flames. The hero's ashes were then gathered into a golden urn and wrapped in a linen cloth; large golden vessels are the preserve of epic poetry, but tomb 1 produced a bronze cauldron containing a cremation, with traces of cloth inside. Finally a great mound of earth was raised over a Homeric hero's tomb, like the vast tumulus over tomb 3.

For each one of these practices, taken singly, contemporary parallels can be cited from different lands; but when viewed together their close correspondence with Homeric descriptions of funerals must be more than mere coincidence. One could hardly see in them a conservative adherence to the old Mycenaean practices, since cremation had been foreign to Mycenaean tradition, and no earlier chariot burials are known from Cyprus. It is more likely that the Salaminian burial customs represent a revival of interest in the great deeds of the Mycenaean past, inspired by the circulation of the Homeric and other epic poems. This was the way in which the Greek-Cypriot Kingdom of Salamis chose to honour its dead princes, scions of the heroes who had once ruled over the Aegean island to which the Kingdom owed its origin and its name.

IV

THE ARCHAIC PERIOD

750-475 BC

Dr Veronica Tatton-Brown

The prosperity of Cyprus in the 8th century has already been illustrated by the rich grave goods from the 'Royal' tombs at Salamis. In 750 BC, the beginning of the Archaic period, Assyria began to show increasing aggression towards her neighbours. Under King Tiglath-Pileser III and his successor, Sargon II, Assyria extended her influence in Palestine, Syria and Phoenicia, and Cyprus was eventually reduced to submission in 709 BC.

Sargon II erected a stele at Kition to record this event, describing how seven Cypriot kings paid him homage. In later Assyrian records we read of ten kingdoms and by the 5th century there were eleven, namely: Salamis (the most important), Paphos, Soloi, Kourion, Kition, Kerynia (or Kyrenia), Lapithos, Marion, Amathus, Tamassos and Idalion. These city kingdoms were autonomous and towards the end of the 6th century first struck their own coinage. As Persia was by this time in overall control of the island, the individual coinages adopted the 'Persic' weight system and Persian denominations. The designs and lettering reflect the mixed Cypriot, Greek and Phoenician origins of the population.

It was in the Archaic period that the division of language became more apparent. This, like the coinage, illustrates the mixed population of the island where the Phoenicians were still in control at Kition and the indigenous people at Amathus. The Cypriot syllabic script was used to write both Greek (that is Arcado-Cypriot Greek, probably introduced at the end of the Bronze Age) and Eteo-Cypriot. The latter is still undeciphered but it appears to be a pre-Hellenic and pre-Semitic language probably related to the native Cypriot tongue surviving from the Bronze Age. Most inscriptions in this language come from Amathus and the immediate vicinity. At Kition the majority of inscriptions are in Phoenician and the script is found on both imported and locally-made vessels. The Greek alphabet, which appeared occasionally in the 6th century, was apparently officially introduced by Evagoras I of Salamis in the late 5th century, but it was not widely adopted until nearly a century later.

Assyrian domination lasted less than fifty years and from about 663 BC Cyprus enjoyed a hundred glorious years of independence during which her own civilisation and culture flourished and devel-

Jug, Bichrome ware decorated in the 'freefield' style with a bull sniffing a lotus flower; from Arnadi; H 23.5 cm; 750–650 BC (Nicosia, Cyprus Museum)

oped. Many of the finest Iron Age remains and artefacts date from
that period.

Ordinary people were buried in simple rock-cut chamber tombs
often used on more than one occasion. The 'Royal' tombs at Salamis no doubt served the kings and aristocrats. Splendid tombs built
of well-dressed ashlars with rectangular chambers with saddle or
trapezoidal roofs approached by stepped dromoi (entrance passages) dating from the 7th and 6th centuries have been found at other
city sites including Tamassos, Amathus, Kition, Idalion and Soloi
and elsewhere as at Patriki and Trachonas. The finest are those at
Tamassos built about 600 BC whose architecture in stone imitates
in detail wooden construction. The roofs of the chambers are
beamed. Certain elements are of Phoenician origin like the volute
capitals surmounting the pilasters supporting the entrance doors
and the blind windows in one tomb whose sills are decorated in
relief with a version of the eastern 'Tree of Life' a favourite ornament in several media in Archaic Cyprus.

Another tomb in the 'Royal' necropolis at Tamassos was a

Some of the 2,000 terracotta
figurines from a sanctuary
at Ayia Irini; 750–500 BC
(Nicosia, Cyprus Museum)

67

simple rock-cut chamber tomb, but remains of horses and bronze trappings found in the dromos recall the Homeric practice of sacrificing chariots, horses and slaves prevalent in the 'Royal' tombs at Salamis (see Chapter III). Further evidence for a cult of the dead comes from the Cellarka cemetery at Salamis in use from about 700 to 300 BC and situated south of the 'Royal' necropolis on a low ridge of hard limestone. The tombs here evidently served the ordinary population, being simple rock-cut chamber tombs, occasionally with carved entrances, often used for more than one generation, the earliest burials being pushed aside to make room for the later ones. In the dromoi of some tombs, or close by, pyres were discovered containing in the ashes a number of offerings, all burnt, including vases evidently smashed after a libation had been offered. The practice may have been copied from Athens, although there is no evidence for cremation in the Cellarka cemetery such as was associated with the Athenian pyres.

When the Assyrian Empire finally broke up, at the end of the 7th century, Egypt emerged as the major power and in the middle years of the 6th century held political control over Cyprus. Direct Egyptian influence on Cyprus during the period of domination is not always very apparent, but to this era belongs an interesting tomb on the outskirts of the Koufomeron cemetery at Salamis. The short dromos cut in the rock leads to a rectangular chamber built of fine

Egyptian bronze situla with an inscription in Egyptian hieroglyphs and also an inscription in the Cypriot syllabic script; from Kourion; H 11 cm; 663-525 BC
(Nicosia, Cyprus Museum)

Terracotta model of a shrine with free-standing columns crowned by lotus flower capitals either side of the entrance; from Idalion; H 21 cm; *c*. 7th century BC
(Paris, *Musée du Louvre*)

68

Ox-shaped flask (askos), Black-on-Red ware; from Kourion; H 19 cm; 7th century BC (London, British Museum)

limestone blocks with a vaulted roof and paved floor. The whole of the interior of the chamber is painted like the inside of an Egyptian sarcophagus: the decoration in blue and purple is applied directly to the surface of the stone; on the side walls are lotus flowers and buds on long stems and the ceiling is covered by a network-pattern with rosettes and crosses at the junctions.

In 526/5 BC the Cypriot kings submitted to the Great King of Persia. They had to pay him tribute and place their forces at his disposal, but they retained a certain measure of independence. Four years later Persian control was tightened by including Cyprus in the Fifth Satrapy of the Persian Empire. The island therefore shared the same fate as the East Greek cities of Ionia (on the west coast of modern Turkey). Freedom of movement within the Persian Empire intensified contact between Cyprus and Ionia and Cypriot art became increasingly susceptible to East Greek influence. When the Ionian revolt, an attempt by the East Greek cities to rid themselves

Terracotta female figure wearing a *polos* (tall head-dress) and with upraised arms, perhaps a goddess. Painted decoration in red and black; from Palaepaphos; H 36 cm; 7th century BC (London, British Museum)

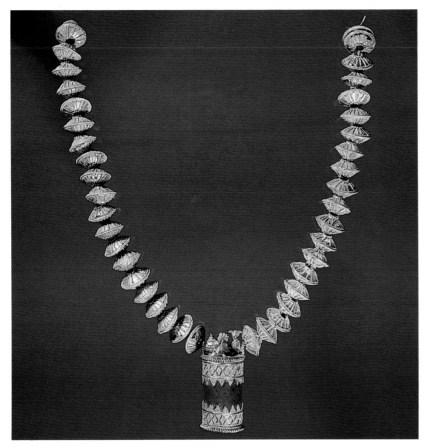

Gold necklace with agate pendant; from the sanctuary of Aphrodite at Arsos; 7th century BC
(Nicosia, Cyprus Museum)

of Persian rule, broke out in 499 BC all the kingdoms of Cyprus except for Amathus joined in at the instigation of Onesilos, the King of Salamis, who had recently dispossessed his brother of the throne. The Persians sent a military force to the island and, having heavily defeated the Cypriots in the field, proceeded in 498 BC to lay siege to the cities which still held out against them, including Paphos.

Excavations at Palaepaphos have graphically revealed the story of the siege. The Persians erected a huge mound against the northeast gate of the city, composed of rubble and broken limestone statues and monuments from an open sanctuary nearby, on to which they drove up their siege engines. The inhabitants meanwhile dug long passages and tunnels underneath the wall leading into the mound in an attempt to undermine it by setting it on fire and they hurled stone missiles on to their attackers. All their efforts were, however, in vain and the city was taken. Soloi also surrendered after holding out for five months and all the cities in Cyprus were finally reduced.

Terracotta statuette of a woman with a syrinx (Panpipes); from Arsos; 650–600 BC
(Nicosia, Cyprus Museum)

The city kingdoms were well fortified, their walls built of mud-brick on stone foundations. At Palaepaphos the wall had towers at intervals and the north-east gate developed slowly from the familiar oriental type with twin rectangular bastions projecting outwards from the city wall flanking a narrow passage. About 500 BC, shortly before the siege, both the wall and gate were considerably strengthened, the mudbrick faces being revetted with limestone blocks and a developed system of berm, ditch and glacis was introduced.

Domestic buildings likewise were generally built of mudbrick on rubble foundations set in mud mortar. Rooms were rectangular or apsidal. Public buildings were constructed of fine ashlar masonry with mud mortar and the ability of Cypriot architects and masons of the period is well illustrated by the built tombs. In the sanctuary within the walled city of Tamassos some of the structures were wooden, including a stoa; Phoenician influence is visible in the half-column capitals (evidently supported by wooden shafts) as it was in the architectural decoration of the 'Royal' tombs. Phoenician influence in Cypriot architecture is also apparent in some temple plans, as we shall see, but it was particularly strong on free-standing votive monuments, pillars and pilasters dedicated in sanctuaries. To the 6th century, when Cyprus came into closer contact with the Greek world, belong a few Greek architectural fragments but the evidence for Greek temples or public buildings is very slight.

Religion played an important part in Cypriot life at all periods in antiquity. Many archaic sanctuaries containing quantities of votive offerings have been discovered. They are often situated outside the settlements to which they belong; the larger cities usually had several shrines. The typical archaic Cypriot sanctuary consisted of a *temenos* or open court enclosed by a wall with small cult buildings perhaps including a chapel and altars. Only a few temple-like buildings are known and these are situated within the city walls. At Kition the Phoenician 'temple' of Astarte continued in use as did the two smaller 'temples' rebuilt by the Phoenicians. The Astarte 'temple' retained its tripartite Holy-of-Holies approached by a partly-roofed courtyard supported by piers. Another temple-like building with a tripartite plan, recalling the arrangement of Solomon's temple in Jerusalem, stood within the walled area of Tamassos. It was dedicated, according to a later inscription, to Aphrodite-Astarte. Soloi and the neighbouring town of Paradisotissa had small temples on the Greek plan with *pronaos* and cella, but these are very rare in Cyprus. According to legend Soloi derived its name from the Athenian law-giver, Solon, who was said to have visited the town in 570/560 BC.

In the Archaic period the Cypriots became acquainted with a number of foreign gods and goddesses. The principal deity re-

Terracotta figurine of a three-bodied warrior (? the mythical Geryon). The helmets and shields are of Cypriot type but modified under Greek influence; from Pyrga; H 24 cm; late 7th century BC (London, British Museum)

mained the Great Mother Goddess, a fertility goddess, who was identified above all with Aphrodite, the Cypriot goddess *par excellence*. In the poems of Homer of the 8th century BC and the slightly-later works of Hesiod she is already described as 'the Cyprian'. Cypriot gods included a principal deity (who was to merge later with the Greek Zeus) and various local deities such as Hylates (of the woodland) and another of music, perhaps originally the deified Kinyras, the legendary founder and first King and priest of Aphrodite at Paphos, her most famous shrine. The Phoenicians introduced their own deities. The goddesses Astarte and Anat (both sometimes identified with Aphrodite) and the gods Baal, Eshmoun, Reshef, Mikal, Melqart and Shed were worshipped. It seems that the Phoenicians were also responsible for the introduction of Egyptian gods such as Bes, Ptah, Hathor and Thoeris who often served as amulets and good-luck charms to ward off evil. They were known before the period of Egyptian rule, during which the only evidence for direct influence on religion is a contemporary imported situla from the sanctuary at Kourion shown by later inscriptions to belong to Apollo Hylates. Alongside the syllabic inscription 'to the god' it bears in Egyptian hieroglyphs a dedication

73

to the Egyptian goddess Isis whose worship is not otherwise attested in Cyprus before the Hellenistic period.

The Cypriots believed that the god or goddess was resident in the sanctuary and therefore participated in their religious rites, which included sacred banquets and ritual dances accompanied by musicians playing lyres, double pipes or the syrinx (Pan-pipes) and tambourines. Worshippers offered a number of gifts appropriate to the deity, such as the dove for Aphrodite. Animals were sacrificed and incense burnt. From the sanctuary of Baal-Hamman at Meniko a lively terracotta group of the 6th century portrays two men

Terracotta group of two men and a bull; from Meniko; H (of bull) 28.5 cm; 6th century BC (Nicosia, Cyprus Museum)

74

leading a bull to sacrifice. The priests wore bull or other animal masks and the people dedicated numerous statues of limestone and terracotta representing themselves or the deity to act as substitutes for themselves as continuous worshippers. At Ayia Irini more than 2,000 statues and statuettes, dating mostly from the Late Bronze Age to the end of the Archaic period, were found grouped around the altar in the sanctuary. The identity of the deity, which may not be recorded epigraphically at this period, is reflected in the dedications. In the sanctuaries of male gods statuettes of horsemen and war chariots are common, while in those dedicated to the female

Terracotta figurine of horse and rider; H 21 cm; 6th century BC
(Nicosia, Cyprus Museum)

fertility goddess bearers of offerings, mostly women, worshippers (or the goddess herself) with raised arms, and musicians predominate. As in the Late Bronze Age the religious leaders evidently had control over the all-important copper industry at least at Kition, where a copper workshop was built close to the Astarte 'temple' around 600 BC and remained in use until about 450 BC, and at Tamassos, where copper installations within the Aphrodite-Astarte and Cybele sanctuary were in use from the third quarter of the 7th century until the Hellenistic period.

The main sanctuaries had their own terracotta workshops and terracotta figurines were also buried in tombs. A vast number were produced, illustrating aspects of both religious and daily life. The techniques vary but several are painted in bright colours of red or purple and black or brown. Figures of the 6th century from Salamis and Kazaphani wear cuirasses with pictorial decoration in the same style as contemporary vases. Moulds for terracottas may have been introduced by the Phoenicians at least at Kition in the mid-9th century, but it was from the 6th century that they were in wider use in the island. Thereafter the head or the whole figure might be cast

Interior of a bowl of Bichrome ware decorated with pairs of women; they wear long robes, with their hair falling down on the nape of the neck, and stand on either side of 'lotus flower trees', sniffing the flowers; from Achna; D 34.3 cm; 6th century BC (London, British Museum)

Polychrome terracotta figurine of a centaur (part human, part horse) holding a quiver; decorated with red, black and white paint; unknown provenance; H 16 cm, L 11.2 cm; 6th century BC
(Nicosia, Cyprus Museum)

in a mould, and in some respects they follow in style the contemporary sculpture. The women have wig-like hair and, if the body too is moulded, wear either a transparent tunic or, like the syrinx player from Arsos, a more elaborate costume consisting of a robe with a sash, underneath a cloak pulled up over the head. Many of the small Cypriot terracottas were still entirely hand-made by the 'snowman' technique. Others have trumpet-shaped or conical bodies either solid and formed by hand or hollow and thrown on a fast wheel with a hand-made or moulded head.

Monumental sculpture in both the local limestone and terracotta began in the early years of independence, around the middle of the 7th century. Some remarkable colossal statues were produced in both media. The large terracotta statues, often over-life-size, were

Limestone male statue
holding a thunderbolt (?),
perhaps Zeus Keraunios
(the Thunderer); from
Kition; H 56 cm; *c.* 500 BC
(Nicosia, Cyprus Museum)

Limestone head from a statue of a bearded youth wearing a headband decorated with rosettes; H 32.5; *c.* 500 BC (Nicosia, Cyprus Museum)

formed of separate pieces, usually hand-made, joined together. There are a number of early examples among the Ayia Irini dedications. Figures from Tamassos look like Assyrians with their long square beards. The Cypriot sculptor in limestone was always constrained by the nature of his material. The softness of the stone precludes elaborate carving of details, although this was partly remedied by the use of paint and engraving. Right into the Hellenistic period the backs of the statues were often left virtually flat and unworked. The earliest (Proto-Cypriote) style was essentially a local creation, although it shows some eastern influence. The faces are usually triangular or oval with severe expressions and large protruding eyes with feathered eyebrows. Both men and women wear their hair long down the back of the neck. The men usually have long beards and wear helmets. The women are often bedecked

Upper part of a colossal limestone statue of a bearded man; a worshipper or priest or Apollo; from Idalion; H 104 cm; *c.* 490–480 BC (London, British Museum)

with jewellery including necklaces, earrings and earcaps and may wear a turban or a low crown. The normal dress for both men and women is an ankle-length robe, partly covered by a a cloak for the men. They stand with their feet together. One arm is by the side and the other is held across the body, tucked in a fold of the cloak for the men, often with an offering. By the early 6th century Cyprus's involvement with other Mediterranean powers led to the development of a new style that shows both Egyptian and East Greek influence. The sculptures now usually have their hair arranged in an Egyptian klaft (wig), the features are softer and there is a slight Greek 'Archaic smile' on the lips. The men sport long beards, sometimes square and artificially curled, like those of their earlier Assyrian rulers. They wear a variety of helmets usually derived from Near Eastern types. Others are dressed in 'bathing trunks' often decorated with rosettes and wear headbands with similar decoration. Also common is a costume comprising a long tunic and often a mantle draped over one or both shoulders. The women continue to wear rich jewellery; their dress is usually a long plain tunic. The head is often simply covered by a veil but turbans may also be worn. The Egyptian rulers left few legacies of material culture directly attributable to the period of their rule, but may have inspired the production of some strongly Egyptianising bronze statuettes.

The intensification of contact with the East Greek world brought about by the inclusion of Cyprus in the Persian Empire had a noticeable effect on Cypriot sculptors in the last fifty years of the Archaic period. Statues of women still wear traditional Cypriot jewellery but their features show strong Ionian influence and there are some fine copies of East Greek *korai*. Likewise the men may still have long hair, now usually arranged in spiral curls, and long beards, and wear oriental helmets or headbands as before (or wreaths), but their soft rounded features and 'Archaic' smiles betray Greek influence. They now usually wear a *chiton* (tunic) and *himation* (cloak), typical dress of the East Greek school. Others wear Egyptian crowns and kilts perhaps reflecting a Phoenician fashion for Egyptianising statues, stimulated in part by the Phoenician population resident in Cyprus. There are exceptions like a statue from Kition, probably representing Zeus Keraunios (Zeus throwing the thunderbolt) whose tunic and aegis recall the costume of earlier figures. Only a few Cypriot *kouroi* (standing youths) are naked in the mainland Greek tradition. An imported example of marble dating from around 520 BC was found at Marion.

The vases in particular illustrate the regional differences in Archaic Cyprus. In the south and east a flourishing school was established continuing and developing the pictorial style which had its beginnings in the Geometric period and drawing its inspiration from Syrian and Phoenician textiles and metal and ivory work. The shapes were mostly developed from their precursors. The favourite fabrics were still White Painted with the ornaments in matt black on buff or greenish-white slip (coating) and Bichrome, which adds decoration in matt red or purple. Elaborate geometric and floral motifs including the guilloche, lotus flower, open palmette and 'Tree of Life' are combined with figures of humans, animals or mythical creatures to form compositions of a wide variety, of which the liveliest and most original belong to the years of independence. Jugs are often decorated in the 'free field' style with no ground line. Birds are a favourite motif. On a jug from Arnadi a

bull is sniffing a flower like the sphinx on the Hubbard amphora.
Amathus again stands apart and the vessels form a particular group.
Belly-shaped amphorae decorated with closely-packed ornaments
were popular there. In the north and west the potters concentrated
on producing elaborate compass-drawn circle designs and also
preferred more intricate vessel shapes. Black-on-red ware is more
common in this region. Not all foreign influence came from the
Near East. Greek pottery was imported and some attempts were
made to imitate it locally. At first it came from the East Greek area
but, as Athens had won all the foreign markets for pottery by the
second half of the 6th century, the later Archaic Greek pottery

found in Cyprus as elsewhere is mainly Attic. Some Attic vases were made in Cypriot shapes, apparently specifically for the Cypriot market.

Jewellery for the most part continued the types which were by now well established in the Cypriot repertoire, but it is generally of higher quality using finer techniques. Granulation (grains of metal soldered on to a background) was a popular decoration. Statues of limestone and terracotta wear earrings, necklaces and bangles, many of which can be matched by actual finds. An example is a magnificent gold necklace from Arsos of ribbed lentoid beads with an agate pendant decorated with granulation and surmounted by a bee and two *uraei* (snakes) wearing Egyptian crowns. Earrings with tapered hoops, more elaborate versions of a type first known in the Late Bronze Age, may have pendants attached. Other earrings are boat-shaped with a hollow hoop, a type of Syrian origin known also in East Greece, and pendants are attached to some of these. Gold mountings probably originally forming a *polos*, a Near Eastern headdress, continued a tradition established in Cyprus at least from the 9th century. They are decorated in repoussé with Syrian motifs. Cyprus introduced the type to Rhodes in the 7th century.

The Archaic period was the zenith of Cypriot civilisation in the 1st millennium BC. The island had three overlords in fairly quick succession but also enjoyed a century of independence during which she was able to develop art and culture in her own right. The stimulus provided by contacts with her neighbours, whether through trade or submission to their rule, led to the production of works of art with a definite Cypriot quality. In this period models were not slavishly imitated, but rather adapted to suit the Cypriot taste and purpose. Cyprus also played an important role in the transmission of goods and ideas, above all to the Phoenician centres in the western Mediterranean, the East Greek cities of Ionia and the islands in the eastern Aegean. The individual city kingdoms grew powerful and were able to make a stand, albeit unsuccessful, against the Great King of Persia. Their final defeat in 498 BC was a turning point in Cypriot history and it was in the turmoil of Greek and Persian politics that the Classical period began in about 475 BC.

V

THE CLASSICAL PERIOD

475-325 BC

Dr Veronica Tatton-Brown

Participation in the Ionian revolt had brought Cyprus into the conflict between Greece and Persia and throughout the Classical period she was poised between these two major powers. The defeat and subjugation of the city kingdoms in 498 BC had left Persia firmly in control. Twenty years later they were freed momentarily by an allied Greek fleet, but Achaemenid Persian rule was soon re-established. In the middle of the 5th century a major expedition was launched to secure Cyprus as a Greek base, but after the death of its commander, Cimon, the Greek and allied fleet sailed for home without completing the task. Thereafter, until the takeover by Alexander the Great, King of Macedon and leader of the Greeks, Achaemenid control was not disputed except by Evagoras I of Salamis.

As before the Persian overlords did not alter the political system in the island. The kings continued to pay tribute to the Great King and had to contribute ships to the Persian fleet in time of war, but were still allowed to issue their own coinage. Persian rule was evidently facilitated by the political disunity reflected by the different ethnic origins of the kings and the conflicting aims and divided interests of the city kingdoms. Phoenician dynasts ruled at Kition which, following the annexation of the Kingdom of Idalion, achieved with Persian help in the middle of the 5th century, grew in power and importance. Phoenician influence throughout the island increased. About this time a Phoenician exile even seized the throne of Salamis, the most powerful kingdom, hitherto ruled by a Greek dynasty that traced its ancestry back to Teucer, the city's legendary

84

founder. There was also it seems a Phoenician dynasty at Lapithos and Kition gained further in political and economic control in the 4th century with the acquisition of Tamassos and its copper mines, sold by its bankrupt last King. Greeks ruled the important Kingdom of Paphos and for most of the time at Marion.

View of Vouni, with part of the north-eastern corner of the palace complex. The palace was built in the early 5th century BC

During the Classical period the despotic form of government of the city kingdoms became fully developed. All power was concentrated in the King, who was supported by 'princes' and 'princesses'. Together they formed a supreme court with wide responsibilities including security. At Paphos, the home of the most important shrine of the Cypriot goddess Aphrodite, and possibly also elsewhere, the King also acted as High Priest. At Idalion, before its capture by Kition, the system was slightly more democratic with the King and people on a more equal footing. In 411 BC Evagoras I seized the throne of Salamis from the Phoenician ruler and restored it to the Teucrid dynasty. He was to dominate Cypriot politics for the next forty years, his principal aim being to extend the rule of Salamis over the whole of Cyprus. The Athenians honoured him by a decree in 410 BC and, after their victory in the battle of Cnidus in 394 BC which ended Spartan domination of the sea, acknowl-

Limestone sarcophagus decorated in high relief: one long side showing advanced guard and the two leading chariots in a procession continued on the other side; from Amathus; H 157.5 cm; L 239.4 cm; *c.* 460–450 BC
(New York, Metropolitan Museum of Art, Cesnola Collection)

edged the help of Evagoras by erecting a statue of him alongside one of their commander, Conon, and next to a statue of Zeus Liberator, in the Stoa Basileios in Athens. After his death he was the subject of a panegyric by the Athenian orator Isocrates. With the help of Athens he gradually increased his control over the island so that by 391 BC he had virtually achieved his goal. However, under the peace of Antalcidas in 386 BC the Athenians, in return for the freedom of the East Greek cities, agreed to recognise Persian sovereignty over Cyprus and the island of Clazomenae as well as the cities of Asia. Evagoras nonetheless maintained his position and even enhanced it, becoming for a short time master in the eastern Mediterranean. In about 381 BC a Persian expedition was again launched against Cyprus. Salamis was besieged and Evagoras was eventually defeated, but in 380–379 BC he managed to negotiate a settlement whereby he lost control over the cities of Cyprus and agreed to pay an annual tribute to the Great King, but retained the throne of Salamis. Persia had therefore regained control over Cyprus and Evagoras I was murdered, probably in the year 374–373 BC. In 351 BC the city kingdoms joined with Egypt and Phoenicia in another revolt from their overlord. This was suppressed and after a siege Salamis also submitted. The whole of Cyprus was therefore again under Persian control. Meanwhile the Greek forces under Alexander the Great, King of Macedon, were gaining considerable success against the Persian Empire. In 333 BC, after the defeat of the Persians at Issus, the Cypriot kings transferred their allegiance to Alexander. Persian domination was finally brought to an end.

Fortifications continued to be of prime importance to the Cypriot kings. At Idalion, which withstood a siege by the Kitians and Persians a generation before its final capture, the citadel wall of the early 5th century was 10.5 m thick with an inner core of small stones faced on either side by limestone blocks set in mud mortar. A tower, perhaps part of a gate, was built of fine ashlar blocks. At Palaepaphos the siege-damaged fortifications were put in a state of defence again and the Persian siege mound was surrounded by a revetment wall and included in the system. The 4th-century fortifications at Golgoi, constructed as at Palaepaphos of mudbrick on stone foundations, had houses built directly inside with their outer walls resting against the city wall as in the Greek city of Olynthus and, in the Hellenistic period, at Ayia Irini.

A number of important buildings or 'palaces' of the Classical period are known. At Palaepaphos one was built to the east of the gate against the inner face of the city wall leaving a gap of 0.85 m to act as a cushion against another attack. Both in plan and construc-

Limestone sarcophagus decorated in low relief with pairs of warriors hunting animals; from Golgoi; H 95 cm, L 207.3 cm; *c.* 475- 460 BC
(New York, Metropolitan Museum of Art, Cesnola Collection)

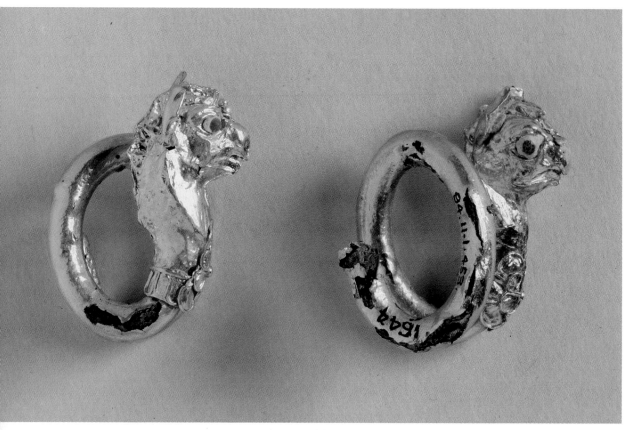

Pair of gold-plated bronze spiral rings for the ears or hair, ending in horned griffin heads with enamel and filigree decoration; from Amathus; L 3.5 cm; 350-300 BC (London, British Museum)

tion the building compares with contemporary Persian structures at Persepolis. The heavy walls were built throughout of masonry with ashlar faces and a rubble core using gypsum plaster also found in parts of the contemporary city wall. There are two storeys, the narrow rooms and long corridors of the ground floor probably used for storage while the main accommodation was evidently above. The walls of the palace of Soloi were similarly constructed with a rubble core faced by ashlar blocks. The same technique was used in part at the neighbouring palace at Vouni, although most of the walls were of mudbrick on stone foundations.

The Vouni palace occupies a magnificent position on a hill over-looking the Bay of Morphou and the city of Soloi. It was built in the early 5th century and, as at Palaepaphos, its original plan was of oriental type. The front of the palace faced south-west, where the main entrance was situated which led into the state apartments (rooms 48-56) consisting of tripartite complex of rooms, the 'liwan' type (so called from a characteristic feature of Persian architecture). From here stairs descended to an open central court surrounded by columns around which the private rooms including bathrooms were arranged. Slightly later than its first construction a sudatorium (sweating room) was added, one of the earliest known. In the mid-5th century rooms for administration and storage were added and the entrance was transferred to the north-east so that the state apartments were located at the rear of the central courtyard. It seems that emphasis was now placed on the administrative functions of the palace; it was finally destroyed in about 380 BC. Some of the walls of the Vouni palace were covered by gypsum plaster. White gypsum plaster was also used to cover the walls of public buildings at Idalion. Structures in the sanctuary of Aphrodite-Astarte and Cybele at Tamassos had doors and windows framed with wall plaster painted in red and maroon. The monumental buildings at Idalion also illustrate other construction techniques. In the earlier stage the walls were built of sandstone ashlar blocks cemented with gypsum plaster but later they were built of dry-laid limestone blocks. Roof tiles have not been found on Cypriot sites and it seems likely that the roofs and ceilings were backed with cane and, at least at Idalion, covered by gypsum plaster. Floors could be made of fine concrete.

Private houses were naturally of more modest proportions, although the plan of the town associated with the sanctuary at Ayia Irini was laid out with three principal streets running from north to south at this period. Mostly the houses were built of mudbrick on stone foundations but at Carpasia, a flourishing harbour town on

Pair of gold-plated bronze bracelets, open-ended and terminating in rams' heads; from Kourion; D 8.4 cm; 475-400 BC (London, British Museum)

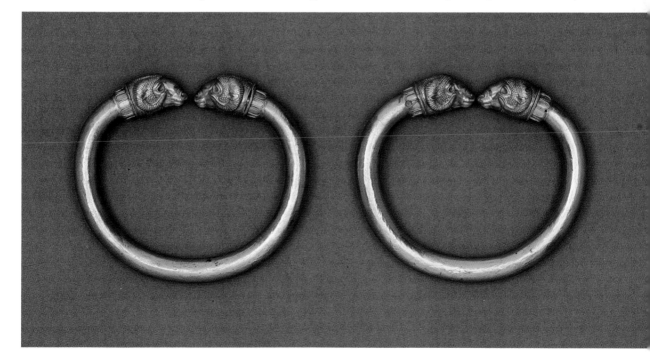

the north of the Karpass, the architecture shows Phoenician influence. The walls of houses originally built at this period are constructed of rubble on ashlar foundations with square blocks at the angles and also acting as uprights at intervals along the walls. As in contemporary buildings on the Phoenician mainland and in the Phoenician colony at Motya in Sicily the technique is derived from timber-framed buildings.

Worship for the most part continued in the open sanctuaries as in the Archaic period and in the Phoenician 'temples' at Kition and Tamassos. At Vouni in the mid-5th century a 'temple' was built dedicated to Athena, but this bears no resemblance to Greek temples. Rather it is a more elaborate version of the typical Cypriot sanctuary with its two open courtyards and the sanctuary buildings leading off the innermost. While religious rites continued as before there is now more epigraphic evidence to identify the deities by name. Aphrodite as the great fertility Mother Goddess was still supreme. Paphos remained the principal centre of her cult and she appears on coins of that city and also of Salamis in the 4th century. In Paphian inscriptions she is simply called 'the Queen', in other cities she may be named 'the Paphian'. In the 4th century she became identified with the Phoenician Astarte and Anat. Anat was also identified with Athena who was worshipped at Vouni, as we have seen, and also at Soloi and elsewhere; she too appears as a coin type. It was in the 4th century that Greek cults became widespread in the island. The principal god was henceforth known as Zeus, at least at Salamis. The Phoenician Reshef and the Cypriot Hylates (of the woodland), both became identified with the Greek Apollo and there were many other local cults of Apollo. At Kition the cult of the Phoenician Eshmoun became the cult of the Greek Asklepios. Artemis, the Greek huntress goddess, perhaps associated with the

90

eastern 'mistress of the animals', was also worshipped; a colony of Kitians established a sanctuary of their own Artemis Paralia in the Athenian port of Piraeus in 333–332 BC.

In burial customs there were also few changes. The tradition of built tombs for the wealthy was maintained but the majority continued to be buried in rock-cut chamber tombs. Sarcophagi were found in the splendid built tombs at Tamassos but in general they were rare in the Archaic period. In the Classical period they became more common and simple versions, either monolithic or built of slabs fitted together, are found in the graves of ordinary people. Two splendid sarcophagi locally made in Cypriot limestone, with elaborate relief decoration in a mixed oriental and Greek style and dating from the middle years of the 5th century, must have been made for aristocrats or kings. Mummy-shaped sarcophagi of marble were imported from Phoenicia in the 5th and earlier 4th centuries; Phoenicians at Kition made their own versions locally. Graves may now be marked by statues or tombstones. Some of the gravestones are purely Cypriot in style but others follow Greek models; some of those made of imported marble may have been carved locally. The cult of the dead continued with evidence of libations being offered in tombs at Amathus.

The struggles between Greece and Persia for supremacy in Cyprus and the different sympathies within the island had their reper-

Bronze statuette of a cow, perhaps a copy of Myron's statue; from Vouni; H 25 cm, L 25 cm; 475–400 BC (Nicosia, Cyprus Museum)

91

Bronze head of Apollo (the Chatsworth head) made in Athens; from Tamassos; H 31.7 cm; *c.* 460 BC (London, British Museum)

cussions on Cypriot art. Contacts were now with mainland Greece and Achaemenid Persia. Attic (Athenian) pottery continued to dominate the market. The vigorous pro-Greek policy of Evagoras I and his successors led to the adoption of certain Greek forms. Influence from Classical Greece is apparent in several media, although there is a certain stagnation in Cypriot styles.

Sculpture in limestone, terracotta and bronze illustrates the different trends. There is a marked contrast between the intentional imitations of Classical Greek models and work in native styles which admitted little new outside influence.

Numerous dedications were still offered in sanctuaries. Many of the statues continued the Archaic Cypro-Greek style which gradually became stagnant and repetitive; the later pieces are very poorly carved. Some marble sculpture was imported and works like a fine marble head of the second quarter of the 5th century, probably from Lapithos, no doubt inspired sculptors to follow Attic models. A good example of this group is a limestone head from Idalion dating from the second half of the 5th century and therefore contemporary with works of famous Classical Greek sculptors like Phidias and Polyclitus. Among the immigrants at Salamis during the reign of Evagoras I were Greek sculptors, one of whom was probably responsible for a beautiful marble head of a goddess, perhaps Aphrodite, dating from the early 4th century BC. It was found re-used as building material in the Roman gymnasium. Other imports which must have had an impact on Cypriot artists of the period include a magnificent bronze head of Apollo from Tamassos, known as the Chatsworth head because of its long sojourn in Chatsworth House in Derbyshire. The head was cast hollow and much of the hair was cast separately and attached; the eyes were originally inlaid. It was made in Athens in 470-460 BC at the time when Greek sculptors, breaking away from the rigid

Terracotta group made by a Cypriot craftsman representing Athena in a four-horse chariot; from Mersinaki; H 36 cm; *c.* 450 BC (Stockholm, Medelhavsmuseet)

Limestone gravestone
following Greek models
with an inscription in the
Cypriot syllabic script
naming the deceased
(Aristila); from Marion;
H 92.5 cm, W 41.5 cm; c.
420 BC
(Nicosia, Cyprus Museum)

Archaic style, were attempting to reflect the perfect human form and give their own works expression and movement. Bronze sculptures of the 5th century from the temple of Athena at Vouni are also Greek in style. Among them is a splendid cow, cast solid, which may be a copy of the well-known statue by the Greek sculptor Myron. In addition there are reliefs showing a bull attacked by two lions, exquisite, lively work. Although much limestone sculpture in the round reflected a stagnant style, some fine reliefs were carved in the later 5th and 4th centuries including gravestones following Athenian models. A number of these have been found in the city of Marion including an example in limestone with traces of green paint still visible dating from 420 BC. It shows a seated woman

Marble head of a goddess, probably Aphrodite; from Salamis; H 32 cm; early 4th century BC
(Nicosia, Cyprus Museum)

95

Gold coins of Evagoras I of Salamis (411-373 BC) who was responsible for the island's first gold issue

1
The head of Herakles-Melqart

2 and 3
The forepart and head of a goat

4
The Cypriot sign BA, signifying the royal title of the King
(London, British Museum)

holding a dove and an inscription in Greek syllabic script which reads: 'I am [the stele] of Aristila from Salamis, the daughter of Onasis.'

Some terracotta figures of the 'snowman' type were still hand-made but the majority are now cast in moulds. The moulded terracottas in general follow Greek types; the majority of those found in Cyprus are of local manufacture but some may have been made in moulds imported from Greece.

In pottery the same fabrics continued, notably White Painted, Bichrome, Black-on-Red and Plain White (similar in fabric and slip to White Painted but without painted decoration). Bichrome Red with ornaments painted in white as well as black on a red ground became more popular. Most of the vessels are taller and slimmer versions of the earlier shapes. From the second half of the 5th century, when Attic pottery was imported in particular by Marion and Salamis, Cypriot potters borrowed some Greek ornaments to decorate their vases. Favourite vessels are pitchers with a Greek *kore* (maiden) on the neck pouring from a small jug which acts as a spout.

In the palace at Vouni a treasure of silver vessels, jewellery and coins was found deposited in a terracotta jar under a staircase leading to the upper floor, apparently hidden deliberately at the time of the final destruction by fire of the palace in 380 BC. The finds therefore date from the 5th or very early 4th century. Among the coins are Persian gold darics and silver coins of several cities especially of Marion, Kition and Paphos. The jewellery includes open-ended bracelets of solid gold terminating in goats' or calves' heads and silver snake bracelets similar to examples probably from Marion. These are familiar in Achaemenid Persia. The gold bracelets are the oriental version of this type with a depression in the hoop. Like other craftsmen Cypriot jewellers and silversmiths were now more dependent on outside models than before but they usually adapted rather than slavishly imitated them. A good example is a deep silver bowl, again from the Vouni treasure. In shape it is typically Near Eastern and similar bowls are well known in Persia; but the Cypriot artist has added a Greek egg and dart motif below the rim. It is not always easy to distinguish items of certain Cypriot manufacture from imports at this period since Classical Greek jewellery is better known from places like Cyprus outside Greece itself. The workmanship is generally of a high standard and filigree (metal wire soldered in patterns on a background) became more popular than granulation for decoration. Enamel is used for inlay, sometimes bordered by filigree. Silver became more common than pure gold. Cypriot jewellers often worked in gold-plated bronze: animal-headed bracelets in this material, similar to the Vouni examples but copying the Greek versions of the type without a depression in the hoop, were made locally. Certain other favourite types were also evidently of Cypriot manufacture. Among them are spiral rings, probably for the hair rather than the ears, terminating in female or animal heads executed in repoussé and attached by collars with filigree ornament around the bottom sometimes bordering enamel inlays. Intricate pieces of pure gold like elaborate earrings with fine filigree decoration were probably imported from Greece. Also popular were necklaces with pendants in the form of vases or of acorns, perhaps of cornelian with a gold cap.

The political situation in the Classical period left little peacetime in which the Cypriots could develop and foster their own material culture. The island, however, as we have seen, did have an important role to play and although Classical Cypriot art is more dependent on its models some fine works were produced and the Cypriot character was maintained. The Cypriot kings changed sides to support Alexander the Great in 333 BC and assisted him in his naval siege of Tyre in the following year, but they did not foresee the consequences. Cyprus was to become part of the Hellenistic world and thereby lose some of her individuality.

VI

THE HELLENISTIC PERIOD
Cyprus Under the Ptolemies

325-30 BC

Dr Veronica Tatton-Brown

While they were under Persian control the city states had retained a certain amount of freedom, but this was lost when Alexander the Great took over in 333 BC. He replaced the local coinage with his own imperial Macedonian coinage and also introduced Greek weights and denominations. After the death of Alexander in 323 BC his generals, struggling to inherit his fragmented empire, used Cyprus as a battleground and destroyed the city kingdoms of Kition, Lapithos, Marion and Kyrenia. Subsequently in 294 BC Cyprus was annexed by Ptolemy I, Alexander's general who had taken control of Egypt. Apart from a short period in the second century, she remained in Ptolemaic hands, usually as part of the Egyptian kingdom, although occasionally independent, for two and a half centuries; the city kingdoms ceased to exist and Cyprus was part of the large Hellenistic state of Egypt. There was comparative peace in the island although she was subject to attacks by the Seuleucid kings of Syria. In 168 BC Antiochus IV Epiphanes, King of Syria, conquered Cyprus but Roman envoys intervened and forced him to withdraw. Thereafter Rome, by now a major power in the eastern Mediterranean, became increasingly involved in Cypriot affairs. In about 80 BC the Ptolemies partly withdrew from Cyprus to appease Roman fears over the size of their empire but left a member of their family in control.

In 58 BC Cyprus was first annexed by Rome. The Roman Tribune, P. Clodius Pulcher, a partisan of Julius Caesar, carried a law, implemented by Cato, which reduced the island to the state of a province at first attached to the province of Cilicia on the south coast of modern Turkey. During the civil wars of the Roman republic Cyprus was returned to Ptolemaic rule by Julius Caesar, who gave the island to his mistress, Cleopatra VII. In 36 BC this transfer was confirmed by Mark Antony, Cleopatra's husband. Six years later Octavian, later to be Augustus, the first Roman Emperor, took the Egyptian capital, Alexandria. Cleopatra committed suicide and Cyprus reverted to Rome, becoming a Senatorial Province in 22 BC.

The Ptolemies' chief interest in Cyprus was as a source of supply of copper, corn and timber and as a shipbuilding centre. By the early 2nd century the capital had been transferred from Salamis to Nea Paphos. This was an ideal capital for the Ptolemies: its location on the south-west coast made it very accessible to Egypt; the area was richly forested and had a fine harbour (the one at Salamis had

Miniature bronze head of Zeus Ammon; the eyes were inlaid with silver; from Soloi; H 5 cm; 3rd to 1st century BC (Nicosia, Cyprus Museum)

99

by now silted up) and it was therefore an excellent site for ship-building. Cyprus's continued role in international trade is illustrated by a Greek ship which sank off the coast of Kyrenia at the end of the 4th century. Its cargo included Rhodian wine amphorae, millstones from the island of Nisyros and 10,000 almonds which had probably just been collected from Cyprus.

The last quarter of the 4th century saw the end of the political organisation of Cyprus into autonomous city kingdoms. Under the Ptolemies it was organised as a military command under the overall control of a *strategos* (governor-general) who was responsible to the King of Egypt, except when the island was an independent kingdom. From the time of Ptolemy V Epiphanes in the early 2nd century the *strategos* also received the title of High Priest, which enabled him to enrich the royal treasury with revenues from all the sanctuaries on the island. During the reign of Ptolemy VIII Euergetes II as sole King (146-116 BC) the *strategos* also became admiral. All the *strategoi* were of the highest rank in the Egyptian court and were described as 'kinsmen' of the King. Under the *strategos* there was a commander-in-chief of all the forces and the individual regiments had their own commanders. The important towns housed their own garrisons and the population was swelled by a large mercenary force stationed in Cyprus.

Although the Ptolemies abolished the city kingdoms some forms of liberty were preserved and certain democratic forms of internal administration were introduced. In the first three-quarters of the 3rd century minor Phoenician dynasts were tolerated at least at Lapithos in the north; but for the most part the cities were governed by city commanders who, like the *strategoi,* were always foreigners and members of the Ptolemaic court. As in Hellenistic cities elsewhere public education was in the hands of the gymnasiarchs and the gymnasium was the focus of loyalty to the regime. The coinage of Cyprus was under the control of the *strategos* and incorporated in the Ptolemaic coinage. The island's silver mines were exploited for the very active mints at Paphos, Kition, Salamis and, in the late

The designs on this Cypriot silver coin were inspired by a victory won in 306 BC by Demetrios the Besieger, one of Ptolemy I's rivals for power, in a sea-battle off Salamis; on the obverse Victory, on the prow of a war-galley, blows her trumpet; on the reverse Poseidon hurls his trident (London, British Museum)

Idealised female head of
unbaked clay; from
Salamis; H 25.7 cm; end of
4th century BC
(Nicosia, Cyprus Museum)

3rd to 2nd century, Amathus.

In the late 4th century Nikokles, the last King of Paphos, pro-
moted the cults of the Greek deities or of local deities assimilated
with Greek gods. Under the Ptolemies, themselves of Greek origin,
the Greek cults continued to flourish and the gods are portrayed and
mentioned in inscriptions. Aphrodite remained the most important
and the Great Mother Goddess continued also to be worshipped as
Astarte. At her most famous shrine at Palaepaphos the two goddesses were equated. Other Greek deities worshipped included
Artemis, Zeus, Pan or Melanthios, Apollo and Dionysos. Cyprus's
religious institutions were inevitably affected by Ptolemaic rule.

The dynastic cult was of prime importance. Arsinoe Philadelphus, the wife of Ptolemy II Philadelphus (285-245 BC) was deified on her death in 270 BC. Her cult enjoyed great popularity in Cyprus, probably beginning during her lifetime, and she was frequently identified with Aphrodite. Cities were founded in her name, including that on the old site of Marion destroyed by Ptolemy I in 312 BC. An Arsinoeion was built at Idalion, one of the centres for the worship of Aphrodite. Other Egyptian gods like Serapis and Isis were also introduced and some were equated with Greek deities as the Libyan god Ammon with Zeus, represented on coins and by a miniature bronze head from Soloi whose eyeballs were inlaid with silver.

Dedications continued in many of the open sanctuaries. The construction of new temples is recorded, but the only known example on the Greek plan with typical Hellenistic architecture is the famous temple of Zeus at Salamis which was probably built on

Upper part of the torso and head of a large terracotta statue of a woman, perhaps a portrait; from Paphos District; H 40 cm; early 3rd century BC
(Larnaca, Pierides Foundation Museum)

its high podium in the late Hellenistic period. Three 'temples' were dedicated to Aphrodite, Serapis and Isis on the Cholades hill at Soloi, but these consist of a roofed cella (main room) leading onto one or more courtyards, sometimes surrounded by porticoes, plans developed from that of the Athena 'temple' of the Classical period at Vouni. Excavations have shown that the sacred precinct within the walled area at Tamassos was entirely rebuilt in a magnificent style after its destruction by Ptolemy I in the late 4th century, but few details are known yet.

Many of the public and domestic buildings of Hellenistic Cyprus have been obliterated by later Roman constructions and by the earthquakes of 15 BC and AD 76/77, but epigraphic evidence records gymnasia, the focus of loyalty to the Ptolemaic regime, at Salamis (predecessor of the splendid Roman one), Kition and Kou-

rion. At Kourion the theatre was originally built in the 2nd century BC on a Greek plan very similar to the theatre at Priene in Ionia with an *orchestra* greater than a semi-circle and a high *proskenion* (stage) supported by half columns. These public buildings, as shown by the remains at Idalion, were sometimes constructed of fine ashlar masonry. Others, perhaps of two storeys, had a super-structure of mudbrick supported on thick foundation walls with an outer face of ashlar blocks revetting a mud backing and an inner face of rubble. Roofs were supported by columns. The walls of the palace at Soloi were decorated with painted stucco in the Alexandrian manner. Occasionally buildings had pebble mosaic floors. A fine example was discovered at Nea Paphos dating from the time of its foundation in the late 4th century and another at Kourion perhaps from the heroon of Pnytagoras the last King of the city, whose ship was sunk while taking part in Alexander's siege of Tyre in 332

BC. The Paphos mosaic, composed of small black and white pebbles, shows the legendary Skylla as a fish-like monster with the bust of a female figure and the foreparts of three dogs springing from her waist depicted in white with reddish hair on a black background; before the monster are two dolphins and in the foreground is a fish; the panel is bordered by a meander. The Kourion mosaic is more fragmentary but it too is composed of black and white pebbles and the main preserved section is a panel bordered by a geometric pattern in which are portrayed a vessel, a dolphin and a fish in black on a white ground. Private houses were generally rather small with rectangular rooms; at Idalion a two-roomed dwelling was reduced to one in the later Hellenistic period. In the settlement at Ayia Irini the architecture, as at Carpasia in the Classical period, was derived from timber-framed buildings. Here the houses were larger and provided with bathrooms and little workshops.

While ordinary people continued to be buried in irregular rock-cut chamber tombs there were now more elaborate enlarged versions whose chambers had niches or radiating extensions (loculi). Some of the dead were also buried in simple shafts or pits. Sarcophagi and tombstones are quite common. In the capital, Nea Paphos, impressive rock-cut subterranean tombs, versions of those found in the Hellenistic city of Alexandria, probably served the local aristocracy. Some more elaborate examples have a central peristyle (columned) court in the Doric Order with rooms grouped around it; the court is approached by a flight of steps and carved in the rock face are Doric columns with an entablature of triglyphs and metopes. Recent excavations have revealed more 'Tombs of the Kings' in the same area with different styles of architecture. Some tombs in the northern necropolis have remarkable painted decora-

Bull's head 'capital' of Pentelic marble, probably the plinth of a statue; from Salamis; H 96 cm; 3rd century BC
(London, British Museum)

105

tion, another sign of Alexandrian influence apparent too on the painted tombstones of Amathus.

As part of the Hellenistic Kingdom of Egypt Cyprus became artistically oriented towards the Hellenistic world and her products generally conform to the cosmopolitan tendencies of the period. Much of Cypriot sculpture, however, retained its native quality. This was the result of the continued use of the local limestone and of the purpose of the majority of the statues. Unlike the fine marble products of the Hellenistic world in general the majority were not made as memorials or for the decoration of public buildings, but continued as before to be dedicated in sanctuaries. Marble was imported for expensive commissions and is often used either in pieces or in combination with other materials, a practice that continued until the early years of the Roman Empire. Among the more remarkable marble sculptures of this period found in Cyprus is a sarcophagus of the late 4th century decorated with scenes of the battle between Greeks and Amazons. It was found at Soloi and was perhaps for a prince of that city-kingdom. Another example is a bull's head 'capital' of Pentelic marble found at Salamis but not associated with any building and evidently therefore from a votive

Part of the colonnaded court of one of the subterranean 'Tombs of the Kings' carved in the rock for prominent families of Paphos

monument. Probably dating from the 3rd century BC, with parallels for the type in Persia in the mid-4th century and Delos in the mid-3rd, it now seems likely that, unlike the others, it served as the plinth for a statue rather than the capital of a column. Expressive heads of unbaked clay from the cenotaph of Nicocreon, last King of Salamis, are local work in the style of the 4th-century Attic sculptor, Lysippos. Cypriot sculptors in part respected the current fashions, producing copies in limestone of many deities. Among them their Great Mother Goddess as Aphrodite was naturally predominant. Portraits of Arsinoe often resembled Aphrodite, to whom she was likened. A limestone female head from the sanctuary at Arsos is an impressive attempt by the sculptor to illustrate in his local material the individual and dramatic style of Hellenistic art.

Portraits became fashionable in Cyprus under the Ptolemies as they did elsewhere. The Ptolemies themselves affected the pose of gods and acquired attributes such as the club of Herakles and aegis of Zeus. Many, like a worshipper from the sanctuary of Apollo at Idalion made *c.* 270-200 BC, chose to have themselves portrayed in the Ptolemaic style. Among these votive statues female lyre players and male offering bearers usually wreathed and wearing the typical Greek costume of *chiton* (tunic) and *himation* (cloak) are common in the 3rd and 2nd centuries. Distinctive are statues of small boys found in sanctuaries of Apollo and Aphrodite in particularly large numbers in the Hellenistic period, although the type was known earlier. Known as 'temple boys' they are portrayed kneeling and holding an offering: they wear tunics and usually some jewellery. Their purpose is unclear: they perhaps represent temple servants or prostitutes or they may simply have been dedicated to commemorate the first offering at the shrine. Greek gravestones were copied sometimes rather poorly, but there are some finer versions.

Large-sized terracottas also maintained their Cypriot character, but these are rare; most are rather stiff and stylised versions of Classical types apart from a few following Attic models like the examples from Salamis already mentioned. Minor terracottas for the most part conform precisely to types found throughout the Hellenistic world. For the most part established Cypriot traditions are ignored except for the horsemen who keep the handmade body, although their moulded heads conform to Hellenistic fashions. Apart from these, the terracotta figurines are entirely cast in moulds and hollow. They were usually painted but as the decoration was often applied over a thick lime coat after firing it has usually now disappeared. Deities such as Aphrodite, Eros and Herakles are represented always in their Greek guises. Particularly common among the votaries are standing female figures wearing tight drapery with the cloak sometimes enveloping the head, local versions of the popular Greek 'Tanagra' style.

Terracotta figure of a girl in the 'Tanagra' style; from Amathus; H 21 cm; 3rd century BC
(London, British Museum)

1

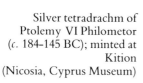

Gilded bronze pin with a
votive inscription; from
Palaepaphos; L 17.8 cm;
2nd century BC
(London, British Museum)

In pottery also the local types were mostly replaced by imitations of forms from other parts of the Greek world, although some fabrics survive, such as White Painted and Plain White. Typical products of the Greek world, like Black Glaze whose red clay is covered by a brilliant black slip and the version with painted decoration known as 'West Slope' ware, were imported and imitated locally. Shapes including *unguentaria* (tubular flasks) and *lagynoi* (squat wine jugs with tall necks) were introduced probably from the eastern Mediterranean, although certain types of amphorae and jugs developed from earlier Cypriot varieties. In the later Hellenistic period after 150 BC imports from the Greek mainland became rare although local imitations are still found made either in Cyprus itself or some other Hellenistic state. Red wares now make their appearance and are indistinguishable from those found elsewhere in the eastern Mediterranean and Asia Minor, some being clearly imitations of metal vessels. Lamps were mass produced in moulds in Cypriot workshops but again conform to general Hellenistic types.

Other arts and crafts tell a similar story. Some fine glasses were imported from Syrian workshops, but of local manufacture were *amphoriskoi* (small amphorae) with S-shaped handles made of coloured glass around a removable core and small female head pendants made by a similar technique. A large amount of jewellery is found in Cypriot tombs of the period witnessing to the fact that after Alexander's conquest of the Persian Empire a great deal of gold became available in the eastern Mediterranean. However, it is not always easy to distinguish articles of local manufacture. Techniques were simpler and both granulation and filigree are rare. An innovation was the practice of inlaying with coloured glass and stone which produced a polychrome effect and a new motif, the 'Herakles' (reef) knot, was adopted by jewellers throughout the Hellenistic world from Egypt. Particularly popular in Cyprus and

Silver tetradrachm of
Ptolemy VI Philometor
(*c.* 184-145 BC); minted at
Kition
(Nicosia, Cyprus Museum)

2

probably of local manufacture were earrings of twisted wire threaded with multi-coloured beads and terminating in animal or human heads. Also common is another well known type of Hellenistic earring decorated with pendants; Eros was a popular motif. Finger rings became mounts for engraved or precious stones or glass set in large round bezels. Other jewellery found in Cyprus such as chain necklaces terminating in animal heads or the 'Herakles' knot and snake finger rings are also common elsewhere.

In the Hellenistic period Cyprus lost her independence and consequently her culture became more cosmopolitan. However, as we have seen, the Cypriot character was not entirely suppressed. The ruling Ptolemies exploited the island's natural resources and exerted strong influence on the political and religious institutions, but the Great Mother Goddess remained supreme and dedications continued in the sanctuaries. One figure of importance of Cypriot birth was Zeno of Kition, founder of the Stoic school of philosophy, who died about 264 BC; but his work was done in Athens not Cyprus. Names of certain other Cypriot philosophers and of historians, writers and poets are also known, but intellectual life in the island was for the most part mediocre. Cypriots did, however, take part in the Olympic games and worshipped at 'international shrines' like Delos and Delphi. Cyprus finally became part of the Roman Empire in 30 BC but even thereafter some of her own traditions survived.

VII

THE ROMAN PERIOD

30 BC – AD 330

Dr Demetrios Michaelides

Most of the ancient ruins that can be seen around Cyprus today date from the Roman era. They include some of the most spectacular relics of the island's past and they clearly reflect one of the most prosperous periods in its history. In spite of this, however, there is little external evidence that would witness to the wealth and prosperity of Roman Cyprus. Except for the Archaic, Classical and Hellenistic periods ancient historians and writers in general are almost totally silent with regard to Cyprus and most of what we know about Roman Cyprus, apart from the monuments themselves, is culled from inscriptions. It is clear that the reason why the island features so infrequently in the ancient sources is that it had and gave no problems. Once the Roman administrative system was brought into action, very little of international purport stirred the tranquillity that reigned over the island. Cyprus, as a matter of fact, was a prosperous, well governed land, but, politically and militarily, it was no more than a harmless backwater.

Roman rule in Cyprus was established in its final form in 22 BC. Rome's courtship of the island (and of Egypt), however, had started about a century and a half earlier, and became always more direct as Rome steadily established herself as a major power in the eastern Mediterranean. By the end of the 3rd century BC, Rome was acting as protector of the interests of the Ptolemies, and so, in 168 BC, when Antiochus IV Epiphanes of Syria took the island (and Egypt, save Alexandria) from the brothers Ptolemy VII

Philometor and Ptolemy VIII, Rome sent an embassy under Gaius Popillius Laenas who obliged Antiochus to withdraw from both Cyprus and Egypt. It was, however, the antagonism between the Ptolemies themselves that gradually opened the doors of Cyprus to the Romans. The two Ptolemies just mentioned were the first to do so. Their co-regency came to an end when, towards the close of 164 BC, Ptolemy VIII drove his brother out of Alexandria. Philometor fled to Rome, where he obtained the Senate's support, and then settled in Cyprus. The differences between the two brothers, however, took a different course and they were eventually settled with the division of the Kingdom into two, before the Roman envoys had time to take action. At the end of the 2nd century BC we find Cyprus included amongst the 'friends and allies of Rome' and a *senatus consultum*, a formal resolution of the Senate, of 100 BC or soon after, advises her rather emphatically not to harbour pirates. The quarrels over the throne of Egypt were getting always more intense, and with all the surrounding lands (Cilicia, Syria and

Marble statue of sleeping Eros; from Nea Paphos; H 26.5 cm; probably 1st century BC
(Nicosia, Cyprus Museum)

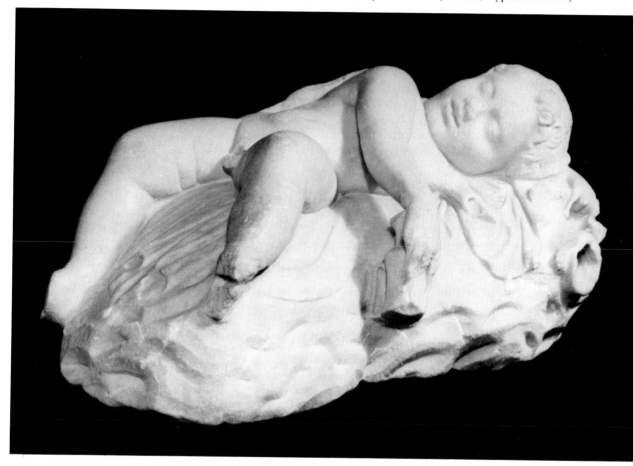

111

Cyrene), with the exception of Egypt, already Roman provinces, it was obvious that the turn of Cyprus was imminent. The Romans claimed to possess a 'will' of Ptolemy of Cyprus according to which the island was ceded to Rome. The excuse was soon found in an incident with Cilician pirates. This gave Rome the chance to accuse Cyprus of being a stronghold of piracy in the eastern Mediterranean, and led the Roman Tribune P. Clodius Pulcher, a partisan of Julius Caesar, to carry in 58 BC a law for the annexation of Cyprus. M. Porcius Cato was appointed to perform this task, and his duties included the confiscation of the royal treasury — the auction of which, incidentally, raised the astronomical sum of 7,000 talents.

Cyprus was made a praetorian province governed by a proconsul in association with the province of Cilicia on the south coast of Asia Minor. In 50/51 BC, the Proconsul was M. Tullius Cicero, the great orator, who tried, rather unsuccessfully, to protect the Cypriots from Roman exploiters. In 48 BC, during the Civil Wars, Julius Caesar restored Cyprus to the Ptolemies, initially allegedly in favour of Arsinoe IV and Ptolemy XIII, the younger children of Ptolemy XII. In the following year however, after the birth of Caesarion, Caesar presented the island to Cleopatra and their son. After the battle of Philippi (autumn of 42 BC), Cyprus came under Mark Antony who confirmed Cleopatra's possession of it. Ptolemaic rule eventually came to an end after 31 BC when Octavian, the future Emperor Augustus, became master of Egypt. Mark Antony and Cleopatra committed suicide and Caesarion was murdered in the following year.

Thereafter Cyprus went back to Rome, and her people who were considered *dediticii,* people who had surrendered unconditionally and had no rights, came under the direct responsibility of Octavian. Finally, in 22 BC, Octavian, now the Emperor Augustus, transferred Cyprus to the rule of the Senate, whereupon, under the *Pax Romana,* the island entered a long period of practically uninterrupted peace. In fact, apart from some frequent natural disasters — a more than fair share of earthquakes and the occasional famine and plague, the most disastrous one being that of AD 164 allegedly brought back from Parthia by the soldiers of Lucius Verus, little seems to have troubled the Cypriots during the next 300 years. Apart from an abortive raid by the Gothic fleet on Cyprus in AD 269, there was only one, extremely serious, event which threatened the peace and stability of the island. This was the Jewish Insurrection of AD 116. The rising started in Cyrenaica and spread to Cyprus, Egypt and Palestine. Cyprus, however, seems to have suffered worst since, being a politically and militarily unimportant province, it had no troops to defend it. The uprising was eventually quelled by extra forces sent to Cyprus under the cavalry general Lusius Quietus, a Moor who had played a leading role in Trajan's

Marble statue of Aphrodite; from Soloi; H 81 cm; *c.* 1st century AD
(Nicosia, Cyprus Museum)

Parthian Wars. In the meantime great damage had been done. The Jewish community of the island was led by a certain Artemion, and the centre of the trouble seems to have been Salamis. According to the historian Cassius Dio (2nd/3rd century AD), the whole of the non-Jewish population of this city was massacred, while the death toll from the whole of the island came to 240,000. Even though this account is wildly exaggerated, there can be little doubt that this was one of the bloodiest and most disastrous events in Cypriot history.

Apart from the Jewish Insurrection which showed up the one weak point − the absence of military forces − of Roman rule in Cyprus, the island was peaceful and well governed. Roman rule, even though designed for exploiting the resources of the island, was not unduly hard or heavy. The government machine was headed by a proconsul, a Roman senator of praetorian status, who held office

'The Blinding of Elymas'; engraving after Raphael (London, Victoria and Albert Museum)

114

C 431

TOMBSTONE FROM TREMITHUSA.

About 280 B.C.

Limestone grave relief showing a young man in the centre, probably the deceased, with his parents (or mother and brother); from Tremithus; H 98.5 cm; *c.* 1st century AD (London, British Museum)

for one year only. The proconsul had a multiple function. Naturally he was responsible for the internal security of the island which, as we have seen, with the notable exception of the Jewish Insurrection, was an easy task. He also had a judicial function and was the official mouthpiece of both the Senate and the Emperor in their legal decisions. He was the head and guide of all affairs aimed at expressing the province's loyalty to the Emperor, and he had a ceremonial function involving the consecration of imperial statues, and buildings either built by or in the name of the Emperor. Some of his other duties included the promoting of public buildings and civic works, such as roads, aqueducts, theatres, public baths, etc., and the restraining of the financial extravagance to which the cities

Bronze coin of the Emperor Vespasian (AD 69-79) issued by the Confederation (Koinon) of the Cypriots figuring on the reverse the statue of Zeus Salaminios (London, British Museum)

were often prone. He was assisted by a *quaestor provinciae,* a financial officer, and a *legatus pro praetore,* a deputy commander, both of whom also served on a yearly basis. The governing of the island fell fundamentally into the hands of these three men, who were undoubtedly aided by their own staff that they brought with them. The position of proconsul was not much sought after since Cyprus, being a minor senatorial province with no army apart from the Governor's bodyguard, gave little scope to men of political or military ambition. Moreover, and this to Cyprus's advantage, the short tenure of all these three posts meant that there was not much opportunity for corruption in the government – especially since the same two men were never together on the island for more than six months, the proconsuls being appointed on the 1st of July, and the quaestors on the 10th of December. After the 1st century AD we find that a *procurator* for the island was appointed by the Emperor, clearly as a means by which the latter could supervise finances and look after his own interests in the senatorially-controlled province. Also in later times a *curator civitatis* was imposed on the cities, again by the Emperor, in order to keep in check their extravagant spending; while considerable control could be exercised in an island always involved with trade through the *limenarcha Cypri* (inspector of harbours for Cyprus).

For the rest, Roman rule in Cyprus had to rely on the good will and co-operation of the old-established cities. In this aspect the Romans had a fairly easy task since, by this time, the cities of Cyprus were practically uniform in constitution, social organisation and language. As before, the cities had a *boule* (council), but it was the *archons* (magistrates) presiding over the *demos* (popular assembly) that did most of the governing. They were assisted in their tasks by a secretary, a treasurer and clerks of the market. There were, moreover, gymnasiarchs who supervised education.

For administrative purposes the island was divided into four districts: Salamis in the east, Lapithos in the north, Paphos in the west, and Amathus (with the central Troodos massif) in the south. The territory was divided between twelve (or thirteen) cities, with, as in Hellenistic times, Paphos as the capital – Palaepaphos with its still world-famous Temple of Aphrodite was reduced to nothing more than the sanctuary of the new capital Nea Paphos. It remained the capital up until the 4th century AD, when it was superseded by Constantia, and as such was the administrative and cultural centre of the island. The other cities into which Cyprus was divided were Kourion, Amathus, Kition, Salamis, Carpasia, Kyrenia, Lapithos, Soloi, Arsinoe (formerly Marion), Chytroi (Kythrea) and Tamassos. As is clear from the above list, with the exception of Chytroi, built near the island's most celebrated spring, and Tamassos, situated near some of the most important mines, all the other large

The Gymnasium of Salamis. The majority of the columns came from the nearby theatre and were used here during the early Byzantine reconstruction

cities of Cyprus were coastal — a clear indication that this was a peaceful period in Cypriot history. In fact, Tamassos, at about 305 m, was the most high-lying city in the island, and, generally speaking, only the lower foothills of both the Kyrenia and Troodos mountain ranges were inhabited. Higher up we have evidence for a temple of Hera at Ayia Moni, a Hellenistic temple that seems to have continued into the Roman period, over 914 m above Ktima, and a temenos of Zeus Labranius near the summit of Adelphi at about 1524 m. Otherwise, little is known above the lower reaches of the mountains.

117

General view of the excavations of Salamis. From Left to right: the gymnasium and baths, the stadium, the amphitheatre and the theatre

The whole island was divided between the twelve cities, and other holdings of land were either minimal or died after the early Empire. For example, it is recorded that the temple of Asklepios on the island of Cos held property on Cyprus in the early Empire. Also, considerable remnants of centuriation, i.e. land-survey, near Salamis must be indicative of some land owned by the Roman state, which, however, is not otherwise well attested. There seem to have been no *latifundia* (large landed estates) or imperial estates.

The Roman emperors took good care to provide the cities of Cyprus with a good water supply, and to link them with an efficient road system. Our evidence for the latter comes from the Peutinger Table, a 13th-century copy of a Roman map, and a substantial number of surviving milestones. These show a ring road

round the coastal cities of the island, and an inland road joining Soloi to Tamassos, then Tremithus and possibly Salamis. Other roads seem to have serviced the Karpass Peninsula and joined other cities across the island. The main part of this road system dates to the early Empire and was due to the Emperors Augustus and Titus. There were later repairs and modifications under the Severan Emperors when it would seem the expenses were paid for by individual cities.

Greek, as in the rest of the eastern Empire, remained the official language, and decrees and edicts were published in Greek. Latin is found used extensively only in the early milestones and in the dedications of buildings. In fact Roman imperial policy in general seems to have had little interest in Romanising Cyprus. The Cy-

119

The restored theatre at Kourion; 2nd century AD

priots on the other hand, who as we have seen came under Roman rule technically as enemies, and perhaps because of this, tried very hard to please their rulers, as is witnessed for example by the oath of allegiance to Tiberius on his accession to the throne, a copy of which was found at Palaepaphos. In this, amongst other things, the Cypriots swear 'to obey alike by land and sea, to regard with loyalty and to worship' the new Emperor. Also the *Koinon Kyprion* (Confederacy of Cypriots), the institution which under the Ptolemies organised the worship of the rulers — thus more a political than a religious institution — was very active again. Through this the province could show its loyalty to the Emperor, as well as organise religious festivities and honour public benefactors with decrees. It also had the right to strike copper coins to serve as change for the imperial coinage in more precious metals. Not only did the Cypriots celebrate the emperor cult very fervently, but they also invented, presumably in order to please Rome, a unique, albeit short-lived, Imperial Calendar which glorified Augustus and his house, the Julii, the legendary descendants of Aphrodite. In spite of all this, however, there are very few signs of reward on the part of Rome. There are noticeably few freedmen and only rarely are Roman citizens attested during the first two centuries of the Empire. It would seem though, judging by the minimal reaction of the Cypriots, that, by AD 212, when Caracalla offered Roman citizenship to all free males living in the Empire, they had lost interest in obtaining it. On the other hand the island seems to have attracted very few Romans of wealth and influence to settle there permanently — although there were certainly Italian trading communities established in the late Ptolemaic and Republican periods at Paphos, Salamis and probably Kition. No colonies, however, were established on the island, and no city was granted either full citizenship or even limited privileges, and all paid taxes. The taxes do not seem to have been very heavy since the island clearly prospered. It was self-sufficient in most ways and continued to exploit timber and minerals as during the Hellenistic period. The mines, which had been royal property under the Ptolemies, had now come under imperial ownership. From Josephus, the 1st-century-AD Jewish historian, for instance, we learn that in 12 BC Augustus leased out half the output of the copper mines of Soloi to Herod the Great of

Part reconstruction of the temple of Apollo Hylates, Kourion; c. AD 100

121

Judaea for the sum of 300 talents. In imperial times the mines were administered by imperial procurators and were famous enough for Galen, the great physician, to visit those of Soloi in AD 166 in order to collect a variety of minerals that could be used in medicine. Moreover, so far as timber and ship-building are concerned, as late as the 4th century AD the historian Ammianus Marcellinus, speaking of the fertility and opulence of Cyprus, tells us that the island could build and send to sea a ship fully equipped from stem to stern entirely from its own resources.

Cyprus was a fertile land and had, as always, a predominantly agricultural population. Pliny the Elder (AD 23-79), in his *Natural History* includes Cypriot wine in his list of highly esteemed wines; the Greek geographer and historian Strabo (*c.* 63 BC to *c.* AD 24) mentions that the island had good wine and good olive oil and was self-sufficient in corn. Flax was also an important source of income and the linen-weavers of Salamis were wealthy and influential enough to erect a statue of Hadrian in the gymnasium of their city. In this trouble-free and prosperous environment it was natural that culture and the arts would flourish, and, as we shall see, there are enough splendid monuments on the island to bear witness to this. Nevertheless the culture of Cyprus remained predominantly insular, and there are extremely few Cypriots who seem to have attained world renown. Perhaps the most important is the Platonic philosopher Bacchion son of Tryphon. A native of Paphos, Bacchion became Marcus Aurelius' first tutor in philosophy, and was honoured by Delphi between AD 150 and 160. Another Cypriot of international repute was the flute player P. Aelius [Ae]lianus, almost certainly a native of Cypriot Salamis, who lived during the Antonine period and was honoured at Delphi. Locally, on the other hand, both sciences and the arts flourished as is recorded by a number of inscriptions. These mention doctors, musicians and philosophers, amongst whom special reference can be made to Plous of Paphos who lived in Augustan times, and who was a philosopher as well as a High Priest of the imperial cult. From an epitaph we also learn of Kilikas, a Homeric poet who was born and died at Kition. There are a fair number of inscriptions mentioning doctors some of them described as *archiatroi;* certainly, though, no other Cypriot doctor can compete with the fame of Zeno of Kition, a namesake and compatriot of the founder of Stoic philosophy. He lived in Alexandria in the mid-4th century AD and became the *archiatros* of that city. He founded his own school of medicine from which three famous doctors of antiquity graduated: Magnus of Antioch, Oreibasius of Pergamon and Ionikos of Sardis. Relatively recent evidence shows that the tradition of medicine in Cyprus, already firmly established in the Classical and Hellenistic periods, with famous doctors like Apollonios of Kition, Onasilos

Marble statue of Asklepios, god of medicine; from the Villa of Theseus, Nea Paphos; H 48 cm; probably end of the 2nd century AD (Paphos, District Museum)

Onasilos Onasikyprou and Syennesis the Cypriot, continued to
thrive in the Roman period. The visit of Galen in AD 166 to the
mines of Soloi in order to collect minerals must more than likely
have been prompted by the local tradition and use of these minerals
in medicine. Much more tangible evidence comes from Paphos
where, apart from the monumental Asklepieion in the city's civic
centre, there is a unique set of clay hot-water-bottles moulded
in such a way as to fit the contours of the different parts of the human body (hands, shoulders, chest, ears, genitals, etc.) on which
they were applied. Again in Paphos a recently-excavated tomb of a
Roman surgeon was found to contain, amongst other objects, a
collection of about thirty iron and bronze surgical instruments and
containers, some still filled with pills and powders.

That the Asklepieion and the tomb of this well-equipped surgeon are found in Paphos is not surprising since it was the capital of the island. In fact, a look at the history of this city will enable us to see and understand how the island as a whole developed during the Roman period. At the beginning of Roman rule, Paphos was simply the *polis* (city) or *demos* (popular assembly) of the Paphians. After the earthquakes of 15 BC, during which the city was very badly damaged, the Emperor Augustus contributed to its rebuilding and granted it the title of *Sebaste,* the Greek equivalent of Augusta. It is not known exactly how and why Paphos came to be called, in the last quarter of the 1st century AD, 'Augusta Claudia Flavia' — a title obviously conferred by one of the Flavian emperors. It has been suggested that 'Claudia' was a result of Nero's artistic tour of Greece; and 'Flavia' was granted by the Emperor Vespasian as a reward for the favourable response given to his son Titus when, on his voyage to Syria in AD 69, the future Emperor stopped at Palaepaphos and was received by Sostratos, the High Priest of Paphian Aphrodite, who assured him of the brilliant destiny in front of him. It is, however, more likely that the latter indicates the esteem and a beneficent interest shown by Titus or Vespasian (as had been the case with Augustus earlier on) in the restoration of Paphos after the disastrous earthquakes of AD 76/77 when Paphos, together with Salamis and a third, unnamed city were completely destroyed. The last and at the same time most glorious title given to Paphos was 'Sebaste Claudia Flavia Paphos, he hiera metropolis ton kata Kypron poleon' (the sacred metropolis of the towns of Cyprus). It is not known exactly when it was bestowed on the city, but it is mainly encountered during the Severan period (late 2nd to early 3rd century AD). This is not surprising since not only in Paphos but throughout the island the surviving monuments, from architecture to sculpture, mosaics to wall paintings, proclaim a period of unprecedented opulence and sophistication — a situation that is also reflected in the wealth and variety of tomb architecture, decoration and offerings.

The prosperity of Roman Paphos, and Cyprus as a whole, seems to have continued for the rest of the 3rd century; but there were already obvious signs of decline. These can be attributed to a number of factors which in one way or another led to the loss of the favoured autonomy within the Roman world that Cyprus had enjoyed up until then. In AD 293, under Diocletian, the Roman Empire was divided into East and West, and Cyprus, together with south-east Asia Minor, Syria and Palestine, went to the Diocese of the East. In this way, Cyprus became subordinate to Antioch since it was no longer governed by a proconsul of its own but by a *consularis* working under the Praetorian Prefect of the Orient residing in Syrian Antioch. There were further changes in the admin-

Over-life-size bronze statue of Emperor Septimius Severus (AD 193–211); from Chytroi (Kythrea); H 2.08 m; *c.* AD 200

Detail of floor mosaic
depicting Orpheus and the
Beasts; from the House of
Orpheus, Nea Paphos; late
2nd/early 3rd century AD

istrative system but Cyprus's subordination to Antioch continued under the Vicar of the Orient and, after AD 331, the Count of the Orient, right up to the 6th century AD when, with Justinian's provincial reorganisation, the Governor of Cyprus ceased to function under the Count of the Orient, and became directly responsible to the central government in Constantinople.

Up until the 4th century AD, Paphos had remained the capital of the island, and as such the political and cultural centre. It was also the centre of administration, as well as the place of residence for the Roman governors. The political reorganisation of the Roman

ΘΙCΒΗ   ΠΥΡΑΜΟC

Floor mosaic representing Pyramos and Thisbe; from the House of Dionysos, Nea Paphos; late 2nd/early 3rd century AD

world in the 4th century AD, however, and Cyprus's new subordination to Antioch and general re-orientation towards the East, was to prove Paphos's undoing. At about this same period Cyprus witnessed a series of natural disasters culminating in the earthquakes of AD 332 and 342 which destroyed Paphos, Salamis and most large cities of the island. Paphos was restored but the strategic interests of the time dictated that precedence was given to Salamis which, rebuilt by the Emperor Constantius II (AD 337-361) and renamed after him Constantia, became, by the mid-4th century AD, the new capital of Cyprus.

It is clear from what has been said up to now, and from what actually survives in the ruins of Paphos and Salamis, that these two cities were the leaders in the development of culture and the arts in Roman Cyprus. Excavations in the other cities, however, show quite clearly that the flowering of the arts was by no means the prerogative of Paphos and Salamis only. The architecture and art of Roman Cyprus is marked by a mixture of local and foreign styles and trends that also characterised the art and architecture of the Hellenistic period. There is, for example, imported sculpture of the highest quality in marble (e.g. the Asklepios from the Villa of Theseus in Paphos) and in metal (e.g. the bronze statue of

Septimius Severus from Chytroi) which clearly belong to mainstream imperial art or at least to the art of world-famous artistic centres. There are also, however, statues in local stone which betray a mixture of characteristically Cypriot style, a continuation of indigenous traditions, and newly imported ideas. In architecture as well, the traditional sacred enclosures of the past continued to predominate, but now we also find more standard forms, like the Temple of Apollo Hylates at Kourion which has a podium and a tetrastyle façade with Nabataean capitals. A similar colonnaded front is found in the Temple of Aphrodite at Amathus where the architectural decoration blends Greek, Egyptian and Nabatean elements.

Of the many important buildings so far excavated or known to have existed in Roman Cyprus, mention can be made of the following: gymnasia, so essential to a Greek city, are attested by inscriptions at Paphos, Kourion, Kition, Chytroi, Lapithos and Carpasia (and must have doubtless also existed at Arsinoe and Amathus), while the colonnaded one excavated at Salamis, probably one of at least two Roman gymnasia in the city, is among the most splendid examples of its type. Theatres are known at Kourion (seating capacity of 7,000), Salamis (seating capacity of 15,000), Soloi seat-

Floor mosaic representing Apollo and Daphne; from the House of Dionysos, Nea Paphos; late 2nd/early 3rd century AD

129

Detail of floor mosaic representing the Triumph of Dionysos; from the House of Dionysos, Nea Paphos; late 2nd/early 3rd century AD

ing capacity of 3,500) and Paphos (apparently the largest of all), while another at Kition is attested by epigraphy. Most of these were earlier foundations modified to suit the changing Roman tastes. Thus the theatre at Kourion was converted under Caracalla (AD 211-217) into a hunting theatre, and that at Salamis was modified in the 3rd century AD to accommodate aquatic games. Buildings of undoubted and characteristically Roman flavour were also constructed, for example the public baths of Salamis and Kourion, the nymphaea of Soloi and Kourion, the Odeon of Paphos, and, above all, the amphitheatres of Paphos and Salamis. These last two buildings, together with an inscription from Ankara, mentioning a procurator *familiae gladiatoriae,* leave no doubt that gladiatorial games were practised in Cyprus − something already hinted at by the mosaic decoration of the House of the Gladiators at Kourion. The houses of the Roman period, such as the Houses of Dionysos and Orpheus at Paphos and the House of the Gladiators at Kourion, follow the traditional plan with the main rooms arranged around an open courtyard, the atrium, but they are of unprecedented size, with a large number of rooms decorated with mosaics, frescoes, sculpture and other works of art. At Paphos there is also the gigantic so-called Villa of Theseus which has more than one hundred rooms and corridors, a plan characteristic of late Roman palaces, and was almost certainly the residence of the Roman pro-consul. Nothing, however, shows better the wealth of Roman Cyprus, and the high standards attained by its artists, than the rich series of mosaics that, from the Severan period onwards, decorate many of the buildings, mostly private (e.g. the House of the Gladiators at Kourion, the House of Leda at Palaepaphos, and the houses in Paphos discussed below) but also public (e.g. the Baths of Salamis decorated with wall mosaics). The evidence so far available shows that the centre of mosaic production was, as is to be expected, Paphos. Here among several isolated, and many unexca-vated, examples there are the magnificent series of mosaics from the Houses of Dionysos, Orpheus and Aion, and the Villa of Theseus. These names have been given to the various buildings after the main mythological character depicted in their mosaic decoration. Thus in the House of Dionysos, of the late 2nd/early 3rd century AD, the most important part of the decoration is occupied by Dionysos, the god of wine, and by themes and motifs associated with him. One of these is the myth of Icarios, the first man to make

Floor mosaic showing Ganymede being carried off by Zeus in the guise of an eagle; from the House of Dionysos, Nea Paphos; late 2nd/early 3rd century AD

131

wine, and the 'First Wine Drinkers', thus described in an inscription written above two drunk men. The house is also decorated with other non-Dionysiac mosaics, amongst which are depictions of the myths of Narcissus, Ganymede, Pyramos and Thisbe and Apollo and Daphne. In the nearby House of Orpheus there are highly accomplished representations of an Amazon, Herakles and the Lion of Nemea, and a magnificent depiction of Orpheus surrounded by beasts, listening to his heavenly music. In the Villa of Theseus there is one of the most masterful illustrations of the story of Theseus and the Minotaur, as well as representations of Neptune and Amphitrite, and the First Bath of Achilles. In the adjacent so-called House of Aion (the exact nature and plan of this recently-discovered building are not yet known) there is one of the most important groups of mosaic panels from the late Roman world. They represent the Birth of Dionysos, the Triumph of Dionysos, Leda and the Swan, the Judgment of Marsyas, and the beauty contest, presided over by Aion, god of eternity, between

Floor mosaic showing
Theseus and the Minotaur,
Ariadne and
personifications of Crete
and the Labyrinth; from the
Villa of Theseus, Nea
Paphos; made in the 3rd and
restored in the 4th century
AD

133

Cassiopeia and the Nereids. From the artistic point of view these panels are of the highest quality, full of baroque-like richness of design and colour. Iconographically, however, they are even more important since they depict, and identify with inscriptions, little-known and even unknown personages and personifications, thus enriching our knowledge of ancient iconography. A coin of Licinius I of AD 317-323 found in the bedding of these panels shows that the floor must have been made towards or after the second half of the 4th century AD. This is the time that Constantine the Great made Christianity the official religion of the Empire but these mosaics, in their glorification of paganism, provocatively ignore all ideas about the new religion.

Whether this was deliberate it is impossible to know. What is certain is that the surviving evidence shows undeniably that Christianity had made very little progress in Cyprus during the first three centuries of our era. This is surprising since the event that had the most long-lasting effect on the history of Roman Cyprus was the visit of St Paul in AD 45. St Paul, accompanied by St Barnabas, a Cypriot Jew who had for some time been preaching the Gospel in Antioch, came to Salamis, preached in the synagogue and then

Bronze coin of the Emperor Caracalla (AD 198-217) issued by the Confederation (Koinon) of the Cypriots, showing the temple of Aphrodite at Palaepaphos (London, British Museum)

ΛΗΔΑ

ΕΥ
ΡΩ
ΑΣ

crossed the island to Paphos. There, as recorded in the 'Acts of the Apostles', they visited the Roman Proconsul L. Sergius Paulus. The Proconsul, after witnessing the miraculous blinding of the sorcerer Elymas Bar-Jesus by St Paul, 'believed being astonished at the doctrine of the Lord'. Despite this, however, and in spite of the Cypriots later proudly claiming that their country was the first ever to have a Christian governor, there is little on the island that is indisputably Christian before the mid-4th century AD. By this time however, after the inauguration of Constantinople in AD 330 and Constantine the Great's recognition of Christianity, the old Roman world came to an end, and Cyprus, like the whole of the Eastern Roman Empire entered the Byzantine era.

Detail of floor mosaic representing Leda and the Swan; from the House of Aion, Nea Paphos; mid-4th century AD

135

VIII

THE BYZANTINE PERIOD

330-1191

Sir Steven Runciman

It was with the reign of Constantine the Great that the Byzantine period can be said to have begun. Not only did he found a new capital for the Empire on the site of the ancient Byzantium, but he allowed the Christians freedom of worship and increasingly gave them his own personal patronage. Within half a century of his death Christianity had become the official religion of the Empire.

The new capital was inaugurated on 11 May 330. Constantine christened it New Rome; but it was generally known, after his name, as Constantinople: though its inhabitants simply called it the *Polis,* the City: which in the form *'s tin polin,* 'to the City', survives in the Turkish name, Istanbul. It was not until the division of the Empire in 396 between the sons of Theodosius the Great that Constantinople became the fixed residence of the emperors of the East; but already the administration of the Eastern provinces, including Cyprus, was seated there. For the Cypriots themselves the change made little difference, except that henceforward the administrators of the island tended to be drawn from the Greek-speaking world, and were more in sympathy with their subjects than their Latin-speaking predecessors.

The triumph of Christianity, however, made a vast difference in the life of the island. The Christian community seems already to have been large, though nothing is known of its organisation. But, as at least three Cypriot bishops attended the Oecumenical Council of Nicaea in 325, only thirteen years after the Edict of Milan had legitimised the Church, it is likely that their sees of Paphos, Salamis and Tremithus were already organised. Twelve Cypriot bishops

136

were signatories to the decrees of the Council of Sardica in 344. By 400 fifteen were mentioned in the letter written by Theophilus, Patriarch of Alexandria, to the Church of Cyprus; and the Metropolitan see by now was fixed at Constantia, that is to say, Salamis.

Traditionally the Church of Cyprus had been founded by St Barnabas, the twelfth apostle who replaced Iscariot. We are told in the *Acts of the Apostles* of two visits that St Barnabas paid to the island, one with St Paul and the other, after he had quarrelled with St Paul, with St Mark. The tradition can therefore be accepted. He was supposed to have been born at Salamis and to have been put to death there by fellow-Jews. The early Cypriot saints, such as St Heracleidius, are shadowy figures. But the 4th century produced three historic figures who had an undoubted influence on the spread of Christianity in the island. The first was St Spyridon, who had been tortured during the Galerian persecution early in the century but survived to become Bishop of Tremithus and to attend the Council of Nicaea. He was sufficiently revered for his body to be removed for safety to Constantinople at the time of the Moslem invasions and thence, on the eve of the capture of the City by the Turks in 1453, to Corfu, where he became that island's patron saint. Next was St Hilarion, a hermit saint whose life was written by St Jerome. He came to Cyprus from Palestine some time in the 330s and settled near Paphos. His body too was not allowed to rest in peace but was taken by pious thieves to Palestine soon after his death. Finally there was St Epiphanius. He also was of Palestinian origin and came as a young man to Cyprus; he was elected Bishop of Constantia-Salamis in 368. He dominated the Cypriot Church till his death in 403, when he was nearly ninety. He was a man of great erudition but cantankerous and obstinate. His main achievement was to hold a Council in Salamis in 401 at which Origenist doctrines were finally condemned.

These saints added to the prestige of the Cypriot Church; but perhaps more influential at a popular level was a visit to the island from that holy archaeologist, St Helena, on her return from discovering the site and the relics of Our Lord's Passion in Jerusalem. According to the accepted story, Cyprus had been suffering from a terrible drought and consequent famine for thirty-six years, which promptly ended when the Empress arrived with some of her relics. Obedient to a divinely-inspired dream she deposited the cross of the Penitent Thief in a monastery that she founded at Stavrovouni and a fragment of the True Cross at the church of Tokhni, close to her landing-place. This fragment was to prove its authenticity by triumphantly surviving an ordeal by fire in the reign of King Hugh IV. It is not possible to decide now between historic truth and legend; but it seems probable that St Helena did in fact visit the island and that the famine, for which there is historic evidence, did cease about the same time; though it had probably been of lesser duration. At any rate, Cyprus was held henceforward to possess Christian relics of the greatest importance.

The establishment of Christianity undoubtedly eased the life of the population. Harsher Roman laws were repealed. The death-penalty became rare. Concubinage was abolished, as was the *patria potestas,* the right of life and death that a father had over his children. Gladiatorial sports were abandoned for the less bloodthirsty sport of chariot-racing. Above all, the Church in Cyprus was always in close touch with the people and was always ready to champion popular rights against overbearing officials. But the new religion did not ameliorate the stern laws which tied labourers to the land on which they were born. Indeed, Constantine, in his anxiety to maintain agriculture, tightened them; and a little later the Emperor Valens imposed heavy punishment on any peasant who left his district. But the imperial control over officials was tightened. They could no longer enrich themselves at the expense of the populace. Measures were taken to see that the taxes, which were heavy, were received in full by the government.

In addition to the drought, for which there is other evidence, though it probably did not last as long as the thirty-six years of the legend, Cyprus suffered in the 4th century from devastating earth-

The monastery of St Barnabas, west of Salamis, is built on the site traditionally occupied by the tomb of the saint; the present church dates from the 18th century

138

quakes. In 332 Paphos was badly hit. When St Hilarion arrived there soon afterwards his biographer, St Jerome, tells us that 'it has now only its ruins to show what once it was'. Salamis was also damaged; and ten years later almost the whole city was destroyed by a still more severe shock, followed by a tidal wave. The Emperor Constantius II relieved its surviving citizens from taxation for four years and organised the rebuilding of the city, on a slightly smaller scale, rechristening it Constantia, though the old name continued in use.

Of the political history of Cyprus in the 4th century little is known. In about 330 Constantine sent an official called Calocaerus to govern the island. Legend relates that he found it infested with snakes, as a result of the drought. He therefore introduced the special breed of cats, which were cared for by the monastery of St Nicholas, near Akrotiri and close to the cape called Gata after them. These cats are mentioned by many medieval travellers to the island. Encouraged, perhaps, by the success of his enterprise, Calocaerus rebelled against the Emperor in 333. Constantine sent his nephew Delmatius to deal with the rebel, who was captured and put to death at Tarsus. The island seems to have passed the remaining years of the century in tranquillity.

This political tranquillity seems to have lasted throughout the 5th

century, during which the Cypriots' main attention was devoted to the establishment of the independence of their Church. The Patriarch Alexander of Antioch wrote in about 410 to Pope Innocent I to complain that the Cypriots were now ordaining their own bishops, contrary to a canon of the Council of Nicaea, which declared that the Patriarch had the right to appoint the Archbishop of Cyprus. Only if winter weather made communications impossible could the Cypriot bishops elect their chief. This canon was undoubtedly forged. The relevant canon, the 6th, merely confirmed the rights of the Church of Antioch 'and of other eparchies', of which Cyprus presumably was one. The Pope ordered the Cypriots to return to their obedience. He received no answer from them. But Antioch was not prepared to let the matter rest. The summoning of an Oecumenical Council to Ephesus to discuss the Nestorian question provided an opportunity. The Metropolitan of Cyprus, Theodore of Constantia-Salamis, who had been a firm defender of Cypriot independence and who had once, when visiting Antioch, been struck on the face by a minion of the Patriarch, had recently died. The Patriarch John of Antioch induced an old friend of his, Flavius

Dionysius, who was now Count of the Orient, to send instructions to the Consular (or Governor) of Cyprus, that he was to insist that if the Cypriot bishops elected a new metropolitan, he and his suffragans must attend the Council to justify their insubordination. Heavy penalties would be imposed were they to disobey the summons.

On receipt of these orders the Cypriot bishops firmly elected a new Archbishop, Rheginus, and he, with three bishops and a *protopapas,* set out for Ephesus. It was on the whole a successful journey. John of Antioch, who supported Nestorius, proved to be on the losing side at the Council; and the Bishops of Curium and Soloi − their colleague of Paphos having died soon after his arrival at Ephesus − gave a spirited defence of the autonomous tradition of the Cypriot Church. But the Fathers of the Council were guarded in their verdict. The 8th canon of the Council pronounced that if, as the Cypriots claimed, it was against the ancient tradition for the Bishop of Antioch to consecrate bishops in Cyprus, then the church authorities in Cyprus should have the free right to consecrate their bishops themselves, according to the canons and the established customs.

At the time this canon seems to have been accepted as endorsing Cypriot ecclesiastical autonomy. But Antioch had not given up the struggle. Within half a century, probably in 488, the Patriarch Peter the Fuller wrote to the Emperor Zeno, who was an old friend of his, to point out that as the Church in Cyprus had undoubtedly been founded from Antioch and as Antioch was undoubtedly an apostolic foundation, Cyprus should be under its authority. Zeno might well have accepted the argument, despite the established Cypriot claim that St Barnabas was the founder of the island Church. Fortunately the Cypriot Archbishop, Anthemius, warned of the attack, had an opportune dream in which St.Barnabas showed him where he had been buried. As soon as possible Anthemius went in procession to the spot, where, under a tree shown in the vision, his workmen opened up a cave, in which the saint's body was found lying in a coffin; and on his breast was a copy of the Gospel of St Matthew. There was a tradition, confirmed by the apocryphal Acts of St Barnabas, that the saint had always carried about with him a copy of the Gospel written in his own hand, and that his devoted disciple, St Mark, had placed the book on his dead body. Armed with the relics Anthemius hastened to Constantinople to show them to the Emperor, to whom he presented the Gospel. Zeno was deeply impressed and delighted with the gift. In return he summoned a synod which confirmed the autocephaly of the Cypriot Church; and he gave to its Archbishop in perpetuity the extraordinary privilege of carrying a sceptre instead of a pastoral staff and of signing his name in purple ink, as only an Emperor might do. These symbols could be held to mean that the Archbishop had temporal authority over the island; but it is doubtful whether this was what Zeno intended. Civil governors were still sent to administer it.

Antioch retained the right to provide the chrism used for the consecration of bishops, as it was now held that such chrism has to be blessed by a Patriarch. This practice lasted till 1860. From 1864 onward the chrism has been obtained from Constantinople. But neither Patriarchate could thereby claim authority over the island Church.

The Church of Antioch accepted the decision. Indeed, a later Patriarch, Severus, recorded that when he visited Constantinople in his younger days, in about 500, he saw and greatly admired the copy of St Matthew's Gospel. The other relics of St Barnabas were returned to Cyprus, to a church that was built over the saint's burial-place.

Of the secular history of the island during the later 5th and 6th centuries we know nothing. There is no record of it having suffered any severe damage from the earthquakes that twice devastated

Floor mosaic in the Annexe of Eustolios at Kourion. It represents Creation (Ktisis) personified as a woman holding a measuring rod; 5th century AD

Antioch in Justinian's reign; and it was spared the destruction that the Syrian mainland underwent owing to the wars against Persia, which resulted in the sack of Antioch. It is probable that the island benefited from the revival of trade across the Mediterranean that followed Justinian's conquest of the West and the elimination of the Vandals: though it never quite recovered the prosperity that it had enjoyed in late Roman times. However, when the secret of the silkworm was brought to Justinian by two monks who travelled from the Far East with worms hidden in their hollowed staffs, Cyprus was one of the areas into which the new industry was introduced. Cypriot silks soon became famous and their export added to the wealth of the island.

This wealth is reflected in the art of the time. The town of Lapithos, on the site of the modern village of Lambousa, was noted for its gold and silver works; and the magnificent treasures unearthed at Lambousa show the high quality of its craftsmanship. The first discovery, made at the end of the last century, produced a number of gold and silver objects bearing the imperial hallmarks of

Tiberius II (578-582), Phocas (602-610), and of Constans II, to be dated between 641 and 651. The second discovery, made in 1902, brought to light a variety of gold objects and a splendid set of nine silver plates bearing imperial marks of Heraclius I that date them between 627 and 630. As Heraclius spent some time in the island in the course of his war against the Persians, it is not unlikely that they were made for the Emperor himself. The repoussé scenes depicted on them illustrate the career of King David and were doubtless intended to symbolise his own struggle against the giant forces of Persia. They are amongst the finest examples of the Christianised Classical tradition that was to last throughout the Byzantine period.

In Cyprus, as elsewhere in the Byzantine world, this was artistically an age of transition. In architecture we find the first domed churches, such as those of St Barnabas near Salamis, St Lazarus at Larnaca, and St Paraskevi at Yeroskipos, though all have been much altered in later centuries. Floor mosaics in the old Hellenistic tradition were still made; but now wall mosaics, made possible by the use of glass tesserae, began to appear on the island. Many of them must have perished during the Arab invasions. Of those that survived, the Virgin and Child, enthroned between archangels, in the church of Panayia Kanakaria, in the Karpass Peninsula, are in the hieratic orientalised art that came into fashion in Justinian's reign. The style is akin to that of the contemporary mosaics in San Vitale at Ravenna. The church is in the Turkish-occupied part of the island and the mosaics were removed at some time after 1974; four fragments were offered for sale in the United States in the spring of

Virgin Mary and Child between two archangels (detail); mosaic in the apse of the church of Panayia Kanakaria, Lythrankomi; first half of the 6th century

145

1989. In a court action brought by the Government of the Republic of Cyprus and the Church of Cyprus they have been recovered and are now back on the island. The similar group in the church of Panayia Angeloktistos at Kiti belongs to a more classical tradition, with more movement and more humanity, foreshadowing the classical style that was to dominate Byzantine art in the centuries after the collapse of Iconoclasm.

It is unknown whether the island was affected by the terrible war against Persia in the earlier years of the 7th century, when much of the Empire was overrun by the enemy. We know that for a short time the Emperor Heraclius minted coins in Cyprus, perhaps when the Syrian mints were closed by the war. We know that under the Emperor a new aqueduct for supplying Salamis was completed. We know too that it was in Cyprus that he first tried out the theological doctrine of Monotheletism − the doctrine that Christ had two natures but one will − which he hoped would heal the rift between his Orthodox and his Monophysite subjects. A decree which he sent to the Archbishop Arcadius spelt out the doctrine, which seems at first to have had some success in the island. Heraclius was of Armenian origin; and the doctrine was in general acceptable to the Armenians, of whom there were large colonies in the island. But it only increased the bitterness between the Orthodox and the

The church of Panayia Angeloktistos, Kiti, first built in the 5th century, largely destroyed by Arab raids in the 7th century, rebuilt *c.* 1000, reconstructed in the 12th century and restored in the 16th

Monophysites; and if the island Church ever officially adopted the doctrine, it was soon abandoned.

Before Heraclius died the whole situation in the eastern Mediterranean world had been drastically altered. The irruption of Arabs from the desert, inspired by the teachings of the Prophet Mohammed, came at a moment when the Christian Empire, exhausted by the long Persian war, was in no condition to oppose them. By 639 all Palestine and Syria were in Arab hands, and by 642 the Arabs controlled Egypt. The Cypriots may have hoped at first that the sea would protect them, as it had done from the Persians. But after their conquest of the Syrian and Egyptian ports the Arabs set about building a fleet. In 649 — the sources also give 647 or 648, but 649 seems the most probable date — the Governor of Syria, Muawiya, obtained permission from the Caliph Othman to use the fleet for an expedition against Cyprus. The Caliph agreed, provided that only volunteers were used. The fleet, which consisted of 1,500 vessels of all sizes and included a large contingent from Egypt, assembled at Acre and sailed to Constantia-Salamis. Muawiya, who commanded it in person, brought his wife Fakhita with him; and his second-in-command, Ubada ibn as-Samit, also was accompanied by his wife, Umm-Haram, a lady related to the Prophet himself and famed for her goodness. Heralds from the fleet ordered

Virgin Mary and Child attended by the Archangels Michael and Gabriel; 6th century; mosaic in the apse of Panayia Angeloktistos, Kiti

the Governor of Constantia to surrender. When he refused, trusting in the city walls, the Arabs landed and laid siege to the city. After a brief resistance the walls were breached and the invaders poured in, massacring vast numbers of the inhabitants and sacking the city so thoroughly that it never recovered. The Arabs went on to pillage the rest of the island but retired on the news that the imperial fleet was approaching. According to an old tradition, in the course of the pillaging the 'righteous lady', Umm-Haram, fell from her horse and died, and was buried in Hala Sultan Tekké.

The expedition had been intended as a raid. The Moslem authorities were too far-sighted to devastate so thoroughly an area which they hoped to incorporate in their empire. But Muawiya seems to have demanded an annual tribute from the island and an undertaking that it would not allow itself to be used as a Byzantine base. In 653 or 654, on the grounds that the latter promise had been broken, he invaded the island again, and again massacred many of its inhabitants. Those who could took refuge in the town of Lapithos, which after a short siege surrendered to him, on condition that all lives should be spared, though all their possessions were

148

confiscated. Muawiya then decided to leave a garrison of 12,000 men in the island, in a town that he built specially for them, and to encourage Moslem settlers.

For the following thirty years life for the Cypriot Christians was uncertain and miserable. Things improved slightly after the failure of the Arabs to capture Constantinople in 677 and the disasters that they suffered on their retreat. In 678 peace was made between the Emperor and the Caliph, which obliged the Caliph to pay an indemnity to the Emperor; and the treaty was renewed in 685. In neither treaty was there any mention of Cyprus; though there is evidence that the Moslem garrison was withdrawn in about 683. But when the treaty was renewed once more, in 688, between Justinian II and the Caliph Abd al-Malik, a special clause regulated the future of the island. It was to be neutralised; that is to say, neither the Empire nor the Caliphate was to keep troops in the island nor to use it as a military base, and the revenues derived from taxation were to be divided equally between the Emperor's and the Caliph's treasuries. So much is made clear by the Moslem historian Masudi and, as regards the taxes, confirmed by the Byzantine historians Theophanes and Constantine Porphyrogenitus. A third clause, attested by the Patriarch Nicholas Mysticus in the early 10th century, required each of the two communities in the island to give help to the other were it attacked from outside. But as the same letter makes it clear that neither community was armed, the help

Hexagonal silver censer. On each side is a medallion containing each of the following; Christ, the Virgin, St Peter, St Paul, St John the Evangelist, St James. On the base is a set of control stamps of the reign of the Emperor Phocas; from Lambousa; D 10.6 cm; AD 602-610 (London, British Museum)

1
Silver plate on footring
with relief of David Slaying
the Lion; from Lambousa;
D 14 cm (plate), 6.5 cm
(footring); AD 627-630
(Nicosia, Cyprus Museum)

2
Silver plate with relief of
David as Shepherd; from
Lambousa; D 14 cm
(plate), 6.5 cm (footring);
AD 627-630
(Nicosia, Cyprus Museum)

2

Silver plate on footring
with relief depicting the
Marriage of David and
Michal. King Saul presides
between them and two
pipers play music on either
side; from Lambousa;
D 26.8 cm (plate), 11.8 cm
(footring); AD 627-630
(Nicosia, Cyprus Museum)

151

2
Bronze follis of the
Emperor Heraclius (AD
610-641)
(London, British Museum)

Opposite
1
Silver bowl with central
medallion representing, in
low relief, the full face bust
of a saint, probably St
Sergius or St Bacchus. On
the underside are five
control stamps of the
Emperor Constans II; from
Lambousa; D 24.7 cm; AD
641-651
(London, British Museum)

2
Silver spoon with the
embossed figure of a ram;
from Lambousa;
L 25.4 cm; AD 600
(London, British Museum)

must have been economic or at least a refusal to give any support to the invader.

This remarkable treaty remained in force for very nearly three centuries, except for a brief period in the late 9th century when, under circumstances that are unknown, the Emperor Basil I sent troops to occupy the island. It did not ensure unbroken peace. The Byzantine and Moslem navies were allowed access to the island's harbours and often made use of them when assembling ships for a naval campaign. Cyprus was too well placed strategically for either side to abandon this convenience. Presumably each naval command would seek a harbour in a district where its co-religionists predominated, but there was no territorial division. There were Moslem villages side by side with Christian villages, though probably the former were more numerous in the eastern areas. For the collection of taxes and the administration of justice there must have been Byzantine and Moslem residents permanently established in the island, presumably with fixed seats of residence; and each must have employed officials to see that the taxes were collected and some sort of civil police. The late 9th-century *Life of St Constantine Judaeus* tells us that there were regular passenger services to the island from Adalia on the Anatolian coast and also from Seleucia; and other evidence shows that there were services to Syria. The pilgrim St Willibald, who visited the island in 723, remarked upon the condominium there between Greeks and Saracens. He was able to travel freely through the island, visiting Paphos as well as Constantia. St Constantine was alarmed when some Moslems entered a church in which he was worshipping; but his fears were groundless.

Justinian II seems himself not to have had much faith in the treaty. About the time that he made it he embarked upon a scheme to transfer a large proportion of the Greek population to the Anatolian mainland, providing a new home for them on the southern shore of the Marmora, near the city of Cyzicus. A new town was built for the settlers, which he called Nova Justinianopolis; and the Archbishop of Cyprus was induced to emigrate with his flock on the undertaking that his new diocese, which was to include the whole province of Hellespont, would continue to enjoy the autonomy that Cyprus had enjoyed, an undertaking that was confirmed by the Council *In Trullo* in 691. But already the experiment was proving to be unsuccessful. The transports sent to Cyprus to collect the emigrants, amongst whom were a number of Moslem prisoners of war, ran into a bad storm on the return journey, and many ships were wrecked, with heavy loss of life. A number of Cypriots defected and made their way home. Other Cypriots fled to Syria to avoid deportation. In 698, after Justinian's dethronement, the Emperor Tiberius III sent the whole colony back to Cyprus and at the same time negotiated with the Caliph to have the refugees to Syria

152

1

2

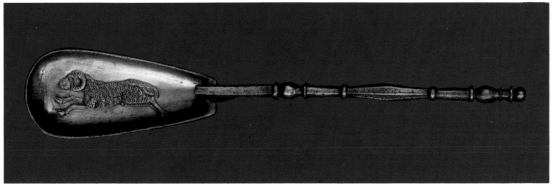

153

returned. The Caliph agreed and sent officials to round them up and to arrange for their transport back to the island.

The paucity of information about Cyprus during the three centuries of the condominium suggests that the island was enjoying a rare period of tranquillity. There were battles off its harbours, as when in 747 a huge Egyptian fleet, assembled to attack the Byzantine mainland, was caught and destroyed by a Byzantine squadron or when in 790 a Moslem fleet, that had assembled in a Cypriot harbour, sailed out and defeated a Byzantine fleet some way off the coast. The Byzantine Admiral Himerius put in to Cyprus on his way to sack Lattakieh in 910. On that occasion some of his men landed and slew a few Moslem officials who were no doubt protesting against their presence. The island did suffer three serious Moslem raids, made in each case because the Cypriot Christians had allegedly broken the terms of the treaty. In 743 the Caliph Walid ordered an invasion of the island and carried off a number of

The Akheiropiitos Monastery, near Lapithos. The church is of the early Byzantine period. A cruciform domed building with a domed narthex and a porch were added later

154

Christians, 'on suspicion'; but we are not told of what misdemeanour they were suspected. His son, Yazid III, sent them back unharmed a year or two later. In 806 a raid on the island was made on the orders of the Caliph Harun ar-Rashid, 'because the people of Cyprus had broken the treaty.' Once again we do not know what they had done. The same excuse was given when the Emir Damian of Tarsus raided the island in 912. Probably this was a reprisal for Himerius' sailors' behaviour in 910; or perhaps the Moslems had come to hear of instructions that had been sent from Constantinople to the Byzantine Resident, the *Archon* Leo Symbaticius, instructing him to find in Cyprus reliable spies who could go to the Moslem ports, Tarsus, Lattakieh and Tripoli, and report on naval activities there. The Patriarch Nicholas of Constantinople wrote to the Caliph to protest against Damian's raid, linking it to Himerius' men's misbehaviour. He pointed out that the Cypriot Greeks could not do anything to help their Moslem neighbours, as they did not have any arms.

The treaty was certainly breached on the Byzantine side when Basil I occupied the island and made it a theme, or province, of the Empire. The circumstances and the date of the occupation are

The five-domed church of SS Barnabas and Hilarion at Peristerona dates from the early 10th century. The iconostasis is dated 1549

155

unknown. It lasted for seven years. Then the condominium was restored.

Little is known of the economic life of the island during the condominium. The few travellers' accounts give the impression that it was modestly prosperous. The silk industry was developed; and it seems that the island exported foodstuffs to Syria. The two communities seem to have lived fairly harmoniously together, though it must have been galling to the Christians, who were far more numerous than the Moslems, to see a large proportion of the taxes that they paid going to the Caliph to make up his half-share of the revenue. Both empires used the island as a place to which tiresome dissidents could be sent. They could do no harm there. The iconoclastic emperors in particular found it a convenient spot to which to exile image-worshipping monks. The Cypriot Archbishop never subscribed to the iconoclastic decrees.

By the middle of the 10th century the Caliphate was sinking into decline. Egypt had seceded and soon, under the Fatimid caliphs, was to annex Palestine and southern Syria. In northern Syria the local emirates were independent in all but name. Under such circumstances there was no more point in the condominium. In 965 the Emperor Nicephorus Phocas reconquered Cilicia and turned his

The monastery of St John Lampadistis, Kalopanayiotis, contains an 11th-century church of St Heracleidius , with next to it another dedicated to St John Lampadistis and a tall vaulted building, perhaps a Latin chapel

attention to Cyprus. The Egyptians also were interested in the island; but, after defeating their fleet off the mainland coast, he sent troops under the Patrician Nicetas Chalcutzes to occupy Cyprus, which once more became a province of Byzantium.

It can be questioned whether the island benefited from the change. It had its advantages. The Christian islanders could now feel themselves to be full citizens of the great Christian Empire. Many of the Moslems emigrated. Others became converts to Christianity and were absorbed into the Greek population. The islanders no longer had to pay half their taxes to the Caliph. But the Byzantine Empire was the most highly taxed state in the medieval world; and the taxes were efficiently collected. The governors sent out from Constantinople were far more powerful than the previous residents; and their power was resented by the Archbishop, who regarded himself as head of the Christian community. There was constant friction between the civilian government and the Church. The island now contained armed forces to protect it against raiders. But the era of the Arab raids was over; and ambitious governors were sometimes tempted to use these forces to defy the central government, thus involving the island in a rebellion.

The first Governor to rebel was Theophilus Eroticus, a man who

Kykko Monastery is said to have been founded *c.* 1100 by a monk named Esaias under the patronage of Butumites. An icon ascribed to St Luke was given by the Emperor Alexius Comnenus

had been Governor of Serbia and had failed to crush a revolt there in 1040. Instead of being retired in disgrace he was transferred to Cyprus by the Emperor Michael IV, with whose family he was probably friendly, as it was on the fall of Michael V, Michael IV's nephew, that he decided to rebel. The *protospatharius* Theophylact, the official in control of judicial and fiscal affairs, refused to join him; so he tried to stir up the populace against the *protospatharius,* whose office was always unpopular. But Constantinople was warned, probably by the *protospatharius.* A naval squadron was sent to the island by the new Emperor, Constantine IX. The abortive revolt was easily put down and Eroticus was brought as a captive to Constantinople. The authorities did not take him very seriously.

They confiscated his possessions and forced him to parade in the
Hippodrome dressed as a woman, then set him free.

It was important to have a loyal governor in Cyprus, as he was
conveniently placed for seeing to the Empire's interests in Syria and
Palestine. He kept a close connection with the Byzantine frontier-
officials in northern Syria, who, when unrest across the frontier
made travel dangerous, would often send pilgrims to wait in Cyprus till conditions improved. Bishop Lietbert of Cambrai and his
fellow-pilgrims were obliged to follow this course in 1055. In their
ignorant arrogance they regarded it as an attempt to sabotage their
pilgrimage, not realising that it was intended for their safety. In
1027 a treaty with the Fatimids entitled the Emperor to rebuild the
church of the Holy Sepulchre in Jerusalem, destroyed by the mad
Caliph Hakim in 1009. The treaty was renewed in 1036; but it was
only in 1045 that work was started. It was the Governor of Cyprus
who was sent to make the final arrangements for it and for the
rebuilding of the walls of the Christian quarter.

The whole situation in the Levant was changed a quarter of a
century later when the Turks, mostly under the leadership of the
Seljuk dynasty, burst into Anatolia after the disastrous defeat of the
Byzantine army at Manzikert in 1071. Within ten years they were in
control of all Anatolia, as far as the Aegean and Marmora Seas,
apart from a few isolated cities and most of the coast. Meanwhile

The monastery of
St Chrysostom belongs to
the Orthodox see of
Jerusalem. The original
building dates from the
11th century and the church
of the Holy Trinity, one of
two attached to the
monastery, was founded in
1110

159

other Turks had invaded Syria and Palestine, causing utter disruption and confusion there. Cyprus was not directly affected; but communications with Constantinople were continually interrupted, especially after the Turkish Emir Chaka occupied Smyrna and built a fleet, with which he began to capture the nearby Aegean islands.

The Empire was saved by a remarkable Emperor, Alexius I Comnenus, who took over the governmnent in 1081, when the Empire seemed unlikely to survive. By the time of his death in 1125 he had recovered all the coastal lands of Anatolia, as well as the islands. He recreated the imperial army to be an efficient fighting-force; but his successes were due more to diplomacy than to warfare. He also depended on the loyalty and abilities of his lieutenants.

He was not always fortunate in them. In 1093 the Governor of Cyprus, Rhapsomates, conspired with the Governor of Crete, Caryces, to revolt against the Emperor, hoping for help from Chaka of Smyrna. Alexius at once sent his brother-in-law, John Ducas, with a fleet to deal with the rebels. At the news of his approach the Cretans rose against Caryces and slew him. Ducas sailed on to Cyprus. When he landed a small body of troops at Kyrenia he found Rhapsomates encamped with the island militia in the hills above the town. But Rhapsomates was a man with little

The church of St Nicholas of the Roof, Kakopetria, dates from the 11th century and a narthex and cupola were added in the 12th. The church interior is entirely covered with wall paintings dated between the 11th century and the mid-15th and some in the 17th century

160

military experience and a lack of decision. Instead of attacking the imperial troops as they were disembarking he hesitated; and when at last he marched down against them, several hundred of his forces went over to the other side and the rest showed little desire to fight. Rhapsomates gave up the struggle and fled towards Limassol, where he hoped to find a ship to take him overseas, but was captured at Stavrovouni and sent to Constantinople. His fate is unknown.

The general in command of the small imperial landing-force was Manuel Butumites, a man who was to have a very distinguished career as a soldier and diplomat. He seems to have acted briefly as Governor of the island, till Alexius sent out a new military commander, Philocales Eumathius, and an official of known probity and modesty, Calliparius, to take charge of the judicial and fiscal administration.

According to a legend which there is no reason to doubt, Butumites when he was in the island was cured of sciatica by a monk, Esaias, whom he encouraged to found a monastery at Kykko. Under his patronage Esaias then visited Constantinople, where he cured a daughter of the Emperor of the same complaint. In gratitude Alexius gave him an icon of the Mother of God, attributed to the brush of St Luke, which remains to this day the holiest icon in the island.

The church of Panayia Phorbiotissa at Asinou, near Nikitari, dates from 1105 and the domed narthex was added c. 1200. The walls are entirely covered with paintings which are considered among the finest in Cyprus

161

Philocales, who succeeded Butumites, was, according to the historian-Princess, Anna Comnena, our chief authority for Cypriot history during these years, a man of high qualities, prudent, generous, pious and loyal. Though no soldier — he could not draw a bow nor wield a shield — he was an ingenious strategist. He seems to have had two periods of office in the island, from about 1093 to 1100 and from about 1105 to 1112. In the interval the Governor was Constantine Euphorbenus Catacalon. Unfortunately Philocales was on bad terms with the Cypriot Church and its Archbishop, Nicholas Muzalon. After his retirement in about 1110, which was perhaps forced by Philocales, Muzalon wrote a long poem describing the sufferings of the Cypriots at the hands of Byzantine officials and blaming in particular a governor who is certainly to be identified with Philocales. It is a hysterical work. It depicts the inhabitants of the island being cruelly tortured if they did not pay taxes that left them starving, and, significantly, it lays most emphasis on the extortions to which the clergy were subjected and the cruel

Makheras Monastery, on the northern slopes of Mt Kionia, was founded c. 1148 with the help of a grant from the Emperor Manuel Comnenus. It was burnt down in 1530 and 1892, rebuilt in 1900

162

punishments meted out to those who disobeyed the tyrannous governor. Particular venom is directed against those clerics who supported the lay authorities. It is true that taxation was very severe and that taxes were collected ruthlessly. But the exaggerated picture of an island reduced to penury by wicked officials is clearly the work of a disgruntled and ill-tempered cleric with a grievance. The island was in fact rather prosperous. In 1097 Symeon, Patriarch of Jerusalem, who had retired to Cyprus when life became impossible in the Holy City, was able to send several consignments of food-stuffs from the island to the soldiers of the First Crusade when they were suffering from hunger before the walls of Antioch. In 1105 the threat to withold the export of foodstuffs to Tripoli was sufficient to make the authorities there comply with the Emperor's wishes. It is unlikely that a starving island should have exported food. If the government had confiscated all the island's produce in order to export it, an enfeebled peasantry would hardly have been in a condition to continue cultivation. It is certain that there had been

extortionate governors, as we know from an anonymous work, the *Logos Noutheticos,* traditionally attributed to Cecaumenus, which mentions Cyprus as a victimised province. Muzalon many years later, in 1147, returned to episcopal life as Patriarch of Constantinople. But his temper had not improved; and everyone was delighted when, four years later, it could be shown that his election had been uncanonical.

Both Butumites in his later career and Philocales when Governor of Cyprus were employed by the Emperor to help to deal with the situation that arose on the Syrian mainland out of the advance and ultimate success of the First Crusade. The Crusaders had at first, despite minor misunderstandings, co-operated fairly well with the Byzantines and helped them to recover much of western Anatolia. But when the Crusade moved into Syria there were difficulties. Till the Turkish invasions Byzantium had controlled northern Syria as

The monastery of Panayia Chrysorroyiatissa on the western slopes of Mt Troodos was traditionally founded in 1152; the present buildings were extensively restored in the second half of the 18th century

far south as Lattakieh and including Antioch; and the Emperor had induced the Crusader leaders to restore the area to him. But the ablest of them, Bohemund the Norman, had seized for himself Antioch and the surrounding country. The Emperor was determined to recover the coastal ports; and for that Cyprus was the obvious base, both militarily and diplomatically. His success was limited. He did not object to the Crusaders establishing settlements farther south, in Lebanon and Palestine. The Cypriot Governor continued to send provisions and military equipment to the crusader army. But it is interesting to note that it was in Cyprus that several Moslem princes, ousted by the Crusaders, sought temporary refuge. The island itself was not directly affected by troubles on the mainland. In 1099 a Pisan fleet conveying the Archbishop of Pisa, Daimbert, who had been appointed Papal Legate for Palestine, after raiding Corfu and other Greek islands on its way, attempted to land on Cyprus; but Philocales had little difficulty in thwarting the landing.

During the first half of the 12th century Cyprus enjoyed a period of tranquil prosperity. The establishment of the Crusader states on the mainland opened up new markets for the produce of the island; and it was admirably placed for taking advantage of the new trade routes. The Venetians, who were now the most active traders in the

The church of Panayia Arakiotissa, Lagoudera, dates from the late 12th century and was re-roofed in the 18th century with a protective steep-pitched roof. Its interior is covered with wall paintings

165

eastern Mediterranean, considered it important enough to demand that the Emperor should grant them the commercial privileges that they had been given, in return for naval help, in other parts of the Empire. The governors sent out to administer the island were all men of distinction, such as Philocales, or Catacalon, who had been a successful naval commander and whose son was married to the Emperor Alexius' youngest daughter, or John Comnenus, whom the Emperor Manuel regarded as his favourite cousin. They now bore the title *Doux,* or Duke; and they governed the island from the city of Nicosia. New towns were arising. Constantia-Salamis had been replaced by Famagusta, as its harbour seems to have silted up. Kyrenia on the north coast and Limassol on the south coast were the other chief ports of the island. Taxation undoubtedly was high but it does not seem to have been oppressive.

The prosperity of the island inaugurated a period of great artistic activity. It is probable that a number of architects and artists arrived from Constantinople, bringing with them the current artistic fashions of the capital. They tended to build churches that were comparatively small, all with a centralised dome, a form that allowed for a number of variants. The interiors were covered with

The church of St Theodosius, Akhelia, is cruciform and the original building dates from the 12th century. It has some 15th-century wall paintings

The small, single-aisled church of the Holy Apostles, Perakhorio, dates from the 12th century

frescoes, so that the worshipper could gaze on the holiest scenes in the story of the Incarnation and could feel that the saints depicted on the walls were close by, worshipping with him. Byzantine art continued to have two main schools, the hieratic, by now chiefly associated with the monasteries and the provinces, and the classical, the art of Constantinople itself and the Court. To judge from what has survived, notably the earlier frescoes in the remarkable church of St Nicholas of the Roof, near Kakopetria, Cypriot painters in the 11th century followed a monastic, hieratic style. But the arrival in the 12th century of officials connected with the imperial court led to a more sophisticated taste, as can be seen in the superb frescoes in the small church of Panayia Phorbiotissa at Asinou, commissioned by a *magistros* called Nicephoros. These reflect the contemporary style of Constantinople, where the classical tradition was beginning to include a touch of poignancy and emotion. These new elements are even more pronounced in the wall paintings in the little church of the Saviour at Aphendrika, attached to the monastery of St Chrysostom at Koutsovendis. Their present condition is unknown; but they included an Entombment of Christ which closely resembles that in the church of St Panteleimon at Nerezi in Macedonia, a painting that is the finest surviving example of Byzantine 12th-century art. The Cypriot version is not quite so sure in its execution as that at Nerezi, which is dated 1164; and many scholars regard it as an earlier work. But the Nerezi frescoes were commissioned by the Governor of the province, John Comnenus, who shortly afterwards became Governor of Cyprus. It is tempting

167

to think that he brought with him to the island a pupil of the painter of Nerezi, a good artist but one who lacked his master's supreme genius.

This lively Cypriot art of the Comnenian period was well enough established to survive the coming of Frankish rule to the island. But it was necessarily muted and confined to country districts, and began to show signs of Western influence.

The tranquillity was cruelly broken in 1156. An Armenian principality had been founded in Cilicia, and its Prince Thoros II, was in constant rebellion against the Emperor. A French adventurer, Reynald of Châtillon, who had become Prince of Antioch by marriage with its heiress, had undertaken to invade Thoros's territory to recapture some land that he had annexed. After defeating Thoros but before he had taken over the promised towns he demanded subsidies from the Emperor Manuel, who told him to wait till the task was completed. Reynald therefore made peace with Thoros and planned to raid Cyprus with his help. King Baldwin III of Jerusalem heard of the plan and sent to Cyprus to warn John Comnenus, the Governor. But before reinforcements could arrive from Constantinople, Thoros and Reynald landed with a large

TAH

force on the island. The island militia tried to intercept them but was hopelessly out-numbered, and its commander, Branas, was captured. John Comnenus himself was captured when trying to defend Nicosia. Then the invaders overran the whole island, burning churches, monasteries and houses, taking anything of value that they could find and rounding up the herds and flocks and, since they were too many and awkward to export, forcing the farmers and peasants to ransom them at a heavy price. Then, before the Byzantine forces could arrive, they sailed away with their booty and their captives.

The raid shocked Reynald's fellow-Franks as much as it infuriated the Emperor. Two years later the Byzantine army marched on Antioch and forced Reynald to make a humiliating apology. But that could not repair the damage done to Cyprus. Many years were to pass before it recovered its prosperity. Severe earthquakes in 1157 added to the misery; and in 1158 an Egyptian fleet raided the island, capturing the Governor's brother and returning home with such booty as they could find. The raid was probably made without the authority of the Egyptian authorities, who hastened to send the

The single-aisled church of Antiphonitis dates from the 12th century and has a vaulted 14th-century narthex. The dome is carried on eight round columns and covers the whole of the nave

169

Governor's brother home with every honour. It is probable that the Governor in question was the Emperor's cousin, John Ducas, who certainly held the post in 1161, when the Emperor Manuel married as his second wife Princess Maria of Antioch. He had first negotiated for the hand of Princess Melisende of Tripoli, a lady later famous as the *princesse lointaine* of the troubadours. Her disappointed brother, the Count of Tripoli, lent the fleet that he had prepared to escort her to Constantinople to pirates, telling them to raid Cyprus and any other important imperial territory that they chose; which they carried out with efficiency.

In 1166 Manuel appointed his cousin Andronicus Comnenus Governor of Cilicia, with rights over the government and revenues of Cyprus. The idea of connecting the island with Cilicia was not new. The Emperor John had in 1142 toyed with the idea of turning southern Anatolia and Cyprus into an autonomous appanage under one of his sons. Andronicus was a man of many talents but unstable and, at the time, more interested in amorous adventures than in administration. He soon went off to Antioch, enriched with the revenues of the island, where he seduced the Empress's sister, Philippa of Antioch, then left her for Palestine, where he seduced and eloped with the Queen Dowager, his cousin, Theodora Comnena. The island was left once more impoverished. These melancholy years saw the emergence of two great Cypriot saints. Nilus, who came to the small monastery of Makheras in 1172, soon made it one of the most influential establishments on the island. He later became Bishop of Tamassos, and was greatly admired for his piety and his care for the oppressed. But he was overshadowed by Neophytus, who had been a novice at the monastery of St Chrysostom, and then a hermit in the hills above Paphos. He was not allowed to remain in solitude for long; in the 1170s he founded for his disciples the monastery of New Zion, better known as the Enkleistra. He made himself an outspoken critic of the misgovernance of the island. There was little that he could achieve; but he was so greatly loved by the people that the authorities could not silence him.

In 1176 the Imperial Army under Manuel was utterly routed by the Turks at the battle of Myriokephalon, a disaster from which it never recovered. The Empire lost its control over southern Anatolia; and Cyprus was isolated once more. Manuel died in 1180. His widow, Maria of Antioch, took over the regency for their young son Alexius II. But her incompetence and the favour that she showed to the Latins soon made her hated. The adventurer Andronicus then emerged from exile and marched on Constantinople to take over the Empire. He was an able administrator who tried to stamp out inefficiency and corruption in the civil service. But he was also tyrannical, suspicious and so savagely cruel that he lost all his popularity. After two years he was dethroned and torn to pieces by the furious population of the capital. In his place they elevated a distant cousin, Isaac Angelus, an elderly, amiable and incompetent man, who in his turn was dethroned in 1193 by his brother Alexius, who was equally incompetent and less amiable.

There was a junior member of the imperial family, Isaac Ducas, who took his mother's surname of Comnenus, and who had been appointed Governor of Cilicia at the end of Manuel's reign. He could do nothing there and was soon captured by the Armenians, who sold him to the Order of the Templars. At the request of his aunt, ex-Queen Theodora, Andronicus' mistress, Andronicus consented to ransom him and to permit him to return to his precarious governorship, lending him a sum of money on the security of two distinguished Constantinopolitan citizens. Isaac used the money to collect a few soldiers, with whom he crossed the sea to Cyprus, armed with forged letters appointing him as its Governor. Once he was established there he threw off allegiance to Andronicus and took the supreme title of *Basileus,* or Emperor. Andronicus in his rage tortured and impaled the two innocent sponsors but perished himself before he could take action against the rebel. His successor, Isaac Angelus, tried to buy back his allegiance, and when that failed sent a naval expedition to recapture the island. The Emperor of Cyprus was warned of its approach. Having no ships of his own and hearing that a Sicilian Admiral, Margarito, was cruising off the Syrian coast, he hired his services. When the expedition landed

The 12th-century church of Panayia Katholiki, Kouklia, cruciform with a central dome, is situated near the Royal Manor and was probably used by the Latin Catholics working on the royal sugar estate

Margarito swept into the harbour. Isaac then had little difficulty in forcing the landing-force to surrender. Its leaders were put to death, except for a few who agreed to take service under him. The common soldiers and the ships' crews were sent back unharmed to Anatolia, while Margarito made off with the ships and the ships' officers.

Independence under its own monarch might have been the best temporary solution for Cyprus. But Isaac had a difficult task. His usurpation was resented by many Cypriots; and he had aroused the bitter enmity of Constantinople. The island was still impoverished after three decades of disasters; and soon its foreign trade was to be disrupted by Saladin's conquest of the Kingdom of Jerusalem, after the battle of Hattin in 1187. This not only deprived Cyprus for the time being of one of its main markets, but it involved a political threat. A Crusade was certain to come east to try to recover the lost lands; and as a base for operations Cyprus would be invaluable to the Crusaders. Isaac was aware of the danger. As soon as possible he entered into relations with Saladin, hoping for his help in the event of a Crusader attack. But it is hard to see how Saladin could have come to his assistance. Nothing came of the negotiations.

Had Isaac been a more popular ruler he might have survived. But his financial exactions, from which the wealthy suffered as much as the poor, lost him the good will of classes that might have supported him. He was personally detested for his ungovernable rages and wanton cruelties. His high-handedness offended the Church and caused St Neophytus to write bitter diatribes against him. It may be that his many enemies exaggerated his crimes. But when the crisis came his only loyal supporters were some, and not all, of

The church of St Anthony, Kellia, probably dates from the 9th century

his troops.

In the spring of 1191 news came that King Richard of England had set out from Sicily on his way to fight in Palestine. At the end of April three ships from his fleet appeared off Cyprus. Two were wrecked on the coast, but the third, containing his sister, Queen Joanna of Sicily, and his betrothed, Berengaria of Navarre, anchored off Limassol. Isaac hastened to the town and invited the royal ladies to come ashore. They refused, fearing to be used as hostages, but asked permission to send ashore for water and provisions. Isaac forbade this and began to fortify the coast. About a week later King Richard arrived with his main fleet. He considered that his sister and his betrothed had been insulted and landed with some troops at a nearby bay and marched on Limassol. The Italian merchants in the town welcomed him gladly and even the Greeks, in their dislike of Isaac, were friendly. Isaac, who had retired to the slopes of Troodos, then offered to negotiate, if given a safe-conduct. He visited Richard's camp and in an interview agreed to pay the King a sum of money, to allow his men to buy provisions free of custom dues, to send a contingent to join the Crusade and to offer his daughter as a hostage. But his visit to the English camp made him think that Richard was not so formidable after all. When he returned to his own camp he repudiated the agreement.

The church of Chrysopolitissa (Ayia Kyriaki), Paphos, believed to be a very early Latin building later converted to the Orthodox rite; it is Byzantine in form and the columns in front are from a much earlier basilica

173

Unfortunately for him, that very day Richard was joined by a number of distinguished lords from Palestine, come to welcome him, and each with his escort of knights. On 12 May Richard married Berengaria in the chapel of St George at Limassol, and on 13 May the remainder of the English fleet arrived. Seeing his mistake, Isaac moved to Famagusta, but realised that he could not hold it against a combined naval and military attack. He retired to Nicosia, sending his wife, an Armenian Princess, and his daughter, his only child, to the castle at Kyrenia, hoping that they might if need be escape to Armenia. In Nicosia he collected all his troops and marched down to meet the English army at the village of Tremithus. After a sharp skirmish, his troops, who were said to have been armed with poisoned arrows, were routed. Isaac fled to Kantara; and Richard entered Nicosia without opposition, many of the inhabitants even welcoming him. There Richard fell ill; and Isaac hoped to hold his four northern castles, St Hilarion, Buffavento, Kantara and Kyrenia, till the King tired of his venture and went away. But Guy of Lusignan took command of the English army and marched on Kyrenia, capturing it together with Isaac's wife and daughter. He then blockaded St Hilarion and Buffavento. Richard, as he informed an envoy from King Philip of France, had no intention of leaving the island till Isaac had been punished; and he pointed out how valuable possession of the island would be for the pursuance of the Crusade.

By the end of May Isaac realised that he was beaten. He surrendered unconditionally, asking only that he should not be put in irons. So he was brought before Richard loaded with silver chains. When Richard left the island a few days later, Isaac was brought with the fleet and later handed over to the Hospitallers. He died, still a captive, in about 1195. His wife and daughter were attached to Queen Joanna's household. Isaac's surrender had left the whole island in Richard's hands. His first act was to extract all the ready money that he could from it. Then he confirmed the laws and institutions that had existed in the Emperor Manuel's time. Latin garrisons were placed in all the castles, and two Englishmen, Richard of Camville and Robert of Turnham, were appointed justiciars, to govern the island till Richard should decide on its fate. The Greeks soon found that they had not gained from Isaac's fall. They were to take no more part in the government of their land. As a symbol of their subservience they were ordered to shave off their beards. A new era had begun.

174

IX

THE FRANKISH PERIOD

1191-1571

Richard the Lionheart 1191
The Templars 1191-1192
The Lusignan Dynasty 1192-1489
The Venetians 1489-1571

Sir David Hunt

In coming under the rule of French-speaking foreigners from the West Cyprus suffered the same fate as did most of the rest of Greece and indeed many other territories in the southern and eastern Mediterranean. The great expansion of Latin power into the Greek-speaking territories of the Empire came thirteen years after Richard's intervention in Cyprus, with the capture of Constantinople by the Fourth Crusade in 1204. Compared with that great event the Western acquisition of Cyprus in the early stages of the Third Crusade was much more of an accident. None of the crusading princes coveted the island. Richard was drawn into the adventure which ended with him having the whole of the island in his hands largely by chance and against his wish. He began at once to take urgent steps to pass it on to someone else, having taken as much plunder as he could, which went towards the expenses of his expedition. Nevertheless there was a certain inevitability about it. The Kingdom of Jerusalem and the other states founded by the Crusaders had for the moment the strongest fleets in the eastern Mediterranean, thanks to the support of the Italian maritime republics; it was natural that Cyprus should yield to their control as it had done in the past to all other powers who had dominated the waters around its shores. Before long, when the strength by land of the Moslem powers had become too great to allow the descendants of the Crusaders to cling to their Syrian coastal strip, Cyprus took over the role of the last military bastion of the Cross against the

The Archangel Gabriel, part of the Annunciation; painting in the north-east pendentive, church of Panayia Arakiotissa, Lagoudera; 1192

Crescent and the great entrepôt of East-West trade. It was rewarded, for a time, by great prosperity. The foreign rulers became notorious for their luxurious living; but their subjects profited little.

The Greeks call this period of their history the *Frankokratia*, the rule of the Franks. There is scope for debate whether it was preferable to the succeeding *Tourkokratia*. The characteristic features of Frankish rule are much the same in all the Greek lands whether in the Peloponnese, the ancestral home of the Cypriots, under a family from Champagne or in Cyprus under a family from Poitou. Both had a feudal system of land tenure and inheritance. In peacetime the Cypriot barons were not quite as turbulent as a favourite cliché of old-fashioned medieval history asserts and as they were in the Principality of Achaia. In war they combined personal courage with military mediocrity. In Cyprus the dynasty was generally successful in avoiding internal dissension and for nearly 300 years maintained a regular succession of legitimate male heirs. There were occasional breaks in the dynastic succession, with queens as regents

Christ Pantocrator;
painting in the dome,
church of Panayia
Arakiotissa, Lagoudera;
1192

for minor heirs. Women indeed play a prominent part throughout,
and often a domineering one. In the end the bright silks and plate-
armour of the reigning houses yield place to the mercantile and
calculating Venetians.

Compared with the Frankish states of mainland Greece Cyprus
was largely free of civil war. There were quarrels among the leading French-speaking noble houses, and between them and some of
the kings, quarrels which gained an added edge when Spaniards,
especially Catalans, became involved, as in 15th-century Cyprus.
Undoubtedly the most destructive influence in the long run was the
intense rivalry between the Italian mercantile cities and especially
Venice and Genoa. Most historians blame the Genoese for weaken-
ing the powers of the Government of Cyprus, and for subordi-
nating its interests to those of their trade with the Moslem states.
Venice, whose arms and intrigues had been mainly responsible for
ruining the Empire of Constantinople, was to Cyprus little more
than the final receiver in bankruptcy.

177

The Ascension; church of Panayia Arakiotissa, Lagoudera; 1192

Richard soon found evidence of what he suspected from the start: that Cyprus would be more of a trouble to him than an advantage. The Greek inhabitants had certainly been glad to be rid of Isaac but they soon rose in revolt against the foreign conqueror. Richard's governor, the Englishman Robert of Turnham, put down the rising and hanged a Greek monk who had been proclaimed Emperor. No doubt this strengthened his desire to disembarrass himself of the unwanted possession. He was pleased to find that he could pass it on to the military Order of the Temple at the reasonable price of 100,000 dinars of which only 40,000 in cash down. The Templars were also faced with a revolt; they took more drastic action and massacred so many Greeks in Nicosia that blood ran in the streets. They also ravaged all the villages of the plains, driving the inhabitants to take refuge in the mountains. This was not what the Templars wanted and they appealed to Richard to cancel the sale. He agreed because it would help him in his complicated but well-intended intrigues to settle the affairs of the Kingdom of Jerusalem if he could bestow Cyprus, on the same financial terms, on Guy of Lusignan. Local bankers scraped together 40,000 dinars and the deed was done. A dynasty lasting 300 years was founded.

The Nativity; wall painting;
Panayia Arakiotissa,
Lagoudera; 1192

Guy of Lusignan (1192-1194) had been King of Jerusalem in right of his wife Sybil, mother of King Baldwin V who died in 1186 at the age of nine. She had married him apparently for love since he had a weak and easy-going character, was poor and disliked by most of the prominent barons of the Kingdom. He came from a reasonably distinguished Poitevin family but was the least distinguished of a large family of brothers. He also managed to get himself captured by the Saracens in the battle of the Horns of Hattin where, according to Chesterton, 'the hope of the world went down' and where, in more sober truth, the greater part of the Kingdom of Jerusalem was lost. He was released in 1188 but his rule over the remaining coastal strip was contested. In 1192 he was ousted in favour of Henry, Count of Champagne; in recompense he took over Cyprus, to hold as a fief from Richard for his lifetime.

Although the other Crusaders thought him stupid ('simplex et minus astutus', by which they meant straightforward but not very bright) he followed a sensible policy in Cyprus. He offered the fullest assurance to the Greek inhabitants that there would be no more massacres and they could all go back to work in security. To gain the support needed for his colonial rule he appealed to the

David, Isaiah, Jeremiah, the
Preparation of the Throne;
wall painting; church of
Panayia Arakiotissa,
Lagoudera; 1192

remaining barons of Palestine who had been made landless by
Saladin, or to their widows and children. Instead of clinging to the
few coastal cities still in Christian hands they should come to
Cyprus where they could hold by feudal tenure wide estates rich in
corn and vines. According to one chronicler he was acting on the
advice of Saladin. If so, it was good and disinterested advice, and
the basis of the constitution of the Kingdom of Cyprus.

Guy reigned for less than two years. He never took the title of
King of Cyprus but regarded himself as still King of Jerusalem. He
was succeeded by his elder brother Aimery (1194–1205). During the
latter's reign a complete new ecclesiastical establishment for Cyprus
was brought into effect whereby the Latin Church took over
administration of the dioceses from the Greek Orthodox bishops.
In 1196 he regularised the international position of his state by
doing homage to Henry VI, the Holy Roman Emperor, and receiving in return recognition as King of Cyprus. A year later he was
able to call himself King of Jerusalem as well, by the same means as

his brother, for he married the heiress to the Kingdom, Isabel, widow of Henry of Champagne. His second crown brought him few advantages; the resources and manpower of Cyprus were used to defend Acre and the remaining territories on the Syrian coast which were exposed to raids by the Sultan of Egypt, al-Malik al-Adil. In reprisal he raided the Delta, but he was glad to make a treaty with the Sultan in 1204 which gave him some advantages in Palestine. On the whole he is the King of Cyprus against whom there is least to say; cautious, prudent, and reasonable the only thing reported to his discredit is that he is supposed to have brought on an early death by eating far too much fish at one sitting.

His son Hugh I also had a short reign, from 1205 to 1218; as he was only ten when he succeeded it lasted effectively for eight years. He took part in the Fifth Crusade, which achieved nothing, and died suddenly in Tripoli at the age of twenty-three. He had been married for eight years to Alice of Champagne, daughter of Henry of Champagne, one of the three husbands of Isabel, Queen of Jerusalem. Hugh's only son, Henry, was born only about nine months before his death. When he succeeded as Henry I (1218-1253) a long regency was certain. That was a state of affairs familiar in the Crusader kingdoms of the Levant because the men, especially if

Limassol Castle was built on the site of Byzantine fortifications. Richard I of England and Berengaria of Navarre were married there and Berengaria was crowned Queen of England. The present building dates from the early 14th century; it was reconstructed in the same century and later by the Venetians

181

Buffavento Castle, in an almost inaccessible mountain position, was already in existence in the 12th century. The Lusignans used it mainly as a state prison for their adversaries

Opposite
1
The magnificent Premonstratensian abbey of Bellapais enjoyed royal patronage and was extended and enriched at various times. The church is from the 13th century, the conventual buildings mainly from the 14th

2
Bellapais Abbey; the cloisters

active in war and politics, died much younger than the women. In the case of Henry I the regency lasted nearly fifteen years and the reign a surprising thirty-five years; but his nature was exceptionally easy-going — he was called Henry the Fat and was as lethargic in spirit as in body — so that the leading men were rarely incommoded by a royal initiative. It was not a successful reign from the point of view of Cyprus. On the other hand it must be admitted that there were later kings with conventionally preferable qualities who caused greater damage.

Queen Alice became Regent of the Kingdom and guardian of her infant son; she was assisted by her two uncles Philip and John of Ibelin in succession. One of her first acts, whose effects were to be long-lasting and damaging, was to grant extensive commercial privileges to the Genoese. It included the right of establishment in

1

2

St Sophia Cathedral (Selimiye Mosque), Nicosia, dates from the very end of the 12th century and is in the Gothic style of central France. The cathedral was used for the coronations of the Lusignans as Kings of Cyprus and some are also buried here

Famagusta, which by the end of the century replaced Limassol as the principal port. The main event of the first part of the reign was the attempt by the Emperor Frederick II to seize the regency in virtue of the homage done to his predecessor by King Aimery. Frederick of Hohenstaufen, known as *Stupor Mundi,* the astonishment of the world, because of his knowledge of languages, poetry and law, married in 1225 Yolande, the heiress of the Kingdom of Jerusalem. By her he had a son, Conrad. It was in right of that son that he sailed for the east in 1228 to take over what remained of the Kingdom of Jerusalem. His journey is sometimes counted as the Sixth Crusade. It resulted in his obtaining from the Sultan of Egypt, by negotiation, possession of Jerusalem, Bethlehem, Nazareth, Sidon, Lydda and some other places and the promise of a ten-year truce. In Cyprus he was in the long run unsuccessful. To begin with he received recognition as suzerain of the island from John of Ibelin, now acting as Regent in place of Queen Alice, and from the principal barons, so that when he returned to the West in 1229 he could leave the direction of affairs in the hands of his adherents, five of whom acted as his 'bailies' or representatives. The Cypriots, under the leadership of John of Ibelin, soon went over to opposition. The wars lasted four years, with a brief intermission. The castles of Hilarion, Kantara and Kyrenia, seized by the Imperialists, were twice besieged and twice captured. A famous battle was fought at Aghirda, at the foot of the pass leading across the Pentadaktylos range, in which John of Ibelin and his son Balian of Ibelin won an unexpected victory over the Imperialists. Throughout these

St Sophia Cathedral; the nave

St Hilarion Castle was originally a Byzantine fortress and greatly strengthened by the Lusignans who used it both as a strongpoint and as a summer residence

struggles, which are written up in the brightest colours of chivalry by the chroniclers, especially by the poet Philip of Novara, King Henry the Fat played no active role. He had been prematurely crowned in 1225 at the age of eight but his supporters took great care that he should not be exposed to danger.

He did take part, when he was thirty-one, in the Seventh Crusade led by King Louis IX of France. He had been host to St Louis since September 1248; the next eight months were spent in Nicosia, in leisurely and repetitive discussions on plans of campaign. In May the two kings embarked at Limassol and sailed for Damietta, for it had been decided that the only way to safeguard the Kingdom of Jerusalem was to destroy the power of the Sultan of Egypt. (This was probably a sound decision; it had been the view of all the sensible Kings of Jerusalem). The Latin Archbishop of Nicosia came too, and died in Egypt. King Henry stayed only briefly, though he left behind a strong force of 120 knights, with their accompanying infantry, under his relation Baldwin of Ibelin. The Cypriots distinguished themselves next year at the battle of Bahr-al-Saghir but in April 1250 were forced to surrender with the whole of the army. Meanwhile King Henry, who had been widowed for the second time, had taken as his third wife, in September 1250, Plaisance of Antioch. He died in 1253 having at last begotten a son, Hugh II, who succeeded at the age of a few months.

Another regency for an infant king may give a good opportunity to break off the dynastic chronicle and consider the nature and organisation of the Kingdom of Cyprus. The most important fact about its nature was that the ruling class was a small stratum of West Europeans, French-speaking and predominantly of French origin, and that the subject population was overwhelmingly Greek with a few Armenians and Syrians. The state was organised on the purest feudal principles. Indeed it had what could be called a written constitution because the fief-holders had brought with them from

Aerial view of St Hilarion Castle

187

the Kingdom of Jerusalem treatises expounding feudal custom which are referred to collectively as the Assizes (i.e. ordinances) of Jerusalem; they are often quoted by English and French historians of feudalism who can find nothing so elaborate and consistent in the looser practice of their own countries. The island was divided into King's land and land held by feudatories on condition of rendering him military service. The King was the sovereign liege of all the barons who had originally received their lands from him; like Guy of Lusignan himself the first barons had come from Palestine, most of them having lost their lands there to the Saracens. The original settlers were said to have numbered three hundred knights and two hundred mounted sergeants. The principal constitutional body was the *Haute Cour* or High Court, which consisted of the whole body of barons. It had executive, legislative and judicial powers. No fief-holder could be punished by the King without its judgment. For

Originally Byzantine, Kyrenia Castle was enlarged during the time of the Lusignans and modernised for artillery warfare by the Venetians

The main doorway of the
church of St Nicholas (the
Bedestan), Nicosia

non-noble Franks there was a Lower Court or *Cour des Bourgeois*.

Contrary to the usual practice in western Europe the Lusignan
kings, throughout the history of the dynasty, never allowed any
nobleman to hold a castle as a part of his fief. At most the nobles
would have possessed fortified watch-towers. All castles were royal
castles except for a short-lived Templar castle at Gastria and a
fortified residence for the Commandery of the Hospitallers at Kolossi. Guy of Lusignan inherited from his Byzantine predecessors

189

13th-century stone relief, probably from a tympanum over a door, showing Christ in Majesty surrounded by a mandorla supported by angels and flanked by scriptural scenes; below, the Virgin Mary *Orans*, the Archangel Gabriel and Apostles (London, Victoria and Albert Museum)

castles at Nicosia, Paphos, Limassol and Kyrenia, and at three strategic points in the Pentadaktylos range, St Hilarion, Buffavento and Kantara. There is hardly anything visible now remaining of the Byzantine buildings, except at Kyrenia and St Hilarion, because the Lusignan kings spared no effort to enlarge and improve these instruments of royal power. The system is an exemplary specimen of medieval military science, an inter-connecting network of strong-points. Though it was firmly in the King's hands it probably was not resented by the nobility since all were conscious of the Moslem menace.

The style of fortification that developed in the Levant, from which it spread to western Europe, derived directly from Byzantine, indeed late Roman, practice. The castles of Cyprus are dramatically picturesque examples of it. St Hilarion, the largest, was used by the kings of Cyprus as a summer palace. Kantara, controlling the Karpass Peninsula, is typical of the mountain-top castles of the Levant; Buffavento, further west along the spine of Pentadaktylos in an almost inaccessible position, was used more as a prison and a lookout than for defence. When the Venetians took over, faced with a more immediate threat from the Turks, they dismantled these mountain castles and the medieval fortifications of Nicosia and rebuilt the castles of Kyrenia and Famagusta according to the most modern precepts of fortification in the age of artillery. The new defences of Nicosia were even more modern, being built in the form of a star fort, reminiscent of Palmanova on the Venetian mainland.

When a Latin hierarchy was imposed on Cyprus it provided itself with buildings which are among the most impressive monuments to be seen today. St Sophia Cathedral at Nicosia was built in the 13th century in a rather old-fashioned style deriving from the central French homeland of the Lusignan dynasty. Famagusta Cathedral, dedicated to St Nicholas dates from the early 14th century; it is in a later style, right up to date and influenced by contemporary buildings in the Rhineland. The west front is the finest example of Gothic art in Cyprus. The cathedral was immediately adopted as a model all over the island, not only by Latins but also for Greek Orthodox churches. In addition there were many Latin monastic foundations, some of them originally dependencies of houses in the Holy Land. All the main orders were represented: Benedictine, Cistercian, Premonstratensian, Franciscan, Dominican, Carmelite and others.

The Entry into Jerusalem; wall painting; church of St Heracleidius , monastery of St John Lampadistis, Kalopanayiotis; 13th century

St Nicholas Cathedral (Lala Mustafa Pasha Mosque), Famagusta, was built in the early 14th century. The architecture is inspired by models from the Rhineland. The Lusignans were crowned here as Kings of Jerusalem

The Greek subject classes were divided into three. The lowest and most numerous consisted of *paroikoi* or serfs who were bound to the soil, paid an annual poll-tax and rendered two days a week forced labour to their lords, who also took one-third of their agricultural produce, and were under the jurisdiction of their lords in all criminal matters except those involving death or mutilation. In the second class were the *perperiarii* (from hyperperon, the standard Byzantine coin) who were so called because they had partly compounded with their lords for their servile dues by paying an annual tax of fifteen hyperpera. The third class was of free men or *lefteroi* who were released from feudal dues either by purchase or by favour and held their lands by free tenure.

Many travellers visiting Cyprus during the Frankish period,

after commenting on the wealth of the ruling class, say that the peasantry get no benefit from it but are wretched slaves, oppressed with heavy taxes. Others describe them as cheerful, indolent people who console themselves with the excellent local wine. It is likely that in fact the peasants were materially no worse off than when under either Byzantine or Turkish rule. But material well-being is not everything. They resented their subjection to the foreigners, for the Lusignans made no effort to bridge the legal and social gulf between themselves and their Greek subjects. The Normans in Sicily and south Italy had been brilliantly successful in creating a real national feeling and a fusion of races — and they had had a third element to assimilate, the Arabs. Other Normans in England achieved even more lasting results in reconciling conquerors and

A woman donor (detail) from the composition of the Virgin and Child; wall painting; church of Panayia Phorbiotissa, Asinou. Her black veil is the type introduced into the island by refugees from Syria after the fall of Acre in 1291 and widely used until the 15th century; 14th century

conquered. It seems that in other parts of France there was a less generous, and less effective, political outlook.

Even more serious to the Greeks than their own reduction in status was the treatment of their Church. The Lusignan kings, faithful to the authority of the Roman see, regarded the Orthodox hierarchy as schismatical. Accordingly Nicosia became the seat of a Latin Archbishop in 1196, with suffragans in the dioceses of Paphos, Limassol and Famagusta. The four sees were endowed by Aimery with lands and tithes. The Greeks, however, could not be left without a proper hierarchy and from 1220 they were allowed four bishops, deemed to be subordinate to the Latin four, who took their titles from and resided at villages in their dioceses. Among the Latin monasteries the best known is the spectacularly beautiful Bellapais, on a mountain spur above Kyrenia. Some Greek monasteries, e.g. Stavrovouni, were taken over but the most important Orthodox monasteries continued and monastic life flourished.

The first eight years of the reign of Hugh II (1253-1267) were dominated by his mother, Plaisance of Antioch, who acted as

194

The Nativity; wall painting; church of St Nicholas of the Roof, Kakopetria; middle of the 14th century

Regent. She appears to have been a woman of strong character and is described by one chronicler as 'one of the most valiant women in the world'. In 1258 she made a dramatic appearance at Acre, where the passion for murderous feuding which obsessed the rival factions in the remaining Frankish territory had reached a peak in an all-out war between the Venetians, the Pisans and the Templars on one side and the Genoese, the Spaniards and the Hospitallers on the other. She threw her weight on the side of the Venetians, then in the ascendant, to achieve the recognition of her son as King of Jerusalem. Before long the title began to lose its value as the Sultan of Egypt took advantage of the Franks' quarrels to pick off their castles one by one. Three years later Plaisance died and the Regency was taken over by Hugh of Antioch, son of Prince Henry of Antioch and Isabel of Lusignan. When Hugh II died childless at the age of fourteen the original Lusignan line became extinct.

Hugh of Antioch changed from being Regent to being King as Hugh III (1267-1284). He adopted his mother's name and thus founded the second Lusignan dynasty.

The ruined church of
SS Peter and Paul,
Famagusta, was built in the
reign of Peter I (1358-1369)
at the expense of a merchant
called Simon Nostrano

Hugh III was one of the best of the kings of Cyprus; the competition is pretty weak. The affairs of Syria pre-occupied him more than Cyprus. This was the time when the approach of the Mongol power out of central Asia, friendly to the Frankish Christians and hostile to the Egyptian Sultan, seemed to offer a new chance of survival. It did; and the rivalry and bitterness of the Christians, especially the Venetians and the Templars, threw it away gladly in exchange for a final chance to harass their enemies, the Genoese and the Hospitallers. Hugh attempted to play a mediating role. At one point he was obliged to throw in his hand and return to Cyprus when the intrigues of the Temple brought the recognition of Charles of Anjou instead of himself; but at the end of his life he was back in Syria, endeavouring to form a united front. All the time the power of the Mamelukes, the white slave rulers of Egypt, was growing, under two successive forceful Sultans, Baibars and Kalaun.

Hugh died in Tyre in 1284 and was succeeded by his elder son John I. He reigned for just over a year (1284-1285) and died in Nicosia. His younger brother, Henry II (1285-1324), was then crowned as his successor, although he was only fourteen. He reigned for almost forty years, but it was an unhappy and ineffectual reign, partly because he suffered for most of it from epilepsy which prevented the usual kingly activity and deprived him of the respect of his subjects. In 1286, with the affairs of the Kingdom of Jerusalem in their customary confusion, he was acknowledged as King and crowned in Tyre. It was only to preside over the downfall of the Kingdom at the hands of the Mameluke Sultan al-Malik al-Ashraf. In spite of his youth and his illness he fought bravely in the final siege of Acre and was among the last to escape to Cyprus from the harbour after the land walls were stormed. Only the island of Ruad remained in Christian hands for another thirteen years until 1303. Three years later Henry was the victim of a coup d'état by his ambitious younger brother Amaury, who deprived him of all authority, had himself proclaimed 'Governor' and finally drove Henry into exile in the Armenian Kingdom of Cilicia. His exile was ended when Amaury was murdered, apparently on personal not political grounds, by one of his closest adherents. The restored Henry II reigned for another fourteen years. His epilepsy had abated but he remained feeble and unimpressive. Why Dante described him in the *Paradiso* as a beast, who made Nicosia and Famagusta lament, is unknown; locally he had a good reputation as a pious ruler and a man of courage.

The disappearance of the last coastal strongholds of the Kingdom of Jerusalem was of great advantage to Cyprus. Its consequences are the principal reasons for the great prosperity which marked the 14th century. To begin with, it was no longer necessary for Henry II and his successors to pour out their money and military resources in vain attempts to preserve the Frankish foothold in Syria. On the positive side Cyprus gained from its position as a Christian stronghold surrounded by Moslem states. It was ultimately untenable, and was almost of necessity bound to fall when the countries to the north, east and west of it came under a single, strong, military state; but two and a half centuries are a good long time. Immediately it became the main entrepôt for oriental trade, equalling in importance Constantinople and Alexandria. The merchants of Famagusta became notorious for wealth and ostentation. The proceeds of trade spread throughout the island; as a result the standard of living of the nobles improved spectacularly. The German traveller Ludolf of Suchen saw them out hunting the moufflon with leopards. 'In Cyprus the princes, nobles, barons and knights are the richest in the world. They spend all their money on the chase. I know a certain Count (Hugh of Ibelin, Count of Jaffa) who has more than 500 hounds and every two hounds have their own servant to guard and bathe and anoint them.' Even the subject classes found themselves living more at their ease.

The insignia of the Order of the Sword, with the motto 'Pour Lealté Maintenir', established by Peter I (1358-1369)

197

Bowl of sgraffiato ware, a type of glazed pottery used in Cyprus in the 14th and 15th centuries AD; H 12.1 cm
(London, British Museum)

Henry II died in 1324 and was succeeded by Hugh IV (1324-1359), son of his brother Guy. His reign illustrates the advantages of the new situation of Cyprus. He preferred to live in peace with his neighbours although he was ready, at the request of the Venetians, to send a naval contingent to the league of Christian powers which they organised. Thus there were Cypriot ships present at the capture of Smyrna in 1344. The King did not travel outside the island, amusing himself with literature and hunting. His only harassment was from pirates who were attracted by the increase in the wealth of Cyprus and in the numbers of the merchant ships using Cypriot ports. Evidence of the same kind is given by the heightened interest of Venice and Genoa; other merchant cities also obtained privileges in the island including Florence and Montpellier. There was a murderous riot between Venetians and Genoese at Famagusta in 1345, but this was the sort of thing that happened all over the Levant and scarcely ruffled the prosperity of this peace-loving King.

His son and successor Peter I (1359-1369) was his precise opposite. It is in keeping with Gibbon's view of history as little more than the register of the crimes, follies and misfortunes of mankind that he is by far the best-known medieval King of Cyprus. Villon in France and Chaucer in England wrote about him; the peasants in the villages of Troodos still sing songs about him.

King Peter was determined to wage war with the infidel in the spirit of a Crusader born out of time. His first expedition was to Cilicia, where he captured the city of Adalia and massacred 'all that ever were within none except' according to Froissart. In preparation for his second he went on a long mission to western Europe to gather support. He was received everywhere with great enthusiasm but little real help. There is a tradition in the City of London that he was feasted there in the winter of 1363 by the Master of the Vintners Company at a banquet attended by the Kings of England and Scotland. He was nearly three years on his travels.

On his return, in 1365, he led a very large expedition to Alexandria. This was in principle, as already remarked, a sensible move. If he could have established himself on the Egyptian coast he might have altered significantly the balance of power in the Levant. This was possibly his intention; but perhaps because he could not control

The Virgin Mary *Orans*, attended by the Archangels; wall painting; church of the Archangel, Galata; 16th century

199

The Presentation of Christ;
wall painting; church of St
Nicholas of the Roof,
Kakopetria; second half of
the 14th century

his troops he made no serious attempt to exploit his rapid success in capturing Alexandria and withdrew the forces to Cyprus after a few days in which the city was thoroughly sacked. The fleet returned with an enormous booty. The report of the sack spread throughout Europe. In the *Canterbury Tales* Chaucer recounts that his knight had been at Alexandria, as previously at Adalia. If so he showed a taste in massacre at variance with the well-known compliments with which he is introduced in the Prologue. A recent work has argued that Chaucer wrote ironically; he did not intend to present the knight as an ideal of chivalry but as a brutal mercenary fighting for pay and plunder. If so his flattering words about King Peter in the Monk's Tale may not represent his genuine opinion.

These warlike exploits brought King Peter the 'renown' of which Villon speaks but they were very expensive. He raised money partly from his own subjects, by selling their freedom to *perperiarii* at a reduced rate, and partly from abroad, which increased the hold of the Venetians and the Genoese on the trade of

Cyprus. He had another side to his character. He was apparently devoted to his wife, Eleanor of Aragon, and took her nightgown with him on his travels when he was parted from her; but he also kept at least two mistresses. His adulteries were resented by the nobles, who in addition feared his increasingly tyrannical treatment of them in flagrant disregard of the laws. One morning in January 1369 three of the leading barons forced their way into his bedroom and stabbed him.

His son Peter II (1369-1382) was mild-mannered and lethargic, and only twelve when he succeeded. For all the contrast with the preceding reign, this one gave Cyprus what was probably its most decisive push on the downward path. The trouble began in 1372, when the King was crowned with the crown of Jerusalem in Famagusta. A quarrel began between the Genoese and the Venetians immediately after the ceremony about who should take the right-hand rein of the King's horse when he came from the cathedral. This privilege had in the past been claimed by the Genoese but on

Wall painting representing the Communion of the Apostles (detail); church of Panayia Podithou, Galata; 1502

201

The Greek Orthodox
cathedral of St George of
the Greeks, Famagusta,
shows a strong Western
influence after it was rebuilt
in the 14th century

this occasion the Venetian Consul took it by force. That night at the
coronation banquet the brawling broke out again. The Cypriots,
who hated the Genoese because they were grasping and arrogant on
land and pirates at sea, took the side of the Venetians. Genoese
shops were looted and burned and many Genoese were wounded
and some killed. In Genoa the affair was written up into a massacre.

The Italian maritime republics believed that they could only
maintain their trade with the Levant and their colonial possessions
there by taking violent reprisals against any state that ill-treated
their nationals. Genoa pursued this policy with particular relish. An
expedition was sent to Cyprus which ravaged the entire island and
plundered both Famagusta and Nicosia. The King and his mother
fell into their hands by a trick involving the most blatant breach of
faith. Venice was unable to help because she saw herself imminently
threatened by what became the War of Chioggia against Genoa and
her mainland allies. The Cypriots were reduced to guerilla attacks
on the occupying force. Finally, in 1374, they were forced to accept
the Genoese terms. These provided for the payment of a tribute of
40,000 gold florins a year, a fine of 2,012,240 gold florins to be paid
in instalments over twelve years, and a down payment of 90,000

gold florins to reimburse the expenses of the fleet that invaded them. When the 90,000 had been paid the Genoese would hand back Nicosia and the rest of the island except Famagusta. The loss of Famagusta marked the end of Cypriot prosperity. As it happened, its possession did very little good to Genoa. The interminable internal wars of the Franks in Greece and the Levant almost invariably resulted in no advantage to either side.

In spite of the ostensible cause for the murder of Peter I his widow, Eleanor of Aragon, pursued his murderers with passionate vindictiveness. She got the Genoese to execute the better-known ones but she was convinced that her brother-in-law John, known as Prince of Antioch, had been a co-conspirator. For six years she let his suspicions die down until he felt it safe to accept an invitation to dinner in the palace. After dinner a covered dish was brought in. The Queen took off the cover and on the dish was the bloodstained shirt of her husband. 'Do you know whose this was?' she asked. It was the agreed signal for some Italians, concealed in the room behind the Prince's back, to rush out and kill him. The King, who had been persuaded of his uncle's guilt, nevertheless soon thought it time to send his mother back to Catalonia. It was the last time he

Kantara Castle, at the eastern end of the Pentadaktylos range, was originally built in the 9th century and enlarged under the Lusignans and the Venetians

asserted himself. In 1382 he died at the age of twenty-five. His lethargy had increased to such a degree that he was the second King of the house of Lusignan to have the sobriquet of 'the Fat'.

Peter II died without lawful issue and was succeeded by his uncle James I (1382-1398) who at the time was a prisoner in Genoa, having been seized by a more than usually perfidious trick. It was three years before the Genoese let him out on very severe terms including the outright cession of Famagusta. The King had also to agree that all ships coming to Cyprus should discharge only in Famagusta. This prohibition was often ignored but it contributed to the ruin of the island's trade. The King's son and heir had been born in prison in Genoa in 1374 and baptised Janus, after the mythical founder of the city rather than the appropriately double-faced god; he was retained as a hostage and only allowed to go to Cyprus seven years after his father, in 1392. To pay off the Genoese demands the King was forced to impose greatly increased taxes. He

solaced himself with hunting. The Lord of Anglure, a French
traveller who visited Cyprus in 1395, described him as a pretty fine-
looking man who spoke French well enough; he praised the King's
skill at hunting. In 1393 he added to his titles that of King of
Armenia, the Kingdom having disappeared and the last King having died in exile. Sir George Hill claims, on rather thin evidence,
that he was the only King of Cyprus to take an interest in the arts.

King Janus, his son and successor, who reigned from 1398 to
1432, was the third of the Lusignan Kings to be described as fat;
however, the chroniclers record that he was also tall, and good-
looking. His first concern, as was natural and necessary, was to
drive the Genoese from Famagusta but in two campaigns, interrupted by treaties in 1403 and 1414, he was unsuccessful. In its
weakened state it was natural that Cyprus should appear a suitable
prey to its external enemies. The Sultan of Egypt sent an expedition
against it in 1425 which ravaged a great part of the south of the

island. A larger one was mounted in 1426. In a battle at Khirokitia
the Mamelukes defeated the full force of the Kingdom. Janus himself was taken prisoner. Nicosia was captured and devastated. After
two years' captivity in Cairo Janus was ransomed at a great price
and returned broken in health and spirit. He had been forced to
accept the suzerainty of the Sultan and to pay a yearly tribute. The
finances of Cyprus were exhausted and Janus, who never recovered
from his humiliation, died poor in 1432.

King John II (1432-1458), Janus's only son, is described by Sir
George Hill as 'effeminate but not unattractive' and by Pope
Pius II, a contemporary, as 'cowardly and vile in spirit though
handsome to look at' and 'living a life of sloth, gluttony and lust.'
He was certainly ordered about by his women, two wives and a
mistress, all Greek or with Greek connections. His first wife was
Medea, of the Palaeologi of Montferrat, and his second Helena
Palaeologina, daughter of the Despot of the Morea and grand-
daughter of the Emperor Manuel II. Her tyranny over her husband,
mitigated only by occasional bouts of ill-health, is celebrated in
popular song and legend. The mistress, Marietta of Patras, is supposed to have been of a milder nature; in a fight with the Queen, in

206

the enthusiastic presence of the King, she had her nose bitten off. However, she was the mother of James the Bastard, loved and spoiled by his father when alive and his eventual successor. Queen Helena, though disapproved of as a virago, was popular with the Greeks inasmuch as she was devoted to the Orthodox Church. It is in this reign that there can be noticed an improvement in the status of the Greek population and a show of greater solidarity with the alien regime at least on the part of the more prosperous of them. The use of French was declining and the use of Greek increasing; in the towns there is evidence from the 15th century of a *lingua franca* in which Greek, French and Italian words were indiscriminately

SS George and Theodore (detail); wall painting; church of St Nicholas of the Roof, Kakopetria; 15th century

John II (wrongly named Philip), King of Cyprus (1432–1458); sketch from the *Diary of Georg von Ehingen* (Stuttgart, Württembergische Landsbibliothek)

Philip vō gots gnaden kűnig: von apern

mixed. Charlotte, the last Lusignan Queen, spoke Greek not French and annoyed Pope Pius II by her excessive fluency in it.

In many other ways also Charlotte, John's daughter, turned out to be one of those forceful women who make the history of Cyprus so entertaining. She intimidated her father and dominated her second husband Louis, son of the Duke of Savoy. As the only legitimate heir she was recognised as Queen-Regnant in 1458, with the right of succession to Louis. Her illegitimate half-brother James was the complete opposite of his father, except in good looks, being active and ambitious. He had been involved in several murders before his father's death and he was not slow to try his hand at usurping Charlotte's throne. Defeated in his attempt he fled to Egypt, where the Sultan was also captivated by him, and, having received from him a promise to be a faithful subject, conferred the Kingdom on him by right of suzerainty and supplied him with ships, soldiers and money to make good his claim. With a fleet of eighty ships under the Egyptian Commander-in-Chief he landed at Ayia Napa in September 1460 and advanced boldly on Nicosia. Charlotte and Louis took refuge in Kyrenia, whose strong castle stood a siege for four years. Next year James began operations against Famagusta. In 1464 he was finally successful on both fronts. Queen Charlotte, showing the strength of character she had inhe-

At Kouklia there was a Lusignan royal manor in the centre of large plantations of sugar cane. The east wing remains, after the destruction of the rest of the manor by the Mamelukes in 1426

209

One of the many versions presumed to be a copy of a lost Titian portrait of Caterina Cornaro, the last Queen of Cyprus (Nicosia, Cyprus Museum)

rited from her mother, went on repeated journeys to the West pleading for support. She was unsuccessful, and Kyrenia Castle, whose garrison had been reduced to famine by the siege, was surrendered by the treachery of its commander. Famagusta was surrendered by its Genoese garrison when attempts to revictual it failed. James II was now established firmly on the throne and controlled the whole island.

To have regained Famagusta meant the end of a parasitic growth which had for long sapped the strength of Cyprus. But it came too late. The revenues had been mortgaged and capital exhausted. The tribute to Egypt was a heavy burden especially when, as was frequently demanded, it had to be paid in coined gold. The morals of the ruling class had been perverted, treachery was everywhere and the political basis of the Kingdom was undermined. Some writers claim that James was popular with the Greeks because he was half Greek on his mother's side. (The same thing was true of Charlotte.) The evidence is late and doubtful. James certainly treated the serfs on his estates very harshly. When it came to the choice of a wife he broke his father's Greek connections and married a Venetian, Caterina Cornaro. The Venetian state, with prudent foresight, adopted Caterina as a daughter; the legal effect would be that if the crown came to her, and if she then died without heirs, Venice would inherit. In fact when James died in 1473 (having reigned since 1460, or 1464 counting from the surrender of Kyrenia) he left the Kingdom to his posthumous child, for Caterina was pregnant, and to her as Regent.

Caterina's child was a son, James III, but he lived only for a year (1473-1474). She herself remained Queen for fifteen years until 1489. It was not a happy reign. There were still many supporters of Charlotte in the island, and the ex-Queen continued her intrigues

Charlotte entering her name in the registry of members of the confraternity of S Spirito; fresco by Guidobaldo Abbatini
(Rome, church of S Spirito)

211

until she died in 1485. (She bequeathed her rights to the Duke of Savoy and the arms of Jerusalem, Cyprus and Armenia still appear in the great shield of the former royal house of Italy.) In addition there was a strong party which supported the aspirations of Ferdinand II of the Aragonese dynasty of Naples, for a large number of Spaniards, especially Catalans, had settled in Cyprus during the past two reigns. In 1473 the last-named party fomented a conspiracy that began with the murder of the Queen's uncle and principal adviser, Andrew Cornaro, and nearly brought the whole island under control; it was put down by the arrival in mid-winter of the Venetian fleet with reinforcements. The party that favoured Queen Charlotte, headed by a Venetian malcontent Mark Venier, plotted to assassinate Caterina in 1479. The conspiracy had gone far, and the King of Naples was ready to send a fleet to assist, when

Pope Sixtus IV receiving Queen Charlotte; fresco, school of Melozzo da Forli. Among the Queen's attendants are Hugo de Langlois and Louis Podocataro; mid-15th century (Rome, church of S Spirito)

The Miraculous Draught of
Fishes; wall painting in the
church of Panayia
Chryseleousa, Emba; late
15th century

it was betrayed in the usual way and suppressed by the Venetians
with their usual ruthless severity. The internal divisions in the
island with the increasing external threat from the Ottoman Empire
now convinced the Venetians that they would do better to assume
direct responsibility. The agent to persuade the Queen to abdicate
was George Cornaro, her brother. Caterina was reluctant. She
evidently had not the same attachment to Cyprus as Charlotte, last
heiress of a long line of kings, but she would have liked to remain a
Queen all her life. After some persuasion, and the promise of the
city and countryside of Asolo in full dominion, retaining the same
civil list that she had had in Nicosia and her title as Queen, she
agreed to yield the Kingdom to the Republic. Her farewell to

Cyprus took place at Famagusta, from where she sailed direct to Venice. Her formal abdication took place in St Mark's. The Saint's lion flag was already floating over all the castles of the island.

The Signory of Venice had the greatest reputation in Europe for wisdom and the state was both rich and also powerful at sea; but in its colonial territories its administration was inefficient and corrupt. One reason for this was that, in their fear of allowing individuals to become too powerful, the controlling oligarchy insisted on restricting the terms of office-holders. In Cyprus the Government was in the hands of a Lieutenant and two Counsellors (collectively known as the three Rectors) and a Captain to command the army. All these changed every two years. The Venetian state also had a reputation

The Presentation of the Virgin; wall painting by Philip Goul in the church of the Holy Cross of Ayiasmati, Platanistasa; 1494

The Virgin Mary, *Orans,*
Blachernitissa type; wall
painting by Philip Goul,
church of the Holy Cross of
Ayiasmati, Platanistasa;
1494

for parsimony. In Cyprus this was shown by the scant numbers and
inadequate training of the defence forces, and the delay in strength-
ening the fortifications of Nicosia and Famagusta. Taxation was
heavy but insufficient, in many years, to meet the costs of administration. On the other hand the profits from the salt monopoly
brought in a large surplus of revenue which went direct to Venice.

The old feudal class and the Greeks were equally discontented.
The former found themselves excluded from power. Although
many of them were more interested in hunting they resented being
placed in an inferior position to Italian officials, especially since the
first act of the new regime was to abolish the *Haute Cour,* the
symbol and safeguard of noble status. The oppression of the Greeks
is described by Martin von Baumgarten, a Tyrolese pilgrim who
visited the island in 1508: 'All the inhabitants of Cyprus are slaves to
the Venetians.' He goes on to describe how they were obliged to
pay to the state a third part of all their profits and to work for the
state two days a week: 'And what is more there is yearly some tax
or other imposed on them with which the poor common people are

215

The Adoration of the Magi
(detail); wall painting in the
Enkleistra, St Neophytus
Monastery near Paphos;
early 16th century

so flayed and pillaged that they hardly have wherewithal to keep
soul and body together.' There must have been some elements of
the population who were better off than this because when the
Venetians, desperate to raise money, began selling off the old
crown lands they found sufficient buyers. Nevertheless the general
discontent was demonstrated in 1562 when two Greeks, a school-
master and a troop commander of the light cavalry, raised a hope-
less rebellion. The colonial masters could not count on the hearty
support of the Greeks even against the Turks. Many serfs had
already made their feelings plain by fleeing to Turkey.

For the greater part of their rule the Venetians tried hard to avert
the Turkish danger, which increased in 1517 when the Ottomans
conquered Egypt, by diplomacy and bribery. It seems likely that
the only effect of this policy was to convince the Porte that they
would never fight. In 1566 Selim succeeded Suleiman the Magnificent as Sultan; it was generally believed that he would try to make
his name by a new conquest, which would also redeem his father's
failure to capture Malta in 1565. For this purpose Cyprus was an
obvious choice since it was now surrounded on three sides by

Ottoman territory. Accordingly in March 1570 he sent an envoy to present a formal demand to the Council of Ten for the immediate cession of Cyprus. The insulting terms of his message were designed to preclude acceptance. The Signory took up the challenge. They also tried to put together a relief expedition with the help of the Papacy and King Philip II of Spain. It was a disgraceful failure for which the Spanish Admiral John Andrew Doria, of Genoese extraction, was mainly responsible, acting on secret instructions from Philip. The fleet got no farther than Castellorizo and turned back in September. Meanwhile in July a Turkish expeditionary force had landed on the south coast. Its Commander was Lala Mustafa Pasha, Beylerbey of Damascus. The number of soldiers he brought with him is unknown. At the siege of Famagusta next year he commanded something like 200,000 all told but it is known that he had received strong reinforcements. Perhaps the first echelon of the invaders was only half as large.

The Venetians had been proceeding in a leisurely way with

The Virgin Mary and Child; wall painting; church of Panayia Podithou, Galata; 1502

217

improvements to the defences of Nicosia and Famagusta since 1567. They gave priority to the latter, which they expected would be the first objective of the enemy. In fact Mustafa moved first on Nicosia. It was ineptly defended by the Lieutenant, Nicholas Dandolo, who was subsequently accused of lacking resolution. He had little competence in military matters but continually overruled his subordinates who had much more. The siege lasted from 25 July to 9 September. After the walls had been surmounted the remnants of the defenders offered to surrender. Dandolo thought, for some reason, that he would receive special treatment. Instead he was massacred with the rest and his head sent to the Commander of

Ayia Napa Monastery was rebuilt and extended in the 15th century and shows Western influence. Although Greek Orthodox, it contains a Latin chapel

Famagusta, to which the Turkish army now transferred.

The Captain of Famagusta, Marcantonio Bragadin, of a distinguished Venetian family, was a commander of a much more resolute character. He was supported by Astorre Baglione, a professional soldier from Perugia. The defence of Famagusta is one of the greatest epics of siege warfare recorded in history. Against Mustafa's 200,000 men, with 145 guns, the Venetians had some 3-4,000 regular Italian infantry, 2-300 cavalry and about 4,000 Greek militia, with 90 guns. The siege lasted from 16 September 1570 to 1 August 1571. On that day the defenders had been reduced to some 400 men and a few barrels of powder. The walls had been

Kiti tower, built in the 16th century by the Venetians

breached so thoroughly that it was said a horse and cart could drive across the moat and into the city; provisions had long been so short that defenders were dying of hunger; in spite of which six full-scale assaults by Turkish infantry had been repulsed. Bragadin offered capitulation. It was accepted by Mustafa in flattering terms. When he and his surviving officers came out, after receiving the acknowledgement of surrender sealed with the Sultan's seal, they were at first received with elaborate courtesy. At a certain moment Mustafa gave the pre-arranged signal for the massacre to begin. Bragadin alone was reserved for a more prolonged fate. Mustafa himself cut off his ears and nose; he was kept waiting for two weeks in this state and then flayed alive. His skin was stuffed with straw and taken to Constantinople in triumph. A patriotic Venetian later stole it and it now rests in an urn in the church of SS Giovanni e Paolo in Venice.

Cyprus was annexed as a province of the Ottoman Empire and Lala Mustafa Pasha became the first Governor.

The buildings of the Frankish period make the biggest impression on the visitor to Cyprus. The walls of Nicosia and Famagusta, the Gothic cathedrals in the two cities, the mountain-top castles of the Pentadaktylos range and the great sea-girt castle of Kyrenia: it is these that are illustrated in tourist brochures and remain afterwards as the most abiding memories. They are, indeed, very fine in their own fashion. The two cathedrals are outstanding examples of the western European Gothic style. The military architecture illustrates

The Sea Gate, part of the fortifications of Famagusta, constructed by the Venetians in the 16th century; pencil drawing

Kyrenia Gate in the
Venetian fortifications of
Nicosia dates from the
middle of the 16th century

the development of the art of fortification as practised in the area
that first gave it birth, from the early period which still reflected
memories of Roman practice down to the age of artillery. The
design and workmanship are also of the highest aesthetic value. But
their fashion is not Cypriot but French or Venetian. For indigenous
art during this period you must look to literature or mural painting.

There is a fair amount of folk-poetry which can be ascribed to the
Lusignan period, some even dealing with themes of the court, such
as the 'Arodaphnousa' cycle which derives from stories about
Queen Eleanor and Joanna l'Aleman, wife and mistress of Peter I.
Of formal literature in Greek the best examples are from the 15th
century, the historical writings of Leontios Machairas and George
Bustron. Both write in a Cypriot dialect of Greek but in a form
closer to French chroniclers, with great vigour and liveliness of
description. It is interesting to note that they are generally sympath-
etic to the Frankish rulers and feel a certain solidarity with them.

Cyprus has preserved more early mural paintings, especially in
remote churches of the Troodos Mountains, than any other part of
Greece. The experts' appreciation of the style of Comnenian and
Palaeologan painting is largely based on Cypriot specimens, many
of which are securely dated. The earliest large-scale series of paint-
ings is to be found on the walls of the Panayia Phorbiotissa at
Asinou, erected between 1099 and 1106. The murals are of the
Comnenian period, probably produced within the reign of

221

Famagusta Gate, in the Venetian fortifications of Nicosia was built in 1567 by Giulio Savorgnano. It opens in the angle of the Caraffa bastion and runs through the walls like a tunnel, surmounted by a central dome

Alexius I Comnenus. The representation of the Dormition of the Virgin above the west door of the nave is one of the greatest triumphs of Byzantine graphic art. The first decorations of St. Nicholas of the Roof are some fifty years earlier; the style of the Entry into Jerusalem and the Transfiguration is connected with that of paintings in Salonica and Kiev. The same two churches contain examples of the style of 14th-century Constantinople; though direct contact was small the inspiration of the Palaeologan school was maintained by the portable icons that were brought to the island. The paintings at Kalopanayiotis in the Monastery of St John Lampadistis are from the first half of the 13th century. Frankish influence is to be detected in a number of details but the essential spirit of the art is Byzantine. The assimilation was in any case very easy because the Romanesque style which dominated western art at the time of the early Crusades drew its inspiration to a large extent from Constantinople.

From the 15th century there is a culminating series in the late Palaeologan style in the monastery of St Neophytus near Paphos. The finest of its scenes shows the departure of the Magi, the three crowned kings riding away on their horses between the hills. There is an illusory third dimension to the composition which gives an air of distance, magic and romance. It may not be fanciful to think of it as figuring the fading out of the Lusignan kings who had come a long way from the plains of Poitou to rule a legendary realm on the wilder shores of the Levant.

222

1

2

Token money issued during
the siege of Famagusta
(London, British Museum)

The monument to
Marcantonio Bragadin,
with his bust surmounting
the urn which contains his
skin
(Venice, church of
SS Giovanni e Paolo)

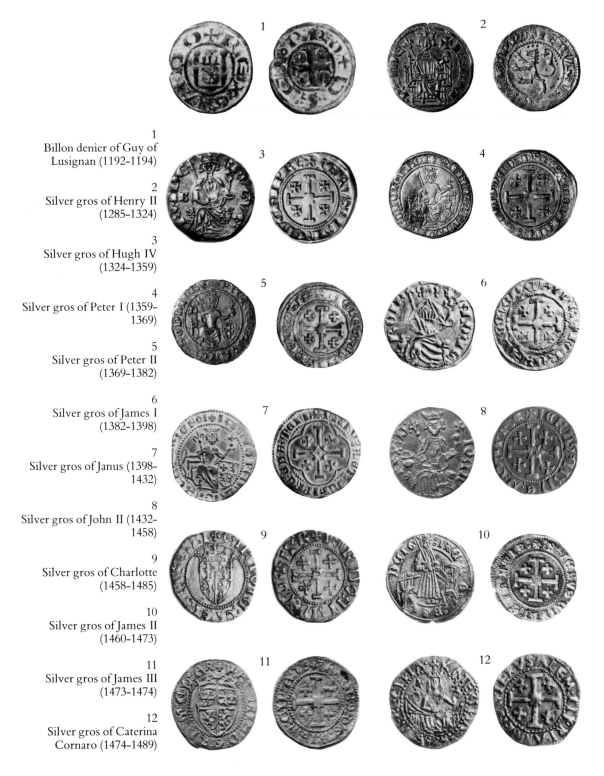

1
Billon denier of Guy of Lusignan (1192-1194)

2
Silver gros of Henry II (1285-1324)

3
Silver gros of Hugh IV (1324-1359)

4
Silver gros of Peter I (1359-1369)

5
Silver gros of Peter II (1369-1382)

6
Silver gros of James I (1382-1398)

7
Silver gros of Janus (1398-1432)

8
Silver gros of John II (1432-1458)

9
Silver gros of Charlotte (1458-1485)

10
Silver gros of James II (1460-1473)

11
Silver gros of James III (1473-1474)

12
Silver gros of Caterina Cornaro (1474-1489)

THE LUSIGNAN KINGS OF CYPRUS

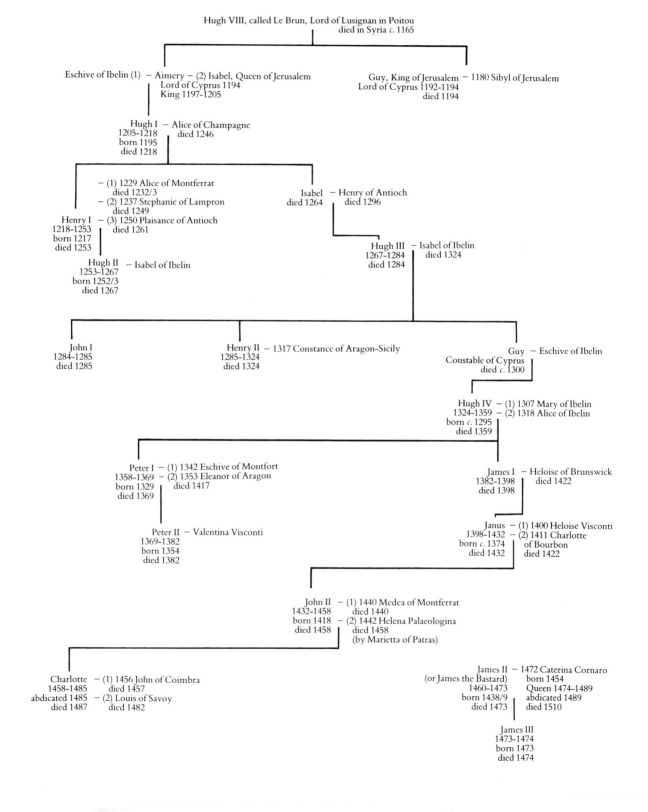

Hugh VIII, called Le Brun, Lord of Lusignan in Poitou
died in Syria *c.* 1165

Eschive of Ibelin (1) — Aimery — (2) Isabel, Queen of Jerusalem
Lord of Cyprus 1194
King 1197–1205

Guy, King of Jerusalem — 1180 Sibyl of Jerusalem
Lord of Cyprus 1192–1194
died 1194

Hugh I — Alice of Champagne
1205–1218   died 1246
born 1195
died 1218

— (1) 1229 Alice of Montferrat
  died 1232/3
— (2) 1237 Stephanie of Lampron
  died 1249
— (3) 1250 Plaisance of Antioch
  died 1261

Isabel — Henry of Antioch
died 1264   died 1296

Henry I
1218–1253
born 1217
died 1253

Hugh II — Isabel of Ibelin
1253–1267
born 1252/3
died 1267

Hugh III — Isabel of Ibelin
1267–1284   died 1324
died 1284

John I
1284–1285
died 1285

Henry II — 1317 Constance of Aragon-Sicily
1285–1324
died 1324

Guy — Eschive of Ibelin
Constable of Cyprus
died *c.* 1300

Hugh IV — (1) 1307 Mary of Ibelin
1324–1359 — (2) 1318 Alice of Ibelin
born *c.* 1295
died 1359

Peter I — (1) 1342 Eschive of Montfort
1358–1369 — (2) 1353 Eleanor of Aragon
born 1329   died 1417
died 1369

James I — Heloise of Brunswick
1382–1398   died 1422
died 1398

Peter II — Valentina Visconti
1369–1382
born 1354
died 1382

Janus — (1) 1400 Heloise Visconti
1398–1432 — (2) 1411 Charlotte
born *c.* 1374   of Bourbon
died 1432   died 1422

John II — (1) 1440 Medea of Montferrat
1432–1458   died 1440
born 1418 — (2) 1442 Helena Palaeologina
died 1458   died 1458
(by Marietta of Patras)

Charlotte — (1) 1456 John of Coimbra
1458–1485   died 1457
abdicated 1485 — (2) Louis of Savoy
died 1487   died 1482

James II — 1472 Caterina Cornaro
(or James the Bastard)   born 1454
1460–1473   Queen 1474–1489
born 1438/9   abdicated 1489
died 1473   died 1510

James III
1473–1474
born 1473
died 1474

X

THE TURKISH PERIOD

1571-1878

Sir David Hunt

The 300 years of Turkish rule left fewer 'footprints' in Cyprus than comparable periods under other rulers. The Ottomans were not interested, at least in this impoverished province, in adorning their new possession with fine buildings; on the contrary they regarded with indifference the slow decay of the architectural heritage left by the Venetians and the Lusignans. Even the strong fortifications of Nicosia, Kyrenia and Famagusta, which the Venetians had re-modelled along the latest lines of military science, and whose value the invaders had themselves experienced, were allowed to crumble. Their garrisons also dwindled and degenerated. In a sense, how-ever, they can be said to have created the image which the 19th century formed of Cyprus: part of the romantic Levant of the Victorian steel engravings which juxstapose the Gothic arch and the minaret in a framework of palm fronds, with a piece of classical ruin to heighten the effect. Time stood still. The island found itself in a backwater of affairs. Surrounded by the possessions of a slowly declining empire it suffered in obscurity from an administration which was not so much actively oppressive as slothful and ineffi-cient. The burdens on the peasantry became heavier and both intellectual activity and commercial prosperity slumbered.

Two consequences of the conquest were to be of great import-ance for the future. The first brought a change in the composition of the population. Grants of land and houses were made to Turks from the victorious army, and other Turks from Anatolia were persuaded, in some cases compelled, to immigrate. Nearly all the statistics of population in the 16th century are unreliable but there seems to be general agreement among historians that the new settlers numbered about 20,000. This includes the permanent garrison whose official strength was 1,000 infantry (janissaries) and 2,666 cavalry (spahis). What proportion this figure bore to the Greek population is unknown but the first census, taken in 1572, is said to have shown a population liable to pay the 'kharaj', or poll tax, of about 85,000. These were by definition Christians, since Moslems were exempt. Included among them were Armenians, Maronites and Roman Catholics of various origins, known for convenience as Latins; all subsequent figures show these made up only about one per cent. In consequence there was for the first time in Cyprus a settled Moslem community, and one whose members were almost entirely of pure Turkish origin.

Copper-plate engraving illustrating the Turkish invasion; published by Balthasar Ienichen in 1571 and based on a map by Hans Rogel, Augsburg 1570 (London, National Maritime Museum)

The second great change was slower to appear: the gradual rise to political power of the Orthodox ecclesiastical establishment. The

Copper-plate engraving of the siege of Nicosia, showing Turkish dispositions; from *Isole che son da Venezia ...*, published by Simon Pinargenti in Venice, 1573. It is a close copy of the one published by Giovanni Francesco Camocio in Venice *c.* 1570 (Venice, Museo Storico Navale)

assumption of political rights and duties by religious leaders was a characteristic of the Ottoman Empire. It was an essential part of their political theory. The Turks were a conquering, military caste like the Normans in England or the Visigoths in Spain. They originated in central Asia and never quite lost traces of their nomadic origins. Their way of life was adapted to continuous warfare and their conversion to Islam provided them with a theological justification for this predisposition. In Islamic theory a state of permanent war with the non-Moslem world was both inevitable and meritorious. Only true believers could take part in it, and the poll tax was the price non-Moslem Ottoman subjects paid for exemption from military duties. For the purpose of tax-paying and to ensure orderly behaviour and security against rebellion each religious denomination was organised into a community known as a *milet*. The largest of them in the Empire was the one that consisted of all Orthodox Christians. This united not only Greeks, though they formed the majority, but also Slavs and Romanians. The titular leader was the Oecumenical Patriarch of Constantinople, the highest ecclesiastical authority in the Orthodox Church. It was with him that the Sultan and his ministers dealt at the capital; the provincial authorities in Cyprus recognised the Archbishop as the responsible leader of the Greek population.

The light in which the Ottoman Government regarded their non-Moslem subjects can be seen from the name of *rayah* which was commonly applied to them: it means 'cattle'. Theoretically they were mere possessions of their rulers, who had, on the same theory, the right to their services and their property. But the prudent herdsman takes good care of his herd. The Turks, who had been notable cattle-grazers in their nomadic life on the steppes, were aware of the desirability, in principle, of keeping their *rayah* contented and prosperous enough to pay their taxes. Mehmed II, the conqueror under whom the system was first elaborated, was partly Greek himself and, though a pious Moslem, wished Chris-

Wood-cut of the siege and capture of Nicosia showing the break-in of Turkish troops in the southern sector of the defences; issued as a separate sheet 'Nicosia Regal(e) Citta Di Cipro Combatuta Da(i) Turchi' with no name of author, date or place of issue

229

Copper-plate engraving of Famagusta under siege by the Turks (north is to the right) showing the fortifications in detail, dispositions of the besiegers and ships bombarding; published by Giovanni Francesco Camocio in Venice *c.* 1571 (Venice, Museo Storico Navale)

tians well. As Sir Steven Runciman comments in his *The Great Church in Captivity,* he wanted them to enjoy peace and prosperity and to be content with his government and an asset to it.

Orthodox patriarchs, archbishops and bishops had been accustomed to the *milet* system since the time when the first Christian cities had been occupied by Moslem conquerors in the 7th century. (It had been copied by the early caliphs from the Persians.) They knew it was their duty to care not only for the spiritual but for the material needs of their flocks, and that usually involved standing up to Ottoman governors against corruption, oppression and excessive taxation. In Cyprus the role of the Archbishop, supported by his suffragan bishops and the abbots of the principal monasteries, went rather further. With the progress of time he became responsible for the collection of tax and, to a large extent, for the administration of the island. He had direct access to the

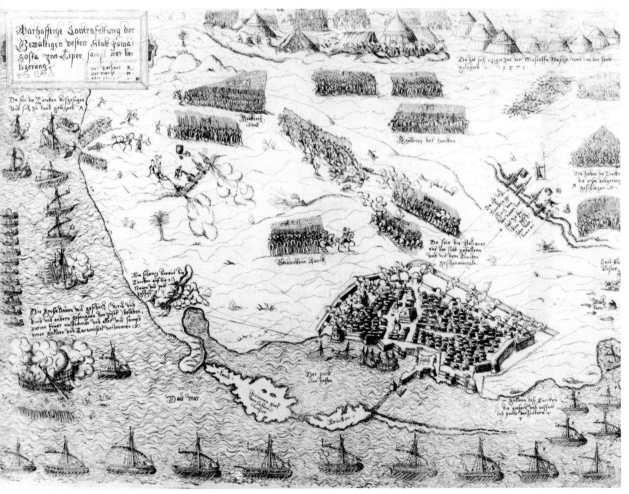

Sultan. He could send messages under his seal — with the impression in the imperial red that Zeno had granted to his remote predecessor — which the Governor could do nothing to stop even though he might himself be impugned in them.

This was only a particularly striking example of a practice common throughout the Empire of leaving civil administration in the hands of subjects, especially Greeks. The sultans of the period of the greatest Turkish successes realised that their Moslem subjects had little aptitude for or inclination towards the management of civil as opposed to military business. They were willing to leave it, as they left commerce, to the Greeks. The highest office in what we would call the Civil Service, that of Grand Dragoman of the Porte, was always held by a Greek. Similarly in Cyprus a Greek was Dragoman of the Serai, the Governor's Palace. The title means literally interpreter; because senior Turkish officials were disinclined to learn Greek they had to use an intermediary, who was never slow to take advantage of his opportunities. There were some notable dragomans, during the 18th century in particular, who grew rich from the exercise of this delegated authority. The Greek Church, which had occupied such a lowly position under the Latins, found

'The Fall of Cyprus, 1571';
oil painting by Bonaventura
Peeters (1614–1652)

The Büyük Khan, Nicosia, built by Muzaffer Pasha immediately after the occupation of the island in 1571 'for the benefit of foreigners'. The rooms are arranged on two floors round a courtyard in the middle of which is an octagonal mosque built over a water tank; pencil drawing

itself under the infidels not merely restored to supremacy in religious affairs but endowed with secular authority as well.

For the Greek Cypriots Turkish rule began well, after the sufferings brought by the conquest. The most noticeable improvement was the reduction of taxes. The Venetian rates were reduced, in some cases by as much as four-fifths, and a number of customs duties and market dues were abolished. This good fortune did not last. The standard Turkish practice was to pay their officials little or nothing as salary, leaving them to squeeze as much as they possibly could from the taxpayers. The most important change, because of its effects in the long term, was the abolition of all feudal tenures. At a stroke the peasant acquired an inalienable and hereditable right

232

to land. Those who for centuries had been mere bondmen on the soil were now on payment of a trifling sum constituted its possessors, with the right of succession to their descendants.

The first Governor after the conquest was Muzaffer Pasha. His title was Beylerbey, or Bey of Beys, and in order to live up to the importance of this rank a proper Pashalik had to be constructed. This was done by adding to the island four districts of the mainland. One of them was the Sanjak of Ichil, thus recreating the old Roman province of Cyprus and Cilicia. Muzaffer was a Pasha of three tails and had under him two pashas of two tails at Famagusta and Paphos. The 'tails', badges of rank in the higher levels of the Ottoman administration, were actual horses' tails attached to a pole

233

as a standard, a reminiscence of Turkish nomad days. This establishment was before long found to be excessive. During the century after the conquest the island suffered severely from locusts and from plague. Many of the *rayahs* had fled the country to Crete and the Peloponnese. The amount at which the island was assessed for tax remaining the same, those who remained had to pay more. A census taken in the 1640s was reported to have calculated that the Christian population had been reduced to 25,000. As a first step the two pashas of Famagusta and Paphos were removed, the establishment of headquarters in Nicosia was reduced and efforts were made to persuade Cypriots who had emigrated to return. It is generally accepted by all historians who wrote of the 17th and 18th centuries that these efforts were unavailing. Travellers comment on the contrast between the potential fertility of the island and the smallness of the population, whereby large areas were left desolate.

As an economy measure the Ottoman administration decided, in or shortly after 1670, to abolish the Pashalik. The island of Cyprus, minus the four Anatolian sanjaks, was put under the Kapudan Pasha, the Commander-in-Chief of the Navy. This meant that it was treated in the same way as the islands of the Aegean or, in the

Kumarcilar Khan (inn of the gamblers), Nicosia; late 16th century; pencil drawing

234

terminology of the time, Rhodes and the Archipelago. As one of these Admiralty properties Cyprus was administered on behalf of the Kapudan Pasha by a deputy, in Turkish a müsellim. He received a fixed salary of 15,000 piastres annually (rather under 2,000 pounds) but since he had had to bid for his post he took steps to extort as much extra as possible during his usually short period of office. Under the new system however, according to the Archimandrite Kyprianos in his history published in Venice in 1788, the Müsellim was not so powerful or so rich as the senior officials in Nicosia, the aghas who controlled the financial administration as tax collectors or tax farmers. Their wealth, their prestige and their influence at Constantinople had made them the real rulers of the island. Another result was jealousy and rivalry among themselves and in about 1680 one of the resulting clashes led to armed conflict. Out of it arose, as self-proclaimed 'leader' of Cyprus, Mehmed Agha Boyajioglou who headed the first rebellion of Cyprus. It was a purely Turkish affair in which none of the Greeks were involved. Kyprianos says his rebellion lasted seven years in all. He made a point of sending the poll tax proceeds regularly to Constantinople, which no doubt delayed the taking of action against him. It could

not have been rapid in any case since one of the facts revealed by the rebellion is that the Sultan had no sufficient force in Cyprus that he could use to assert his authority. It was necessary to bring in troops from Karamania, on the south coast of Asia Minor, under a local commander. After the siege of Nicosia, and a hectic pursuit of Boyajioglou to and fro across the island, he was caught and executed.

The revolt of Boyajioglou, and the reason for it, caused the Ottoman administration to decide that the time had come for another change. With all deliberate speed, that is to say in 1703, about thirteen years after the restoration of order, the island was transferred from the jurisdiction of the Kapudan Pasha and given to the Grand Vizier as a personal fief, for which the Turkish is *hass*. The Grand Vizier was the equivalent of the Sultan's Prime Minister, the head of the administration. It was so powerful a post that, except when held by persons of the greatest strength of character and political shrewdness, it never remained long in the same hands. Cyprus was certainly one of the least of the great man's preoccu-

The fort at the harbour of Paphos replaced a castle built in 1391, and demolished by the Venetians; an incription over the door records its reconstruction by the Turks, 1580-1592; pencil drawing

pations. As the Admiral had done he appointed a Deputy or Müsel–lim who also was the Muhassil, or collector of taxes. The Muhassil was appointed annually by the Grand Vizier, who invariably chose the highest bidder. Alexander Drummond, who was the British Consul in Aleppo not long afterwards, recorded in the course of his visit in 1745 that the current holder of the post had made a profit of 250,000 piastres in his one year whereas the total government revenue of the island was 310,000 piastres.

In the year of Drummond's visit the administrative arrangements were altered again: Cyprus was taken from the Grand Vizier and made an independent province once more under a pasha of three tails. The reason for the change is not known; the Grand Vizier was

The church of St Lazarus, Larnaca. According to Greek tradition Lazarus, after being raised from the dead, came to Cyprus and was the first Bishop of Kition, the ancient town on the site of modern Larnaca. The present church, with porticos showing Gothic influence, dates from the 17th century; pencil drawing

given an annual sum in compensation. The second Pasha of this dispensation, Abu Bekr, is celebrated in history as the only Turkish Governor of whom nothing but good is recorded. Even the violently critical Drummond speaks of 'the old gentleman's public spirit. While he was Pasha of this island in the year 1747 he formed the noble design of bringing water from the spring of Arpera to supply the people of Larnaca. A work worthy of a great and good man, which might have cost him above 50,000 piastres.' The money came from his own pocket in the form of a charitable foundation. The aqueduct was about six miles long and parts of it can still be seen near Larnaca.

The good Pasha had one successor of whom little is known except that he finished the aqueduct in 1750; but shortly thereafter the island was returned to the Grand Vizier who reintroduced the system of muhassils. Taxes both ordinary and extraordinary were exacted with growing rapacity. By general consent Chil Osman Agha who arrived in 1764 was the worst of all the governors. According to Kyprianos he was deeply in debt because he had put in a very high bid for his office. He was determined not only to recoup what he had paid but also to gain 'fantastic wealth' on top of it. Within a few days of his arrival he announced to the Archbishop through the Dragoman that the tax paid by the Greeks would be

Scene in the Mevlevi Tekké, Nicosia, built in the early 17th century as the centre of the Mevlevi sect of dervishes founded by Jalal ad din Rumi, the great Islamic mystic. His followers were known as the 'Dancing Dervishes' because of their ecstatic whirling dances

Ayia Sophia Mosque,
Paphos (Ktima), formerly a
Greek Orthodox church;
pencil drawing

more than doubled. The Archbishop, Paisios, declared that it was impossible for the *rayahs* to pay such a sum; he demanded, and was allowed, to send a delegation to the Vizier. After much delay the delegation returned with a *firman* or imperial order addressed to Chil Osman ordering him, with threats, not to exact more than the sum fixed by the imperial rescript and to repay all that had been levied in excess of it. The order was brought to Cyprus by one of the Vizier's own staff. It should have been read out in court but the Governor asked that it should be communicated to him in the Serai, the Governor's Palace. The Archbishop and the bishops, and numerous senior officials both Greeks and Turks, were summoned to attend the ceremony. Only the first part of the order had been read when part of the floor of the room collapsed precipitating the ecclesiastics and others (including Kyprianos the historian) into a

239

'Aqueduct at Larnaca'; the aqueduct was built by Abu Bekr Pasha in 1747; wood engraving (Illustrated London News)

basement. The Pasha remained in safety on a surviving portion of the floor. Foul play was at once suspected and stories of rafters and columns being sawn through, with ropes to pull on at the right moment, rapidly circulated. At least the interruption came very conveniently. The messenger from the Grand Vizier was not endangered by the collapse as he was sitting too close to the Pasha who consequently had to resort to the supplementary measure of poisoning his coffee. It was frustrated by the timely provision of an antidote.

This spectacular example of political manoeuvring gave immediate rise to the second revolt in Cyprus. The Molla, the Islamic religious head, summoned the Governor to appear before him, as he had the right to do, but when he three times refused the Nicosia mob, Greeks and Turks together, invaded and burned down the Serai and killed Chil Osman with some eighteen others. There was a similar but less violent outbreak at Larnaca. Then came the reckoning. The surviving authorities composed a report which was conveyed to the Vizier by his messenger, who in the light of his own experiences could be relied on to put a fair complexion on events. The Vizier and the Sultan were appeased, a new moderate Governor was appointed; but there was a price to be paid for the rebuilding of the Serai, compensation for looted property and the blood money of the victims. Turks and Christians agreed to allow the new Governor, Hafiz Effendi, to assess the amount required, and the bishops and aghas worked out that it could be covered by a payment of fourteen piastres a head by Christians and seven by Turks. This was accepted by the former but the Turks, accusing Hafiz of deliberate overassessment, broke into open insurrection headed by Khalil Agha, the Dizdar or Fort Commander of Kyrenia.

Khalil's insurrection, which lasted over a year, was a serious

240

affair because he was supported by so many of the Turkish inhabitants. The Archbishop, escaping from the island with difficulty, went to Constantinople to appeal for an imperial force to be sent to restore order. Once again the weakness of the military forces at the disposal of the Governor was revealed since a special expeditionary force from Karamania had to be sent. It took a long time to arrive but eventually Khalil was driven to shut himself in the castle of Kyrenia. For two months it resisted all attempts at a storm. Eventually Khalil was tricked into giving himself up when provisions began to run short. He was executed with the bowstring in violation of his safe-conduct; the heads of 200 of his supporters were sent to the Sultan as proof of the suppression of the rising.

The Russo-Turkish war of 1768 to 1774 affected Cyprus to the extent that the Russian fleet soon gained complete dominance in the eastern Mediterranean after it had destroyed the Ottoman fleet at Cesme, on the coast opposite Chios. The result was not only to hamper the island's maritime trade but also to impose on it extra expense for the maintenance of the military reinforcements sent there. These afflictions were, however, almost forgotten in the extraordinary episodes which marked the period as Governor of Haji Baki Agha. He may not have been the worst Governor but no other was more picturesquely reviled by his contemporaries and by posterity.

Baki was a Cypriot by origin, from the village of Klavdhia, about six miles east of Larnaca. He is described by Kyprianos as a one-eyed, illiterate woodcutter. Obviously a generous allowance must be made for the conventions of Levantine political abuse. His subsequent history shows that he possessed much personal charm, which enabled him to ingratiate himself with persons of influence, and intelligence sufficient to allow him to rise to high office and to administer it with at least as much competence as his predecessors and successors. He cannot have been as ugly as he is described since his first appointment, as Governor of Adalia in Karamania, was allegedly due to having gained the favour of a member of the harem of a notable of the island. His next post was as Chief Magistrate of Larnaca. In 1771 the Governor of Cyprus, Ismail Agha, made him Defterdar, head of the financial administration and the senior Agha of Nicosia. A new Governor arrived in 1775. Allegedly he intended to dismiss Baki because he knew him of old — or because he would have liked to give his post to a nominee of his own; but he died before he could give effect to his intention. Baki's enemies naturally accused him of having poisoned the Governor, and when the Deputy Governor died about a month later this was also supposed to be his work. In spite of these hostile mutterings he had such support from the Turkish senior officials and clergy, and from the bishops, that he became Governor, first on an acting and then on a

241

permanent basis. In the latter capacity he ruled for six years, an unusually long term. The evidence even of his enemies credits him with being a good administrator and if he made a very large fortune by corruption and illegal extortion he did no more than many other governors had done. For some reason, however, he has remained a well-known figure in folk-memory; 'Baki Agha the tyrant' is the very type of the bad governor.

Travellers from Europe who visited Cyprus in the 17th and 18th centuries are eloquent about the heavy taxation imposed. 'The impositions upon the island are such as you never heard of' says Drummond, who goes on to give full details of the poll tax and the other regular taxes. In addition there were always special impositions known as *avanie,* brought in whenever the governors thought they could squeeze something extra out of the peasants. After all, as Drummond has just explained, they were only in office for a year and had had to pay great bribe to obtain it; if they were to recoup these expenses and make a fortune as well they could not afford to be nice in their methods. As Drummond concludes: 'The method of levying these impositions is very strange: no time is fixed for payment, but when the officer empowered shall make his demand if the unhappy man cannot produce the money, he must undergo imprisonment, the bastinado or some other torture; if he is possessed of any effects, houses, lands, cattle or other moveables they are instantly sold at an undervalue to satisfy these cormorants, who set his wife and children adrift without remorse or compunction; nay, they even make sport of their misery.' What made things even more poignant for the Greek peasantry was the prominent part played in the tax-gathering machinery by their own religious leaders, the Archbishop and bishops.

In accordance with the Ottoman theory whereby the religious leaders of the various communities in the Empire were responsible for the secular behaviour of their flocks, it was reasonable that they should have powers to enforce obedience. After all, it was the Archbishop who would be held responsible if the community rebelled or failed to pay taxes. A hundred years after the conquest, in about 1660 according to Kyprianos, the Archbishop and his suffragans were formally recognised as 'official guardians and representatives of the *rayahs.'* To make them effective in this role they were given the right of direct access to the Sultan with petitions and complaints. In 1754 they were made responsible for the actual collection of taxes. They constituted in effect a second source of authority set over against the Governor. They had also the advantage in that the Dragoman of the Serai, the man through whom all official business between the administration and the Greek Cypriots was conducted, was a Greek appointed by the Archbishop. At the beginning of the 19th century the Dragoman Hadjigeorgakis

Kornessios was described as the most powerful and the wealthiest person in Cyprus. This special position of the higher clergy is always commented on by travellers during this period of Ottoman rule. The British diplomat Turner in 1815 goes so far as to say that 'Cyprus is in fact governed by the Archbishop and his subordinate clergy.' The French Consul at Larnaca a few years before had strongly condemned the Archbishop and the Dragoman and their

Cypriot iconostasis of carved, painted and gilded pine-wood; H 4.20 m, W 4.60 m; 1757-1762 (Berlin, Staatliche Museen)

subordinates, the tax collectors, for oppression so serious that they drove the Christians from the island. Sir George Hill takes a more judicious view of the conflicting evidence: although the archbishops often made themselves unpopular with their flocks by their demands for money the best of them took seriously their duty to protect against oppression the faithful committed to their charge.

The consequences of the Greek War of Liberation, starting in 1821, showed the other aspect of the Archbishop's position. In the plans of the *Philike Hetaireia* (Friendly Society), the first movers of the insurrection, Cyprus was naturally included, along with all other Greek territories, among those to be liberated. It was recognised that its position was difficult because of its distance from the Peloponnese, the first focus of the movement, and because it was surrounded on north, east and south by predominantly-Moslem countries. On the other hand the Turkish garrison was small and inefficient and the Greek insurgents had reasonable grounds to hope

This house, in the old part of Nicosia, belonged to Hadjigeorgakis Kornessios (Great Dragoman of Cyprus 1779-1809). A typical 18th-century Cyprus town house incorporating features from earlier periods, including a stone relief with the lion of St Mark; pencil drawing

244

Portrait of Dragoman
Hadjigeorgakis Kornessios
holding a *firman* with the
Sultan's cipher
(Nicosia, Cyprus Museum)

that they could successfully challenge the Ottoman navy. Agents
from the Society came to Cyprus in 1818 and Kyprianos, Archbishop since 1810, was enrolled as a member; he pointed out, however, that for the reasons already given he could contribute no more
than a promise of money, and supplies if ships could be sent to fetch
them. The latter promise was fulfilled when in July 1821 the Greek
naval commander Canaris was secretly revictualled at an anchorage
on the north coast. The Governor, Mehmed Silahshor (known

Hala Sultan Tekké stands on the site of the burial place of Umm Haram, maternal aunt of the Prophet Mohammed. The mosque was built in 1816 by the Governor Seyyid Mohammed Emin; pencil drawing

as Küchük, or Little Mehmed) was aware of what was going on, for it is rare in Cyprus for anything to be kept secret. Greatly alarmed, he asked the Sultan for troops and for permission to execute all the leading Christians in the island. Some 4,000 troops were sent from Syria but the Sultan, for the moment, preferred merely to disarm the Christians. This was done in April and May 1821. Küchük Mehmed began executing Christians in any case and sent a further message detailing 486 prominent persons of whom he would like to make an example. Kyprianos told a British traveller, who has left a moving account of him in his last days — 'highly eminent for his learning and piety as well as for his unshaken fortitude' — that he knew the Governor was only waiting for an opportunity to kill him.

Very shortly afterwards the Sultan — who had just executed the Oecumenical Patriarch — sent his assent to Mehmed's proposal. On 9 July the three bishops were beheaded and the Archbishop was

246

hanged in the square in front of the Serai. Next day the Abbot of Kykko and other clergy were executed. The property of the Church was plundered: that was indeed one of the main motives of the aghas of Nicosia in urging severity on the not unwilling Governor. As a further step an order was enforced that all Christians were to pull down the upper storey of their houses since only Turks were allowed to have houses with an upper floor. This order remained in force until the British occupation in 1878. The French Consul reported on 6 August that in the whole of Limassol there remained only two Greeks, a few porters, and the Governor's executioners.

Massacres continued and became worse when the Sultan felt bound to call on the Pasha of Egypt for help in Cyprus as in the other insurgent Greek territories. The Egyptian troops were as badly disciplined as the Syrians who had preceded them. The number of Greeks fleeing from the island increased; out of this emigration many for the first time went to Egypt. Küchük Mehmed had made so much money from confiscating the property of those he massacred — greed had probably been a stronger motive with him than fear or hatred — that he was able by bribery to prolong his tenure for an extra year.

In 1833 three insurrections broke out, inspired by the sudden imposition by the Governor Said Mehmed of a new, arbitrary and heavy tax. The last known of them is the one called the revolt of the Giaur Imam. It was led by a wealthy Turkish landowner from Tremithus who claimed support among the Christians, from which circumstance he was given the nickname of 'infidel'. He appears to have been driven to it by a personal insult but he capitalised on the resentment aroused by the new tax to occupy the whole district of Paphos. He held out for about three months, murdering people whose wealth he coveted, until finally crushed by government troops who outdid him in atrocities against innocent people.

The Greek War of Liberation marks the beginning of the process which transformed the Ottoman Empire into 'the sick man of Europe'. The 19th century was full of deathbed repentances and promises of reforms. Intentions were good, results were negligible. Sultan Mahmud II began the process but the first codification came with his successor and eldest son, Abdul Mejid I, who in his first year 1839 issued a charter of reforms. These provided for regular and published scales of taxation and the abolition of tax-farming, an improvement in the system of justice and the strict prohibition of bribery and corruption in the administration. None of the reforms were applied in Cyprus any more than in other Ottoman provinces. When in 1856 the Sultan issued another version of the original *Hatti Sherif* or noble writing, the Kadi of Nicosia (the Chief Judge) assured the Turks that it would have no more effect than the earlier version. As Sir Charles Eliot wrote in 1908, in his influential work *Turkey in Europe:* 'The reforms of Mahmud and Abdul Mejid ... and the establishment of parliamentary government by the present Sultan (Abdul Hamid II) were measures which would have revolutionised any ordinary country but they have simply collapsed in Turkey without result and without fuss.'

When in 1840 a new Governor Talaat Effendi was sent with the express purpose of introducing reforms, especially in taxation, the Turks began to arm themselves. Their aim was to intimidate the administration against tampering with the old system from which they had profited. Troops were again brought from Karamania but the intimidation was successful; the introduction of the reforms was indefinitely postponed. So was the promise of the institution of a commercial court in Larnaca. As a result of the confusion the collection of taxes had been suspended and the subsequent demand for arrears caused more emigration of taxpayers. Over the next few

Opposite
'Famagusta, the ancient Venetian port of Cyprus'; wood engraving (Illustrated London News, 1878)

years, however, there came a change in the method of collection.
The Archbishop no longer guaranteed the tax, assessed it and
collected it through his own officials; instead it was collected direct
by the Government. From this period the ascendancy of the hierarchy began to diminish although the Archbishop still remained the
Rayah-Vekili, the representative of the Christian *rayahs,* a title which
the Greeks, stressing race rather than religion, translated as Ethnarch.

From 1849 to 1861 Cyprus was included in the Pashalik of
Rhodes, which was the provincial capital of the islands of the
Aegean. During this period the governors changed rapidly. Some
were octogenarians and some permanently drunk but even the
more competent never had enough time to do any good. After
seven years as an independent province it was transferred to the
newly-formed Vilayet or Governor-Generalship of the Darda-

nelles. This made for even greater inefficiency because the Governor-General had his headquarters at Chanak. Since all important powers were centralised in his hands both administrative and judicial business was subjected to great delay. After two years the island was put back under the jurisdiction of Rhodes. It was to the Governor-General of the Archipelago, with his seat at Rhodes, that Sultan Abdul Hamid addressed the order to transfer Cyprus to British administration in 1878.

There are not many significant remains of the Turkish occupation to be seen in the island. The fort at Paphos is a poor specimen of military architecture and in any case largely based on a Venetian original. Nicosia was the centre of government and the majority of its inhabitants were Turks; the principal architectural remains are here. The Büyük Khan (the Great Khan) built by Muzaffer Pasha in the 16th century is a respectable, functionally designed building.

Cartoon showing Disraeli carrying the Sultan across the tight-rope of the Congress of Berlin. The rockets in the bacground celebrate the Cyprus Convention (Punch, 1878)

The 17th century saw the construction of the Tekké of the Mevlevi Dervishes, now a museum, as a centre for this mystical Sufi brotherhood. Perhaps the most attractive specimen of Turkish architecture in Cyprus it is built in a decent, unpretentious style well suited to the engagingly austere ideology of a sect that has suffered in western eyes from its appellation of the 'Dancing Dervishes'. The small Arab Ahmed Pasha Mosque has its admirers among those who are attracted by Ottoman 18th-century architecture. The best specimen of this is undoubtedly the Hala Sultan Tekké in which is the tomb of Umm Haram, the maternal aunt of

252

Cartoon showing the
Sultan as Humpty-Dumpty
being put back on the wall
(the Asian frontier in
Anatolia) by Disraeli,
assisted by Cyprus
(Punch, 1878)

the Prophet Mohammed. The tomb, built in 1760, incorporates a
megalithic dolmen but the mosque and tekké were added in 1816.
Romantically placed in a grove of palm trees with a salt lake in front
the tekké is the embodiment of the old Levant.

Of all the periods of which there is historical record this is
without doubt the unhappiest and least prosperous. Cyprus was of
no particular importance to the Ottoman Government. It was
neither a frontier province nor of strategic value; for a regime
whose interests were primarily military that meant that it was
regarded solely from the point of view of how much money could

be made out of it. There were, it is true, enlightened sultans, especially in the earlier period of the occupation, who were able to take a long-term view. They might treat their provincial subjects as sheep but, like the Emperor Tiberius, they preferred them shorn not flayed. Their orders were well conceived but always disobeyed. Because the only system of administration they could imagine was based on unrestricted autocracy their civilian officials held on a servile tenure posts which they had purchased by bribery. The interests of these officials were directly opposite to those of the sultans. They could only take short-term views. They must recoup by oppression and corruption, as quickly as possible, the expenditure which had won them their chance of a fortune. The judgment of Captain Saville in 1878 is temperate and reasonable. 'It seems that in Cyprus it is not so much the laws themselves but rather the administration of laws which needs reform. The Ottoman Government is noted for publishing innumerable *firmans,* laws and ordinances, which leave but little room for improvement as regards either completeness or natural equity; and it has been either the disregard or maladministration of these laws which has done so much injury to the country.'

The principal change brought about by the Ottomans, as has been already mentioned, was the introduction of an extraneous ethnic element. The new Turkish settlers, however, rapidly divided into two unequal parts, different both in their own eyes and in those of the Greeks. One the one hand were the aghas, the representatives in Nicosia of the oppressors of the island, and on the other the Turkish peasantry who suffered as much as the Greeks from the exactions of the tax-gatherers, among whom some Greek magnates could be numbered. As many travellers attest, relations in the countryside were as friendly under the Ottomans as they remained until the second half of the 20th century.

XI

THE BRITISH PERIOD

1878-1960

Sir David Hunt

It should not have been a matter for surprise that Cyprus came into British hands in the last quarter of the 19th century. The reasons were strategic and political though that does not imply that it was itself of strategic value. Cyprus appears to occupy a central position in the eastern Mediterranean but in fact is not on the way to anywhere in particular. Its ports are of no great commercial importance. For naval purposes the only one that was thought to have possibilities as a base, Famagusta, was then not capable of being one and was never properly developed into one during the eighty-two years of British rule. The lesson of history is that so far from bringing advantage to a country that seeks to dominate the area Cyprus has always fallen, as though inevitably, into the hands of whichever country was in fact already dominant there. It is not a positive aid but a passive adjunct to power. Britain's acquisition of Cyprus was not for the sake of adding to the Empire and certainly not for the sake of Cyprus itself; it was a commitment accepted to serve other and more distant purposes.

Since the day in 1683 when the flood-tide of Turkish conquest had fallen back from the gates of Vienna the Christian powers in emulous contest had planned the division of the Sultan's European territories. In due course the weakness of the Ottoman Empire began to menace the peace of Europe as much as its strength had done in the past. The first main contestant for the reversionary estate was the Habsburg dynasty under the successive titles of the Holy Roman Empire, the Austrian Empire and Austria-Hungary.

Its aim was to expand its rule into the Balkan Peninsula, much of which had belonged earlier to the Hungarian Kingdom to which the Habsburgs were the heirs. Very soon, however, imperial Russia stepped forward as the chief rival of the House of Othman both because of its sympathies with its Orthodox co-religionists and also because the Habsburgs, unlike the Romanovs, had always had to occupy themselves with western Europe as well. France, allied to the Turks in the 16th century and with long and valuable commercial ties with them, had been stimulated by Napoleon's romantic ideas of oriental conquest; the Bourbon and Orleans monarchies which succeeded him pursued similar policies under the more respectable pretext of protecting the Latin Christians of the Levant. Napoleon III was at times thought to have considered the acquisition of Cyprus. The whole system of conflicting claims was a high concern of European politics under the general designation of 'the Eastern Question'.

The Royal Navy had been actively engaged in the Mediterranean since the 16th century but it was not until the beginning of the 19th that it played a dominating role, especially in the Levant. British policy there differed from that of the other powers by being inspired by extra-European motives. They were imperial motives. Throughout the 19th century the word Empire meant India. Africa was merely an inconvenient piece of land that got in the way of a voyage from Britain to India; the posts occupied on the two coasts for the purpose of suppressing the slave trade were 'millstones round our neck' as Disraeli called them; the only parts of Africa of any interest were those that commanded the way round, the Cape and the isthmus of Suez. The Cape was safe enough. In the eastern Mediterranean British policy would react to any hostile threat but there was one which inspired special fear. The power which was making most of the running against the Turks, Russia, was also the one whose Empire in central Asia was expanding most rapidly. The occupation and colonisation of one independent Asian state after another was bringing the Russians closer every day to the frontiers of India. A series of successes in wars against the Turks seemed to presage a time when the Czar would not be satisfied merely with the annexation of additional Ottoman provinces but would take over, either as a protectorate or in full possession, all the territories of that Empire whose imminent demise Nicholas I had confidently predicted in 1853.

In London strategic opinion was unanimous in holding that any further advance by Russia would fatally endanger imperial communications. The key issue was Constantinople and the straits, that is the Bosporus and the Dardanelles. In consequence, throughout the 19th century it was an axiom of British policy that Turkey should be supported against Russia, preferably by diplomacy only

256

but if necessary by arms. The Crimean War was an example of the latter. It also demonstrated the difficulties of giving military support to the Sultan, for although in the circumstances it was remarkably successful as an amphibious operation, the fact that the British-French expeditionary forces had no base nearer than Marseilles caused grave difficulties of supply. The restrictions imposed on Russia by the Black Sea clauses of the Treaty of Paris in 1856 were satisfactory so long as they lasted, but Alexander II took advantage of the defeat of France in 1870 to repudiate them. In the succeeding decade Russian military strength was augmented (universal conscription was introduced in 1874), the struggles for freedom of the still-enslaved Christian nations of the Balkans became sharper and the highest levels of the imperial government began to espouse with fervour the Pan-Slav cause which called for independence for Serbs, Macedonians, and Bulgars under Russian inspiration and control.

The most serious of the Russo-Turkish wars was the one that broke out in 1877. Its origin was the Russian desire to rescue Serbia and Montenegro, which had been defeated in war by Turkey, and

'General view of the landing place at Larnaca from the anchorage'; wood engraving
(Illustrated London News, 1878)

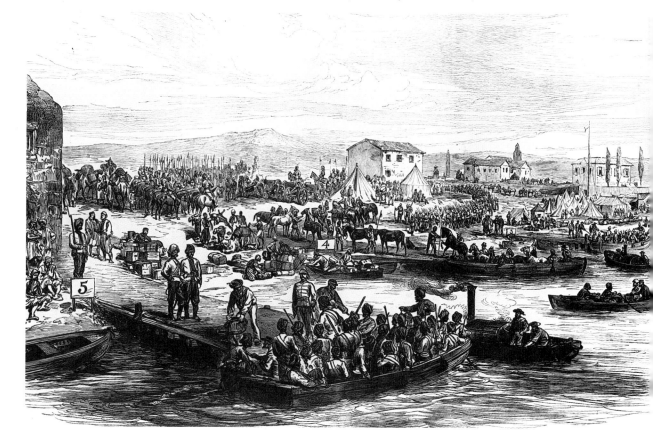

to liberate the enslaved Christian nations of the Balkans; and also, naturally, to exploit the liberation to produce as much political and military advantage as possible. In Britain it found a Conservative government in power under Disraeli with, for the first time in his life, an unassailable majority in Parliament. In spite of a growing wave of public opinion against the Turks, stirred up by reports of the atrocities committed in Bulgaria, he was determined to pursue 'the old Crimean policy'. Besides, on this occasion it looked as though the Russians really would reach Constantinople. The city was within their power. Nothing but the indecisiveness of Alexander II held them back. The British countermove was to send the Mediterranean Fleet through the Dardanelles into the Marmora to anchor in sight of the Seraglio. Troops from the Indian Army were brought to Malta. Plans were made to use them to seize either Cyprus or Alexandretta (Iskanderun) as a base for operations in support of the Sultan. A popular song by G.W. Hunt expressed the mood and added a word to the vocabulary of politics:

> We don't want to fight but, by jingo, if we do
> We've got the ships, we've got the men, we've got the money too.
> We've fought the Bear before and while Britons shall be true
> The Russians shall not have Constantinople.

The Russians flinched from Constantinople but imposed on the Sultan the annexationist Treaty of San Stephano. So exorbitant were its terms that the other European powers insisted on its being submitted to a special congress in Berlin. As with all successful international conferences the main points of contention were the subject of secret, separate negotiations beforehand. Britain and Russia worked out an accord. It allowed the victors a reasonable share of the spoils of war, especially at the eastern end of the Sultan's Anatolian dominions, while reducing their aspirations in the Balkan Peninsula and the region of the Straits. Simultaneously the British and Turkish Governments were conducting a parallel set of preliminary negotiations. For if the old Crimean policy was to be followed and Britain was to protect Turkey against Russian aggression then Turkey must be shown to be worth preserving. Public opinion in Britain was doubtful, on moral grounds, even though an alliance with the Sultan was accepted as being in British interests. Accordingly in the new agreement the British Government's undertaking to assist the Sultan to defend his possessions in Asia (but not in Europe) against any further Russian aggression was balanced by stringent conditions accepted by the Ottoman Government. Not only did they promise reforms of administration for the benefit of their Christian subjects — an easy and by then conventional formality which had already produced several admirably expressed but wholly disregarded constitutions — but they agreed to

Opposite
'Sketches from the British occupation of Cyprus: conveying baggage; camp of Cheflik Pasha; grave of Sergeant Megaw; Minotaur Gate, Nicosia; barracks at Baffo gate, Nicosia'; wood engraving (Illustrated London News, 1878)

CAMP OF CHEFLIK PASHA

MINOTAUR GATE NICOSIA

BARRACKS BAFFO GATE NICOSIA

'Hoisting the British flag in Nicosia; wood engraving (Illustrated London News, 1878)

the appointment all over Anatolia of British 'Military Consuls' who would report regularly on the non-performance of the Sultan's promises. This would give London a desirable leverage. Finally the island of Cyprus was to be handed over to be administered in the name of Queen Victoria while remaining formally part of the Sultan's dominions.

One reason for the acquisition of Cyprus was that the preliminary agreement made by Salisbury, the British Foreign Secretary, and Shuvalov, the Russian Ambassador in London, had conceded Russian territorial claims not only to the fortresses of Kars and Ardahan in the Caucasus but also to the Black Sea port of Batum. So agitated was popular opinion that these concessions, when revealed, would be hard to defend unless there was some positive gain. In this role the Cyprus Convention contributed to the success of the Congress of Berlin. 'This is progress,' said Bismarck when he heard of it. Disraeli commented to the Queen, 'Evidently his idea of progress is seizing something.' The other reason was the practical requirements of this pro-Turkish policy. The announced intention was to use Cyprus as a *place d'armes*: not a strong point or even a naval base but a convenient location where troops could be assembled if they were to be sent to join the Turkish forces in the Caucasus or, a strategic possibility which loomed large at the time, in the Euphrates valley. Experience had shown that Malta was too remote. Many other possibilities were considered but rejected. A fairly strong favourite at one time was Stampalia (Astypalaea), which has indeed an excellent port but not much room for troops.

The link with the Russo-Turkish frontier continued throughout the British period. In the original agreement it was provided that if Russia gave back the two fortresses and Batum Cyprus too would be returned to the Sultan's direct administration. (Kars and Ardahan but not Batum reverted to Turkey in 1921 as part of the terms of a Soviet treaty with Ataturk's government.) At the time of independence in 1960 the link was again in evidence since the NATO commitment towards Turkey was the principal reason why Britain required bases in the island.

Such were the circumstances in which Cyprus in 1878 found itself playing, quite unexpectedly, a leading role in the politics of Europe. It was destined to be only brief. The reasons for this were once more extraneous ones. In 1880 the Conservative government was defeated at the elections and Gladstone became Prime Minister. His ideas on foreign policy were succinctly but sufficiently expressed in the undoing of what he called 'Beaconsfieldism'. He had described the Cyprus Convention as an 'insane covenant' and an 'act of duplicity not surpassed, and rarely equalled, in the history of nations;' he was hardly likely to take serious steps to exploit it. His critics pointed out that he took none either to annul it. His sentiments were strongly anti-Turk, as he had demonstrated during his famous electoral campaign in Midlothian; on the other hand by recalling the military consuls from Anatolia he gave up the best chance of ensuring an improvement of Turkish methods of rule. There was therefore little prospect of Cyprus being used for the purpose for which it had been acquired and only four years had passed when its function as the principal British base in the eastern Mediterranean was finally superseded. In 1882 began the occupation of Egypt, which provided not only the far superior facilities of Alexandria but also direct control over the Suez Canal. Cyprus was by-passed.

The actual process of occupation was picturesque and peaceful. On 4 July 1878, the Channel Fleet under the command of Vice-

Admiral Lord John Hay arrived at Larnaca from Crete. On the 6th he was officially informed of the signature on 4 June of the Cyprus Convention but was given no instructions about what action he was to take. After waiting for another two days he went ashore and met the Kaimakam or local Commander, described as a man of mild and indolent temper; it was evident that there would be no opposition. On 10 July the engagingly-named HMS Salamis arrived from Constantinople with the Ottoman Commissioner, Sami Pasha, who brought with him the imperial *firman,* addressed to the Governor of Cyprus through the Vali of the Archipelago, directing him to hand over the administration of the island. A copy for the Admiral was brought by a British official, Walter Baring, who became Secretary to the Government after the transference of power. Sami Pasha and Walter Baring were sent to Nicosia to inform the Governor and on the 12th Admiral Hay set off for the capital in a wagonette. He overtook on the way a detachment of fifty sailors and fifty marines and drove in unescorted. After calling on the Governor, Ahmed Bessim Pasha, at the Serai he was present the same afternoon at a brief flag-raising ceremony in front of the Turkish army barracks. In a short address to the crowd he promised justice for all on an equal basis. The only other speaker was a Greek Cypriot, George Kepiades, who expressed the joy of the Cypriots at the prospect of liberty and progress.

After the excitement of the diplomatic bargaining table and the battles in the Balkan passes and at the approaches to the Bosporus which preceded them the actual implementation of the Cyprus Convention passed off in a markedly humdrum manner. There was nothing to match the scenes of horror which had accompanied the transfer of power from Venice to the Turks; it was to prove a strange coincidence however that Venice and Britain ruled Cyprus for the same length of time, eighty-two years. Turkish military strength had run down as explained in the preceding chapter; the first British force to arrive was a detachment from the Indian army contingent in Malta 400 strong. The existing Gendarmerie, the Zaptieh, were taken over by the incoming administration and after being purged and retrained were found fully adequate to maintain order in a well-behaved and largely crime-free island. For indeed Cyprus never became a *place d'armes*. Except in wartime and, later, during the EOKA campaign, there was no garrison to speak of, merely a company of infantry borrowed from a unit serving in Egypt. The military nature of the occupation began to disappear very soon. The first High Commissioner was a soldier, Lieutenant-General Sir Garnet Wolseley, who went on to become both a Viscount, a Field-Marshal and Commander-in-Chief of the Army. He served for less than a year and was succeeded by another military man, Colonel (later Major-General) Sir Robert Biddulph; but

thereafter Cyprus, having been transferred from the Foreign Office
to the Colonial Office, was ruled by civilians appointed from the
career service of the latter. Their title reflected the anomalous
position of the island so long as the Sultan's ultimate sovereignty
was upheld. As a post it did not rank particularly high compared
with other colonies. It was not quite the backwater it had been
under the Ottomans but it was no longer a centre of world interest.

The proceedings of the Congress of Berlin are not of a nature to
commend themselves to the more enlightened ideas of today, or

even of 1918 when President Wilson proclaimed as one of his Four Principles 'Peoples and Provinces shall not be bartered about from sovereignty to sovereignty as if they were but chattels or pawns in the game.' (He overlooked this admirable principle when disposing of, for instance, South Tyrol.) Neither the people of Cyprus nor the people of Britain were invited to express their views. On the other hand there was fairly general agreement in 1878, shared and vigorously expressed by Gladstone, that the fewer people under Turkish sovereignty the better. Certainly this was the view of the Cypriots. Turkish rule had been corrupt, grasping and desperately inefficient even when not actively oppressive. The mood in which they looked forward to British rule was expressed by Archbishop Sophronios in his address of welcome to Wolseley: 'We hope, therefore, that from now on a new life begins for the people of Cyprus; a new great period, which will become memorable in the annals of the island. We hope that all shall be instructed without distinction of race or creed, that law is the king of all; that all shall have equal rights and equal responsibility before the law; that all shall be used to treading the good road, that is to say, the road of truth, of duty and of liberty.' The other component of that mood was made clear to Wolseley by the Bishop of Kition, welcoming

'Ruins of the Venetian palace, Famagusta'; wood engraving (Illustrated London News, 1878)

264

him to Larnaca. 'We accept the change of government inasmuch as we trust Great Britain will help Cyprus, as it did the Ionian Islands, to be united with mother Greece, with which it is naturally connected.'

Before taking up the theme raised by the Bishop of Kition, which will dominate the rest of this history, it will be as well to say something about the differences produced by the transition from bad government to good, even if often parsimonious, government. It is notoriously difficult to describe the achievements of administration without going into details. And generalities are liable to sound suspect. Nevertheless the progress made in those eighty-two years is plain to see. Roads were built on a scale unparalleled in other Mediterranean islands where previously there had been one rough track connecting Larnaca with Nicosia. 19th-century travellers had called Cyprus the unhealthiest of all Ottoman provinces: the provision of hospitals and medical services eradicated the endemic diseases, especially malaria, and favoured an increase of

'Greek Orthodox priests blessing the British flag at the Kykko Metokhi, Nicosia, in the presence of the High Commissioner'; wood engraving (Illustrated London News, 1878)

265

population from 186,000 in 1881 to an estimated 660,000 in 1978. One of the most remarkable successes of the British administration was the reafforestation of the mountainous regions and the creation of a Forestry Service that was a model for and a teacher of the other services in the Empire. It fulfils the same role in the Near East of today; and so does the Veterinary Service which has transformed animal husbandry. Legislation against usury and the steps taken from an early date to provide agricultural credit meant that the grip of the moneylenders was lifted from the peasantry. Co-operatives were encouraged: the rise in quality of agricultural products, especially wine, and their successful marketing, are evidence of their value. Cyprus trade unions, most assiduously fostered by the colonial administration, have a stability and responsibility which it is unlikely they would have acquired if their development had been left to indigenous talent. Nor has individual enterprise been behindhand. Greeks are admittedly outstanding as businessmen but the Greek Cypriots under colonial rule benefitted from a stable currency and preferential markets and, of course, were spared from the war, the enemy occupation and the civil war which the mother country suffered.

Education calls for special mention. In 1880 the High Commissioner, in a dispatch to the Colonial Secretary, proposed that for the future all education should be through the medium of English. This was consistent with policy in, for example, India. There, in the formative period of British rule, the authorities had positively favoured oriental languages especially Persian; but Macaulay's famous minute and an advancing self-confidence had discarded Hafiz in favour of Wordsworth and Shakespeare. Lord Kimberley, Sec-

'Reception of a deputation, Trikomo; wood engraving (Illustrated London News, 1878)

266

'The British Kaimakam
hearing an assault case at
Ephtakomi'; wood
engraving
(Illustrated London News,
1878)

retary of State in Gladstone's newly-elected government, would
not hear of such treatment for Greek, which was still one of the two
bases of British higher education. In a decision as important as any,
and taken within two years of the occupation, he insisted that Greek
should be the language of education throughout the island, with
Turkish similarly used in the schools set up for the minority. From
then on the schools for the majority followed the official Greek
curriculum, which was in itself largely modelled on the German
system. As a result the history and the literature which children
studied from their earliest youth were those of the mother country
and the objects towards which their patriotism was directed were
the Greek Royal Family and the Greek flag.

Cyprus was given a constitution on the usual colonial model in
1882. It provided for a Legislative Council of twelve elected and six
official members (the latter being colonial civil servants) presided

'The triumphal entry of Captain Swain into Levkoniko'; wood engraving (Illustrated London News, 1878)

over by the High Commissioner, who had a casting vote. The elected members were divided in proportion to the numbers of Christians and Moslems shown in the census of 1881, viz nine to three. This meant that if the officials voted with the three Turkish members they had an equality with the Greek members and the High Commissioner's casting vote would carry the day. The Council's powers were limited, especially in financial matters; although the annual budget was laid before the Council and voted on it could be enforced whatever the result by the use of the High Commissioner's reserve powers. This constitution remained in force until 1931. It was not affected by the change in status of the island which took place in 1914 when, as a consequence of the state of war between Turkey and Britain, the latter declared that it had been annexed to the British crown. (The change was regularised in 1925, when Cyprus was declared to be a Colony; the title of High Commissioner was changed to Governor). There was justification for the complaint, made particularly by the Greek Cypriots, that they had less control over their own affairs than was the practice in many other colonies where the standard of popular education was much lower. It was not their only or most serious complaint. For in contrast to the Asian or African territories the aspiration of the majority of the Cypriot people was not for greater self-government leading to independence; it was for transfer to another crown than that of the British, for union with the rest of the Greek people. The demand for *enosis,* the Greek word for unification, was the only important issue in politics.

The strength of nationalism as a political emotion was one of the distinguishing features of 19th-century history as exemplified in particular by the struggles for unification in Germany and Italy. The Greeks were no less persistent in pursuit of it. The comparatively small nation-state created in 1831, with its capital in Athens, was inspired from its start with the ambition to bring together all the Greek lands which remained unliberated, and fought several wars with this object; the inhabitants of those lands shared the same ambition. In Cyprus there had been no chance under the Ottomans for public demonstrations of nationalist sentiment. The same was

'The first British High Commissioner, Sir Garnet Wolseley, receiving Turkish notables in the Konak on the occasion of Bairam'; wood engraving (Illustrated London News, 1878)

269

true, for example, of Chios or Mitylene and Cyprus was much more distant from Athens being the furthest removed to the east and south of all the Greek islands. The arrival of the British at once released the Cypriots' inhibitions. There was no danger of the savage repression which had been unleashed in 1821; the new rulers were open to argument, allowed free speech and freedom of the press and had even fostered the Hellenic heritage by their educational policy. Besides, there was always the precedent of the cession of the Ionian Islands to which the Bishop of Kition had appealed in the first days of the transfer of power.

From 1878 onwards the hope for unification never dimmed. It would be tedious to detail all the various, almost annual, manifestations which are recounted at length in Sir George Hill's fourth volume. The wording of resolutions and memorials scarcely varies over eighty odd years. From time to time the memorialists received some encouragement. For example Gladstone twice, in 1880 and in 1897, made public statements in favour of *enosis;* but on both occasions he was in opposition; when in power he took no action. The independence of Crete in 1898 roused great expectations because it was accomplished by concerted action by all the European powers. In 1907 an even greater stimulus was given by the visit of Winston Churchill, then Parliamentary Secretary at the Colonial Office and its spokesman in the House of Commons. In reply to a memorial he declared that it was 'only natural that the Cypriot people who are of Greek descent should regard their incorporation in what may be called their mother country as an ideal to be

270

earnestly, devoutly and fervently cherished. Such a feeling is an example of the patriotic devotion which so nobly characterises the Greek nation.' (He added that he respected those views, but also those of the Moslems, that the British occupation should not lead to the dismemberment of the Ottoman Empire or to the impairing of the sovereignty of the Sultans.) In 1915 the Greek Cypriots discovered, after the event, that their great ideal had come momentarily within their grasp, only to be taken away again. When Bulgaria, joining the alliance of Germany, Austria and Turkey, declared war on Serbia the Greek Government under Venizelos was ready to go to war with Bulgaria as its treaty obligations to Serbia required; but it was unconstitutionally dismissed by King Constantine, who thought Germany was going to win the war. The British Government, concerned about the fate of Serbia, offered to cede Cyprus to

'Marching from Mount Troodos into winter quarters'; wood engraving (The Graphic, 1880)

271

Greece in return for the fulfilment of its obligations. Zaimis, Constantine's stop-gap Prime Minister, refused. Although Venizelos later in the war overthrew Constantine and brought Greece on to the side of the Allies the offer was not repeated.

On every occasion the Greek petitions for *enosis* were put forward representatives of the Turkish minority petitioned in the contrary sense. Occasionally, as in 1907 during Churchill's visit, the Turks mounted riotous demonstrations. Normally, however, they did not feel it necessary to equal the fervour of the Greek Cypriots because they were confident that the British had no intention of relinquishing control. They were content with their status. There was no evidence of resentment when in 1914 they found themselves suddenly British rather than Ottoman subjects in consequence of the annexation. They were spared the upheavals that other parts of the Ottoman Empire suffered. Indeed life in Cyprus continued very much in the old pattern, as it had been in Thessaly or Macedonia or eastern Asia Minor before the Balkan Wars and the First World War had broken it. There were Greek villages and Turkish villages and mixed villages as well; Greek Cypriots and Turkish Cypriots lived amicably as good neighbours. But the minority thought that they might not get on so well if they were forced to become Greek citizens. Some of the better-educated reflected that in Crete, where Moslems had once, in the 18th century, been a majority, they were now not even a minority since the remaining ones had all been obliged to emigrate. It was not, however, a burning question until the second half of the 1950s; for the present the Turkish Cypriots were content with their prosperity

'New pier and government offices at Limassol'; wood engraving (Illustrated London News, 1878)

272

'The new iron pier and customs house, Larnaca'; wood engraving (The Graphic, 1882)

and confident it would continue.

The Greek Cypriots were naturally also aware of their increasing prosperity. They did not however allow it to distract them from the pursuit of their national aims. The politically-conscious element kept them constantly before the mind of the public. British officials often expressed surprise at this disregard of the economic factors to which modern political theory tends to attribute predominant influence; but in this they showed a lack of understanding of the Greek national character. One British Governor was reported as declaring, with puzzled emphasis, that he had never met anyone who could show that the Cypriots would be better off if united with Greece. Whether this was true or not, personal advantage was not the moving force for *enosis*.

In October 1931 there took place the most serious demonstration up to then in favour of *enosis*. The guiding organisation was a recently-formed 'National Radicalist Union' which declared as its principal aims 'the fanatical pursuit of the union of Cyprus with the Greek political whole.' A leading role was played by the Bishop of Kition, who addressed a meeting in Limassol calling for civil disobedience. In Nicosia the principal part was played by the chief priest of the Phaneromeni Church, Dionysios Kykkotis, who unfurled a Greek flag and declared 'I proclaim the revolution.' A march on Government House resulted in a riot in the course of which it was burned down. The authorities reacted by bringing in a company of troops from Egypt; order was restored in a comparatively short time. Ten Greek Cypriots, including the Bishops of Kition and Kyrenia, were deported. The constitution was suspended, political parties were forbidden and the press censored. The flying of the Greek flag was prohibited by law.

For the rest of the 1930s the expression of support for the cause of *enosis* was restricted almost entirely to London, Athens and New York. In Athens it was discouraged by the Venizelos government.

273

The London Cypriot Committee was especially active. A change of mood in the island and among the political organisations abroad came with the Italian invasion of Greece in October 1940 as a result of which Britain and Greece became allies. Recruitment to the Cyprus Regiment rapidly increased; in all some 30,000 Cypriots are recorded as having served in the forces. The Greek flag was flown in triumph to celebrate frequent Greek victories in Albania. After the German invasion in April 1941 had rescued the Italians and occupied the whole of the country including Crete it appeared that Cyprus was in imminent danger. The appearance was misleading because Hitler, unsettled by the very heavy casualties in Crete, had personally forbidden any further parachute operations; but this could not be known at the time. In spite of the threat the Cypriot population showed no sign of wavering in its support for the Allied cause. In recognition the prohibition of political parties was rescinded; in October 1941 a meeting at Skarinou led to the foundation of AKEL, the Progressive Party of the Working People. Before long it was joined by a Cyprus National Party (KEK) and a Pan-Agrarian Union of Cyprus (PEK). In 1943 municipal elections were allowed in the principal cities. Throughout the war, however, the national aspirations for *enosis* were not strongly pressed.

The British Labour Party, returned to power in 1945 at the end of the war, was naturally anxious to introduce representative government in a colony which had been under direct rule for fourteen years. A non-career Governor was appointed in the form of Lord Winster, who had been a Labour Member of Parliament and a Minister. The Secretary of State for the Colonies announced proposals for a democratically-elected legislature, a ten-year plan for economic development and social progress, and an amnesty. The Government's intentions were described as aiming at the establishment of a more liberal and progressive regime. It was an intention fully in line with the Attlee declaration of August 1945, that Britain regarded itself as under an obligation to develop self-government in all its colonial possessions. To other colonies the policy was welcome, and it has been duly implemented; but to the Cypriots it was unacceptable. The recently-elected Archbishop, Leontios of Paphos, declared on 13 July, 1947, that any deviation from the enotist solution of the Cyprus problem would mean the prolongation of an unbearable servitude. He ended his proclamation with the slogan '*enosis and only enosis*', which he appears to have been the first to formulate. Two days earlier the newspaper *Eleftheria,* not one of the more extreme, had declared in a leading article that the people of this Greek island would reject even the most perfect constitution if it did not provide for *enosis*. This attitude was generally maintained against later constitutional proposals though there were occasional critics who would have

Opposite
The old Government House, Nicosia, before and after it was burned down in the riots of 1931 (Illustrated London News, 1931)

274

1

2

275

favoured self-government as a stage to *enosis*.

.In August 1948 the constitutional proposals were abandoned in the face of general opposition. Lord Winster resigned as Governor and was succeeded by a career colonial official. No effort was made to impose a constitution, as some had feared and others secretly hoped; the initiative was left to the Cypriots. It was seized by the Church. Archbishop Leontios died only a month after his enthronement and was succeeded by Makarios II, who had been Bishop of Kyrenia. The election was regarded as a triumph for the right; his predecessor had been strongly supported by the left but Makarios was vigorously anti-Communist and a veteran nationalist who had fought as a volunteer with the Greek army in the Balkan War of 1912. At the end of 1949 he announced that the Church would organise a plebiscite throughout the island on the question of *enosis*. The proposal appears to have been brought forward at the suggestion of the Bishop of Kition, later Archbishop Makarios III. Voting in the plebiscite took place from 15 to 22 January, 1950; it was held

View of the gardens of Government House, now the Presidential Palace. The arches in the foreground were taken from the Bedestan

in the churches and women cast votes for the first time. The qualifying age was eighteen. The vote consisted of signing a page of a register under the rubric 'I demand *enosis*' or on a separate page to indicate opposition. The result was highly favourable to the organisers: out of 224,747 on the electoral role 215,108 or 96 per cent voted for *enosis*.

The 1st of April 1955, marked the beginning of the campaign which led directly to the transformation of Cyprus to its position today. The aim was to persuade the colonial authorities, and the government in London, that it would be impossible to maintain their position in the face of the demands for unification. The attack began on that day with explosions directed at government buildings and continued with attacks on officials and on Cypriots who were considered collaborators. The organiser, Lieutenant-Colonel (later Lieutenant-General) George Grivas was a Cypriot by birth who had served in the Greek army from 1916 to 1945. He adopted the code-name Dighenis; his followers were known as EOKA, the National Organisation of Cypriot Fighters. In 1950 the Bishop of Kition had been elected Archbishop at the early age of thirty-seven and took the name of Makarios III. He took seriously his duties as Ethnarch to direct the political aspirations of his flock. In 1956 he was deported to the Seychelles. This was shortly after he had opened negotiations with Sir John Harding, a distinguished soldier who had been appointed Governor. The interruption of these negotiations was unfortunate since the two men appeared close to agreement.

The struggle of EOKA continued throughout 1956, during which time Cyprus was used as a base for the Anglo-French operation against Egypt. (This was the only time during the British period that it was used for the military purposes for which it was ostensibly acquired.) At the end of the year further constitutional proposals were put forward, based on a study by Lord Radcliffe. They provided for a very full degree of self-government and have on occasions since 1960 been regarded by Greek Cypriots with retrospective favour and regret; at the time they were unacceptable because *enosis* was excluded. In 1957 the new British Prime Minister, Harold Macmillan, released Makarios from the Seychelles but banned him from Cyprus. He was given a hero's welcome on arrival in Athens. Not long afterwards Macmillan took the decision that it was not necessary in British interests to retain the whole island as a base; it would be sufficient to have bases on the island.

In their pursuit of union with Greece Grivas and his followers formed an opinion which later proved mistaken about the likely views of the Turkish Cypriots and the Turkish Government; the same was generally the case with their sympathisers and supporters in Athens. The Turkish Cypriots were contented with the *status quo*

Sir John Harding, Governor of Cyprus, visiting The Wiltshire Regiment at Aghirda Camp

and strongly averse to being forced into Greek nationality. They feared that they would become second-class citizens; they would certainly find themselves a tiny minority in the whole population of Greece after having been a respectable one in Cyprus. It was not necessary, as many Greek Cypriots then and later suspected had happened, for British officials to point out the disadvantages of *enosis,* at least to the educated class of political leaders. As for the Turkish Government both Greek Cypriots and Greeks held firmly that it had no right whatever to intervene. They were no doubt correct on this point, as a matter of international law, but they also held that Ankara was not in the least likely to intervene. This was an error. Whether or not the Turks were moved by ethnic solidarity they had serious strategic objections to an extension of Greek territory to a position off their south coast within easy reach of their ports of Mersin and Alexandretta. Once seized of this point — which may have been fallacious if the arguments given above about Cyprus's minor strategic importance are valid — they were able, thanks to their geographical position, to block the solution that appeared the most natural outcome of the anti-colonialist struggle and prevent Cyprus from following the precedent of Crete.

The original demand of the Turkish Cypriots was that if the British withdrew Cyprus should be transferred to Turkish sovereignty. Subsequently the solution favoured was the partitioning of the island between Greece and Turkey, which was commended under the name of 'double-*enosis*'. (The dividing line usually proposed by the Turks was the thirty-fifth parallel of latitude, which would produce an almost equal bisection.) Both these solutions were regarded with horror by the Greeks. Nevertheless these were

278

the slogans chanted by the Turkish rioters both in Turkey and in Cyprus during 1958. Meanwhile the government in Athens was coming to the conclusion that an end must be put to the conflict at whatever cost. In 1957 Sir John Harding was succeeded by Sir Hugh Foot, a regular colonial officer, as Governor.

The vital negotiations which led to the creation of the independent Republic of Cyprus were between Athens and Ankara. They were concluded in Zurich in February 1959. Later in the same month they were embodied in the agreed result of the London Conference, but the essential principles had already been accepted before either the British or the Cypriots joined in. Cyprus was to renounce both *enosis* and partition and there were to be stringent safeguards for the minority. There could be no doubt that the Head of State must be Greek, nor, for that matter, that he would be Makarios, but the Vice-President was to be Turkish. More productive of contention, but considered vital for purposes of stability, the minority would have a veto on tax laws and there should be separate Greek and Turkish municipalities. The Greek, British and Turkish Governments entered into a treaty of guarantee to maintain this settlement. After months of argument two areas became British bases under full sovereignty; their territory was restricted by exquisite bargaining to ninety-nine square miles.

Archbishop Makarios and Dr Fazil Küchük were elected President and Vice-President of the Cyprus Republic. Grivas left the island, unsatisfied, for further retirement in Athens. On the night of 15 and 16 August 1960, the Union flag was lowered and the flag of Cyprus was raised. Cyprus had become independent once more after 470 years and for the first time since 1191 was under a Greek ruler.

The traces of British rule, thirty years after its end, are naturally manifold. English is an official language. The law courts and the administration are British in inspiration. The largest colony of Cypriots abroad is in Britain, not Greece, mainly concentrated in London. Of material remains, such as an archaeologist of the future will unearth, the principal features will be sought in the infrastructure: bridges, dams, hospitals and the best road system in the Levant. The Presidential Palace, once Government House, has been lovingly reconstructed on the original design after its destruction in 1974. A handsome building, suited to its purpose and reminiscent in its architecture of the best local styles, it serves as the best monument to what a contemporary historian has called 'Britain's moment in the Middle East.'

XII

INDEPENDENCE
AND INVASION

1960 –

Sir David Hunt

Cyprus, Reluctant Republic is the title of a book by Stephen Xydis, one of the more serious works on the achievement of Cypriot independence. The adjective is well chosen. The majority of the population was glad to see an end to the conflict between the established forces of order and the patriotic resistance but surprised to find what the final result had turned out to be. It was not for an independent republic that EOKA had struggled; its martyrs had died in the hope that their sacrifice would hasten the day when Cyprus became a province of the Kingdom of Greece. Many consoled themselves with the thought that self-government, though rejected earlier on as a danger to *enosis,* might still be used to achieve the national aims, no doubt after a shorter or longer period of transition. The obstacles, however, were formidable. A complicated constitution entrenched the rights of the Turkish-Cypriot minority. Contingents of troops from mainland Greece and Turkey were stationed on the island. An international treaty to which the parties were Cyprus, Greece, Turkey and the United Kingdom provided that Cyprus should maintain its constitution and its independence, to the exclusion of either *enosis* or partition. In the event of a breach of these provisions Greece, Turkey and the United Kingdom undertook to consult together. A declaratory clause added that each of the three guaranteeing powers reserved the right to take separate action to restore the *status quo* if concerted action proved impossible. So far as the written word could prevail, therefore, all possible steps had been taken that could render permanent the results of the international agreement which had given birth to the Republic. Some hoped and some feared that they might not prove adequate.

The Constitution which formed the basis of this settlement provided that the executive power should be vested in a Greek President and a Turkish Vice-President, elected by their respective communities. The Council of Ministers was to consist of seven Greeks and three Turks; one of the latter must be given the portfolio of either foreign affairs, defence or finance. The legislative power was vested in a House of Representatives of thirty-five Greeks and fifteen Turks, also communally elected. The Turkish members were given in effect a veto over all legislation dealing with electoral law, finance or municipalities. Two Communal Chambers were to deal with religious affairs, education and culture and communal activities. The five main towns were to have separate Greek and Turkish municipalities with their own elected Councils. In the civil service the same proportion of seventy:thirty for Greek and Turkish officials was prescribed as in the House of Representatives; in the army the proportion was to be sixty:forty. Both these ratios were favourable to the Turkish Cypriots since the demographically-correct proportion was eighty-one:nineteen. A Supreme Constitutional Court was established under a neutral president to decide on the validity of legislative or executive actions which might be

Sir Hugh Foot, last British Governor, signing the Treaty granting independence to Cyprus; on his right Archbishop Makarios, President of the new republic and on his left Dr Fazil Küchük , Vice-President

281

challenged as unconstitutional. The Constitution could be amended if two-thirds of both the Greek and Turkish members of the House of Representatives voted in favour.

In November 1959, over six months before independence, Archbishop Makarios was elected as the first President of the future Republic by the voters on the Greek communal roll. He had a majority of two-thirds over his opponent, John Clerides. For the office of Vice-President Dr Fazil Küchük was returned unopposed. On 31 July 1960, elections were held for the House of Representatives. Thirty of the Greek-Cypriot seats were won by the party sponsored by the Archbishop known as the Patriotic Front; the other five went to AKEL, the Progressive Party of the Working People, whose candidates were, by agreement, unopposed. All the fifteen Turkish seats went to Dr Küchük's Turkish National Party. On 16 August Cyprus became independent. On 21 September it was admitted as a member of the United Nations on the sponsorship of Greece, Turkey and the United Kingdom. On 16 February the House of Representatives voted by forty-one votes to nine to apply for membership of the Commonwealth and this was agreed by the other members on 13 March. In 1961 Cyprus, in vindication of its claim to a share in the foundation of European civilisation, became a member of the Council of Europe.

Archbishop Makarios was the dominating figure in Cypriot politics in the 60s and 70s. He was born in 1913 into a peasant family living in a village on the south-western slopes of Mount Troodos. He was destined for the Church and became a monk in Kykko Monastery; from 1938 to 1948 he studied theology in Athens and Boston. In 1948 he was elected Bishop of Kition and Archbishop in 1950. After leading the struggle against the colonial administration he was President of the Republic from 1960 until his death in 1977. His easy ascendancy and unchallengeable authority did not derive only from his office, although as Archbishop and Ethnarch (and later Head of State) he combined both spiritual superiority and political leadership; it came from his strength of character and intellect. He had an exceptionally powerful mind which was quick to follow logical connections and to forecast the future. In his public speeches he had a lucid eloquence whose effect was reinforced by his dignified and benevolent appearance. The principal criticism made of him as President is that he did not do enough to restrain extremists, whose behaviour contributed to the feeling of insecurity of the Turkish-Cypriot community.

The Archbishop quickly launched himself into international affairs. At the United Nations Cyprus joined the Afro-Asian group and played an active role in group discussions. At that time President Nasser was Makarios' closest associate. He also joined the non-aligned nations and was a prominent figure at the Belgrade and

Cairo summits in 1961 and 1964. He did not, however, overlook his Commonwealth connections which to some extent duplicated, and strengthened, his attachment to the Third World. These newly-found associates were prepared to give whole-hearted diplomatic support, but only to a completely independent Cyprus; they were not likely to agree to their newly-liberated comrades being swallowed up by Greece, a NATO country. Some of the more conventionally-minded Greek Cypriots thought that Makarios' foreign policy might as a result work against the pursuit of national aims; indeed some people, who had suspicions about the depth of his attachment to *enosis,* thought that this contradiction was in his eyes one of its attractions. These suspicions were never wholly laid to rest during his first fourteen years as President.

In internal affairs Makarios' influence was equally paramount. (In this sphere his activities were hampered by precisely opposite suspicions held of him by the Turkish-Cypriot leaders: that he was under the control of the Greek Government and intended to bring about *enosis* as soon as possible). Economically the island's prosperity not only remained but increased; politically the first three

President Makarios with General Grivas (right) and Glafkos Clerides (centre)

Group photograph of Commonwealth Heads of Government, Buckingham Palace 1977. President Makarios is on the Queen's right

years were marked by a growing estrangement between the Greek-Cypriot and the Turkish-Cypriot communities. It proved impossible to operate the elaborate provisions of the constitution. Having been imposed from outside on the Greek Cypriots they were regarded by them with dislike and ill-will, while the Turkish Cypriots obstinately clung to every detail. The latter used their veto to prevent the passing of financial measures; in February 1963 the Supreme Constitutional Court declared that the Government had no right to collect income tax or customs dues. The provisions about the apportionment of posts in the civil service were not put into effect. In fact the Constitution appeared to have broken down entirely. At the end of November 1963 Archbishop Makarios put to his Vice-President Dr Küchük thirteen proposals for its amendment. In the meantime both communities were secretly organising clandestine military forces.

Makarios' thirteen proposals, which would have had the effect of reducing the safeguards provided for the minority community, were indignantly rejected by Ankara on 16 December before any

284

reply had been made by Dr Küchük, who at the time was believed by the Greek Cypriots to be not wholly hostile to them. A week later, in the early morning of 23 December, fighting broke out in Nicosia between the two communities. It later spread to other places. On Christmas Day both sides agreed that they would observe a cease-fire which would be supervised by British troops from the Sovereign Base Areas. This agreement was formalised on the 26th. It is from then that the 'Green Line' in Nicosia dates, a neutral zone between the Greek-Cypriot and Turkish-Cypriot areas of the city to be guarded by the British and subsequently by UN troops. These last began to arrive in March 1964, by which time their presence was required throughout the island. The force was known as United Nations Forces in Cyprus (UNFICYP) and included contingents from Canada, Denmark, Finland, Ireland, Sweden, and the United Kingdom under an Indian commander. Originally they were to serve for three months, but they were still in the island after thirty years had passed.

Many Greek Cypriots left places which had come under Turkish control and there was an even greater influx into them of Turkish Cypriots who felt it unsafe or inadvisable to remain in the more extensive areas still controlled by the Government. The result was that for the next ten years the authority of the Government of the Republic extended over by far the greater part of the island but there were definite Turkish-Cypriot areas where that authority was not respected. The largest extended from the northern half of Nicosia almost as far as the northern coast, but there were similar enclaves in all the main towns except Kyrenia, and also others in inland districts. On the north coast the Turkish Cypriots held the area around Kokkina and Mansoura; this was their closest point to Turkey and there was an evident danger of the landing places there being used to bring in arms and troop reinforcements. The Government decided to eliminate this enclave, using the newly-formed National Guard. General Grivas returned from Greece and was allowed to take over command of it. The attack, in August 1964, was only partially successful. Mansoura was cleared but the smaller enclave of Kokkina held out, assisted by the intervention of the Turkish Air Force. It continued to exist, under close blockade of all the landward approaches, for the next ten years.

This was the last serious fighting for some time although both sides strengthened their military capacity with the aid of troop reinforcements from Greece and Turkey. In addition the two 'mother countries' supplied officers and NCOs to train and command the Greek-Cypriot and Turkish-Cypriot local forces. The contingents of UNFICYP patrolled the borders of the enclaves. A proposal for a settlement was produced in March 1965 by the mediator appointed by the Secretary-General, Señor Galo Plaza, a

Intercommunal meeting in 1977 between President Makarios and Rauf Denktash under the auspices of UN Secretary-General Dr Kurt Waldheim

former President of Ecuador. Its principal features were that Cyprus should in effect revert to the form of state provided by the 1960 constitution with additional written safeguards for the minority and a further declaration against either *enosis* or partition. The demand that *enosis* should be formally renounced might have caused embarrassment both in Nicosia and in Athens but fortunately for them the Turkish Government took only a few hours to denounce it and declare that Galo Plaza was unacceptable as a mediator. This rejection came before the Turkish-Cypriot leadership had been able to make any comment.

In November 1967 a serious clash near Kophinou between Greek-Cypriot forces under the direct command of Grivas and the local Turkish-Cypriot forces was followed by an ultimatum from Ankara to Athens. The Greek Government consisted of a military junta which had seized power in a coup d'état in the preceding April. It accepted the Turkish demands with only minor exceptions to save face. In consequence Grivas was again banished from the

island and all the Greek mainland troops who had been introduced clandestinely to the number of about 7,000 were likewise withdrawn. One result of this show-down was a greater tranquillity; another was that on the Greek-Cypriot side the Archbishop was accused of having compromised *enosis*. His critics were joined by all three of his suffragan bishops. Nor did Grivas remain inactive in his second Athenian exile even though his advancing years might have excused him from taking the field again. In 1971 he returned in secret to Cyprus and established what he called EOKA-B, the Second National Organisation of Cypriot Fighters. His operations had no positive result and in January 1974 he died, still in clandestinity, at the age of seventy-five.

It was in that year that, for the first time, a Greek government took the lead in a course of action to further the union of Greece and Cyprus. Hitherto it had been the Cypriots who had expressed their enthusiasm for the achievement of their national aspirations while the Greeks, though making their own feelings clear, had refrained

Intercommunal meeting in 1979 with UN Secretary-General Dr Kurt Waldheim, President Spyros Kyprianou and Rauf Denktash

from anything that might look like undue influence. The initiative may have derived from internal exigencies of the junta. Their popularity had long before disappeared; they possibly hoped to restore it by a triumph such as no earlier government in Athens had been able to achieve. They had the means, since the Cyprus National Guard was still commanded by Greek officers who would accept their orders. Makarios had some advance warning; on 2 July 1974 he wrote to the President of Greece to demand the withdrawal of the Greek officers. The challenge was accepted. On 15 July troops of the National Guard attacked the Presidential Palace. The violence of the attack, which laid the building in ruins, made it evident that the intention was to kill Makarios. In this the conspirators were unsuccessful. He made a daring escape; while Nicosia radio was announcing his death he got safely to Paphos and from there broadcast to the people of Cyprus. Undiscouraged the conspirators proclaimed as the new President Nicos Sampson, who had played an active part in the original EOKA.

Discussions, under the auspices of UN Secretary-General Señor Pérez de Cuéllar, between President Dr George Vassiliou and Rauf Denktash, in 1989

The Turkish Government, purporting to act under the Treaty of Guarantee, ordered intervention by its armed forces. On 20 July the first landings began in the neighbourhood of Kyrenia. The Sampson regime immediately collapsed. Glafkos Clerides, who under the Constitution was the person authorised to act in the President's absence, was sworn in. Makarios had by then gone to the United Nations to rally support. The Turkish bridgehead was expanded to cover the greater part of northern Cyprus. The area seized, which is still in their hands sixteen years later, amounted to forty per cent of its productive capacity. Greek Cypriots fled to the unoccupied zone in numbers estimated at 200,000. There was heavy loss of life both in the course of military occupations and in attacks on civilians. Property was destroyed and looted; the same is true also of cultural monuments and antiquities. Since the invasion immigrants from Turkey have been brought in. The northern half of Cyprus has lost both its Hellenic character and its prosperity. This forcible partition of the island has been maintained until the

Group photograph of Commonwealth Heads of Government, Nicosia, 1993

present day. The unoccupied zone has, in contrast, shown a remarkable economic recovery. The standard of living remains high and is rising.

The case of Cyprus was brought before the Security Council of the United Nations in July 1974 and has been taken up again on frequent occasions in the years that have followed. The Council has not shirked its responsibilities but has passed judgment on the case in a series of resolutions. The essential element in these can be briefly expressed. As the highest organ of international law it has declared that justice requires that all states in the world should respect the sovereignty, independence and territorial integrity of the Republic of Cyprus and has called for an immediate end to foreign intervention and the withdrawal without delay of foreign troops. These are demands which are fully within the competence of the Security Council whose decisions all members of the United Nations are pledged to respect.

Archbishop Makarios returned to Cyprus in December 1974 and resumed his duties as President of the Republic. The next two years were occupied in talks, under the auspices of the United Nations, between representations of the two sides in Cyprus culminating in meetings in early 1977 between Makarios and the Turkish-Cypriot leader, Raouf Denktash, at which a basis was agreed which, it was hoped, would guide towards a solution. In August 1977 Makarios died and was succeeded by the President of the House of Representatives, Spyros Kyprianou, as Acting President. Kyprianou was subsequently elected to the Presidency in 1978 and in 1983 but in the Presidential elections of 1988 he was defeated by Dr George Vassiliou. In 1992 Glafkos Clerides was elected President.

For the past twenty years the two communities, Greek-Cypriot and Turkish-Cypriot, have conducted a series of talks, usually with United Nations assistance, to see whether agreement can be reached on a new form of constitution for the island which would leave it independent and free from foreign intervention. The atmosphere was impaired in 1983 by the sudden declaration by Raouf Denktash that the Turkish-occupied section of the island was now an independent country under the name of the Turkish Republic of Northern Cyprus. Only Turkey and no other state gave any recognition to this declaration; it was condemned by the Security Council. In spite of this negotiations continued and are still continuing to determine what constitutional arrangements would be acceptable to allow the two communities to live together in amity when the military occupation has been lifted.

EPILOGUE

Nine millennia have left many footprints in the soil of Cyprus. The first Cypriots whose culture the ordinary man can grasp are the stocky, round-headed inhabitants of Khirokitia with their village of circular houses on the slope above the bed of the river Maroni. It stands by the side of a main road; it has been most intelligently excavated; the walls of the houses are palpable and their functions clearly to be perceived. If ever a neolithic civilisation can be said to speak plain to the ordinary layman it is here in Cyprus. But with this exception the Stone Age is something to be studied in books or in museums. As with the succeeding Early and Middle Bronze Age there are ingenious and beautiful artefacts to be admired; speculation can play on the evolution of international relations, and maritime trade, in the eastern Mediterranean at the turn of the 3rd and 2nd millennia; but it is from the 14th century BC that the continuity of the history and culture of Cyprus really begins, with the coming of the Greeks.

The land to which they came was the same in geographical outline as the present Republic, apart from the differences in coastal areas that have been caused all over the Mediterranean by variations in sea level. The climate was no doubt much the same although when the island was still covered with its original vegetation this would have produced milder summers than the austere heat that strikes the dried-up plains of the 20th century. There was more water, retained by the forest cover; there were even running rivers. It was a rich land for agriculture, and brought riches to the miner too, as soon as the great copper deposits began to be worked. It was well provided also with harbours, the sea-level being higher; in fact Enkomi and Kition, for the shipping of their time, gave better shelter and easier access than do the commercial harbours of today. They were close to the coasts opposite where a higher civilisation was already in full development in Phoenicia and Egypt. It was a

291

desirable land for colonisation, a sweet land to borrow a phrase from Leontios Machaeras, whose attractions for Arcadian settlers from the Peloponnese outweighed those of the Ionian coast or the precarious trading outposts of Cilicia and the Levant.

The political history of Cyprus begins with the Greeks. The word itself attests that origin since it means the science, or art, of conducting the affairs of the *polis,* the city. There were, indeed, two or three Phoenician cities also before long but the dominating stamp was given by the Greeks. And this is where continuity begins. Down the centuries the line runs true, with minor and occasional deviations. Though interested parties have from time to time attempted to draw a distinction between the Cypriots and the inhabitants of the rest of Greece, the testimony of history is too plain to allow the attempt any plausibility. There are of course certain interesting variations to be noted; this was only to be expected since Greek states, wherever they were situated, never followed the Egyptian pattern of solidifying into a rigid mould. Thus monarchies survived in Cyprus longer than in other Greek states — if you except Sparta and Macedonia. At the turn of the 8th and 7th centuries they seem to have been swept by a passion for Homeric poems — the same could be said of Chios. At about the same time they acknowledged for a brief space the supremacy of the Assyrian Empire. It does not appear to have incommoded them any more than the Ionians were by their subjection to Lydia. They came under the Persian Empire a century and a half later; so did the Greeks of Asia Minor, Thrace and Macedonia. They joined the Ionian Revolt. Defeated, they fought under Xerxes's banner in the campaign that ended at Salamis and Plataea; so did the Thebans. When Alexander destroyed that empire and set himself on the Great King's throne the Cypriots found that their traditional monarchies were back in fashion again. It was not long before they were to come under another monarchy, the Macedonian dynasty of the Ptolemies, just as though they had been any other province of Greece that had fallen under the domination of one of the deified kings who claimed part of the fractured succession to the universal monarchy of Alexander.

The Ptolemies yielded to the arms of Caesar's heir. The most vigorous of a line famous for the martial prowess of its women, Cleopatra VII, after she had vainly staked on a throw for the mastery of the world all the wealth of Egypt and the Roman legions that her captive Antony could command, poisoned herself rather than allow herself to figure in a Roman triumph. Her realm of Cyprus had already come under the grasping rule of the Roman Republic. Cicero, most eloquent of the Latins, had ruled it, unwillingly indeed but more than competently. As an imperial province of the unarmed class, to which Augustus assigned it to gratify the

Senate and preserve a constitutional appearance, it conformed peaceably to the same pattern as the other Greek-speaking provinces. When St Paul went to Paphos he felt himself as much in Greece as when he went to Corinth. It would not have occurred to him to think he was anywhere else. Nor did the Cypriots notice anything different when the Empire was divided and they found themselves under Constantinople rather than Rome. They did not regard themselves as Byzantines — they could hardly do so since that technical and scholarly term had not yet been invented. They did not then call themselves Hellenes either, since the theologians had given that name the meaning of pagans. They knew that they were Romans; they also knew they were Christians.

In coming under the rule of the Franks the Cypriots once more kept company with the other Greeks. There was a Frankish King of Cyprus, just as there was a Frankish Duke of Athens and a Frankish Prince of the Morea. The Cypriot subjects of the Lusignans continued to call themselves Romans. If they ever thought of their co-religionists in the Peloponnese, from which their ancestors had come 3,000 years earlier, they might have reflected with justice that while they in their sea-girt isolation had remained unmixed in blood the Moreotes were in large measure derived from Slav and Albanian invaders. This *limpieza de sangre* may have carried with it some difference in character, a thing quite customary in isolated communities. The language is to this day a little archaic, as in West Virginia. The Hellenic character survived the experience, again shared by Cyprus with all the other Greek lands, of incorporation in the Ottoman Empire.

The Ottoman occupation of Cyprus was not in essence any different from what happened in, for instance, Thessaly or in Crete which, like Cyprus, had been conquered by the Turks from the Venetians. The British occupation was more unusual but that experience too had been shared by the Septinsular Republic of the Ionian Islands. Even the deployment in a Greek island of an international peace-keeping force had been seen in Crete in the years following 1898. In fact throughout the centuries since the 14th before Christ nothing happened in Cyprus which could not be paralleled elsewhere in Greece. There was nothing to modify the essential character of the Great Greek Island.

As in other countries of Greek speech the vicissitudes of history left many splendid monuments in Cyprus. The remains of the public buildings of the Greco-Roman city of Salamis, the theatre of Curium, the mosaic floors of the imperial Governor's palace at Paphos, are reminders of that splendidly homogeneous culture which marks the Roman lands from Newcastle-on-Tyne to Jordan. The painted churches which nestle in the valleys of Troodos are inspired by the same spirit as their sister churches from Sicily to

Serbia to the Ukraine. The first wholly exotic element enters with the Lusignans. The cathedrals of Nicosia and Famagusta are examples of western European Gothic architecture. Their conversion into mosques has preserved them from the hand of the restorer. The great castles hold so much of the spirit of romance that if it had not existed the word would have had to be invented to describe Hilarion, Kantara, Kyrenia, Buffavento whose names fall upon the ear like the echo of a vanished world.

The British legacy is on the surface the most visible today, from the pillar-box on the street-corner to the thrifty architecture of public buildings. Government House, now the Presidential Palace, is an exception because more magisterial; but it too is in a romantic Cypriot-Gothic style. It has so taken the fancy of the Cypriots that after one Greek faction had burned it down the restored republican government rebuilt it and set over the entrance porch once more the strongly-carved royal arms and cipher of their previous sovereigns of the House of Windsor. The real British legacy is to be sought in the very widespread knowledge of the English language, in the uniforms of the police and to a great extent in their behaviour, in the traditions of an impartial civil service and an incorrupt and principled administration of justice, and in the confidence and ability of the commercial and financial community. Cypriots now look on good government as the normal thing, which it is certainly not elsewhere in the Near East; they have a standard against which to measure shortcomings. Countries such as Lebanon admire Cyprus as an example and value it as a refuge in times of trouble.

It would be too gloomy a task to speculate about what will be the mark left on the island by the period which begins with the Turkish invasion of 1974. The brutal partition, enforced by an army of occupation which has repeatedly shown itself capable of deliberate destruction of monuments, has swept away much that had remained unchanged for centuries. A way of life has ceased to exist. The villages where the bell-tower of the church and the minaret of the mosque rose side by side have changed utterly. A piece of the old Levant has been brought violently into the divided Near East of the 20th century. For Europe the lesson is clear. Justice denied to one country flashes a warning signal to all the others. The funeral bell for Cyprus, to borrow John Donne's phrase, tolls as well for the other nations of mankind.

CHRONOLOGICAL TABLE

c. **8500 BC**
EPIPALAEOLITHIC

c. **8500 BC.** Hunter-gatherers on south coast.
Extinction of pygmy hippopotamus.

7000–5300 BC
NEOLITHIC

7000–5300 BC. (?) Colonisation of Cyprus by farmers from
Syria or Cilicia; deer herding(?)

4500–4000 BC. Earliest pottery-using groups and signs of
regionalisation.

4000–2500 BC
CHALCOLITHIC

4000–2500 BC. Emergence of metal-users.

2700–1900
EARLY CYPRIOTE (EARLY BRONZE AGE)

2700–1900 BC. Arrival of people from Anatolia.
Ox-plough cultivation starts.
Sporadic exchanges with Levantine mainland.

1900–*c.* 1600 BC
MIDDLE CYPRIOTE (MIDDLE BRONZE AGE)

1900–*c.* 1600 BC. Beginning of contacts with the Aegean.

1900–1750. First mention of Alasia (probably Cyprus) and its
export of copper in Near Eastern historical records.

1650. Start of large-scale pottery export to Levant and Egypt
Fortifications and development of urbanisation in Cyprus.

c. **1600–*c.* 1050 BC**

LATE CYPRIOTE (LATE BRONZE AGE)

c. **1550.** Development of Enkomi as major port.

c. **1400.** Large-scale imports of Mycenaean pottery begin.

c. **1375–1350.** References to Alashiya in Tell el-Amarna
documents.

c. **1220.** Enkomi and Kition destroyed by 'Sea Peoples';
rebuilt shortly afterwards.
First settlement at Maa-*Palaeokastro*

c. **1190.** Second settlement at Maa-*Palaeokastro*.
Beginning of immigration of Achaeans.
Foundation of Palaepaphos.

c. **1150.** Second wave of Achaean settlers.

c. **1050.** Enkomi abandoned.

c. **1050–950 BC**
CYPRO-GEOMETRIC I

1050–950 BC. Consolidation of Cypriot kingdoms.

950–850 BC
CYPRO-GEOMETRIC II

950–850 BC. Obscure period

850–750 BC
CYPRO-GEOMETRIC III

850–750 BC. Phoenician colony at Kition.
Royal tombs at Salamis, first burials.

750–600 BC
CYPRO-ARCHAIC I

709 BC. Seven Cypriot kings pay homage to Sargon II of
Assyria.

709-*c*. 663 BC. Assyrian domination.

673/672. Ten Cypriot kings pay homage to Esarhaddon of Assyria.

***c*. 663-569.** Cypriot kingdoms independent.

600-475 BC
CYPRO-ARCHAIC II

570-560 BC. Amasis of Egypt takes control of Cyprus.

570/560-526/525 BC. Egyptian rule.

560-525 BC. Reign of Evelthon of Salamis

526/525 BC. Persian annexation of Cyprus.
Beginning of Persian domination.

***c*. 521 BC.** Included in the fifth satrapy of the Persian Empire under Darius.

499 BC. Outbreak of Ionian revolt against Persian rule. Participation of all Cypriot cities except for Amathus, at the instigation of Onesilos, King of Salamis.

498 BC. Reduction of Cypriot cities.

480 BC. Cyprus contributes 150 ships to the Persian fleet for their naval war with Athens.

478 BC. Momentary freedom for the Cypriot city kingdoms, but Persian rule soon re-established.

475-400 BC
CYPRO-CLASSICAL I

***c*. 450 BC.** Annexation of the Kingdom of Idalion by Kition with Persian assistance.

450-449 BC. Cimon's expedition to liberate Cyprus from Persia; mission aborted after his death and Cyprus left under Persian control.

411 BC. Evagoras I becomes King of Salamis.

400-325 BC
CYPRO-CLASSICAL II

By 391 BC. Evagoras I master of virtually the whole of Cyprus.

386 BC. Peace of Antalcidas.
Athens recognises Persian sovereignty over Cyprus.

***c*. 381 BC.** Siege of Salamis by the Persians.

380-379 BC. Evagoras I loses control over Cypriot cities other than Salamis under a peace concluded with Persia.

374/373 BC. Murder of Evagoras I.

351 BC. Cypriot kings join Egypt and Phoenicia in revolt against Persia.
Siege of Salamis, revolt suppressed.

***c*. 350 BC.** The King of Tamassos sells his kingdom to the King of Kition (and Idalion).
***c*. 335 BC.** Birth of Zeno, founder of Stoic school of philosophy, at Kition.

***c*. 333 BC.** End of Persian domination.
Cypriot kings support Alexander the Great after his victory over the Persian forces at the battle of Issus.

332 BC. Cypriot ships take part in Alexander's naval siege of Tyre.

331 BC. Nicocreon becomes King of Salamis.

325-150 BC
HELLENISTIC I

323 BC. Death of Alexander the Great.
Cyprus becomes involved in struggles among his generals over the division of his empire in the course of which a number of the cities are destroyed and their kings imprisoned or executed.

***c*. 310 BC.** Zeno founds school of Stoic philosophy in Athens.

305 BC. Ptolemy proclaimed as Ptolemy I Soter, King of Egypt.

294 BC. Annexation of Cyprus by Ptolemy I.
Cyprus becomes part of the Hellenistic state of Egypt marking the final end of the city kingdoms.

***c*. 264 BC.** Death of Zeno.

168 BC. Attack on Cyprus by Antiochus IV Epiphanes of Syria.
Withdrawal on intervention of Rome.

150-30 BC
HELLENISTIC II

***c*. 106/105-88 BC.** Cyprus ruled as an independent kingdom by Lathyrus (Ptolemy IX Soter II) after his expulsion from Egypt.

88 BC. Lathyrus restored as King of Egypt.

88-80 BC. Cyprus returned to Egyptian rule.

80 BC. Death of Lathyrus.
Ptolemies partly withdraw from Cyprus.

80-58 BC. Reign of Ptolemaios in Cyprus (brother of Ptolemy XII Auletes of Egypt).

58 BC. Cyprus reduced to the state of a Roman province.
Suicide of Ptolemaios.

***c*. 47 BC.** Cyprus returned to Egyptian rule by Julius Caesar.

30 BC. Suicide of Cleopatra VII of Egypt.

30 BC-AD 330
THE ROMAN PERIOD

30 BC. Cyprus comes under the Roman Empire as part of the Province of Syria.

22 BC. Cyprus a separate Senatorial province under a proconsul.

15 BC. Paphos almost completely destroyed by earthquake.

45. Missionary journey of SS Paul and Barnabas and conversion of the Proconsul L. Sergius to Christianity.

47. Second missionary journey by SS Barnabas and Mark.

69. Titus, the future Emperor. visits the oracle at Palaepaphos.

76/77. Serious earthquakes cause damage throughout Cyprus.

116. Jewish Insurrection.

164. Heavy loss of life from the plague.

269. Abortive raid by the Gothic fleet on Cyprus.

293. Cyprus, together with south-east Asia Minor, Syria and Palestine transferred to the Diocese of the East

313. Edict of Milan grants freedom of worship to Christians.

325. Cypriot bishops attend the Council of Nicaea.

330-1191
THE BYZANTINE PERIOD

330. Inauguration of Constantinople as capital of the Roman Empire.

c. **330.** Empress Helena said to have visited Cyprus; foundation of Stavrovouni Monastery.

332. Paphos ruined by an earthquake.

342. Salamis ruined by an earthquake and a tidal wave. Rebuilt as Constantia

431. Council of Ephesus. Cypriot Church given conditional autonomy.

488. Discovery of relics of St Barnabas; Emperor Zeno grants Cypriot archbishop full autonomy and privileges.

c. **550.** Establishment of silk industry in Cyprus.

649. Arabs invade island under Muawiya. Death there of Umm-Haram, relative of the Prophet.

653-654. Second Arab Invasion. Arab garrison placed in Cyprus.

688. Treaty between Emperor Justinian II and Caliph al-Malik neutralising Cyprus.

689. Numbers of Christian Cypriots moved to Bithynia.

698. Cypriots in Bithynia return to Cyprus.

723. English pilgrim Willibald visits the island.

743. Arabs complain of breach of Treaty and raid Cyprus.

806. Raid on Cyprus ordered by Caliph Harun ar-Rashid.

c. **870-877.** Temporary Byzantine occupation of the island.

910. Byzantine Admiral Himerius lands on the island. His sailors molest Moslem villagers.

912. Emir Damian of Tarsus raids island as a reprisal.

965. Byzantines re-occupy Cyprus under Emperor Nicephorus Phocas; it becomes a province of the Empire.

1043. Unsuccessful revolt of Theophilus Eroticus, Governor of the island.

1093. Revolt of Cypriot Governor Rhapsomates, put down by John Ducas and Butumites.

1094. Kykko Monastery founded by monk Esaias, under Butumites' patronage.

c. **1093-1100.** Philocales Eustathius governs the island.

c. **1100-1105.** Constantine Euphorbenus Catacalon, Governor.
Church of Panayia Phorbiotissa, Asinou, decorated under his patronage.

1105-1112. Philocales Eustathius' second governorate.

1157. Severe earthquake in Cyprus.

1158. Egyptian fleet raids the island.

c. **1170.** St Neophytus founds monastery at Enkleistra.

1185-1191. Isaac Ducas Comnenus takes over the government of the island and declares himself independent.

1191-1571
THE FRANKISH PERIOD

1191
RICHARD I (THE LIONHEART)

1191. King Richard I (the Lionheart) of England defeats Isaac Comnenus and takes possession of Cyprus.
He sells the island to the Templars for 100,000 dinars.
Richard marries Berengaria of Navarre in Limassol, where she is crowned Queen of England.

1191-1192
THE TEMPLARS

1192. The Templars resell Cyprus to Richard I, who transfers it at the same price to Guy of Lusignan.

1192-1489
THE LUSIGNAN DYNASTY

1192-1194. Guy of Lusignan, Lord of Cyprus (m. Sibyl of

Jerusalem).

1194-1205. Aimery, brother of Guy, succeeds (m. (1) Eschive of Ibelin, (2) Isabel, Queen of Jerusalem); he later obtains royal title from Emperor Henry VI.

1197. Coronation of Aimery.

1205-1218. Hugh I(m. Alice of Champagne).

1209. Foundation of Cathedral of St Sophia, Nicosia.

1217. Hugh I takes part in Fifth Crusade.

1218-1253. Henry I (m. (1) Alice of Montferrat, (2) Stephanie of Lampron, (3) Plaisance of Antioch).

1220. Orthodox Archbishop and Bishops replaced by Latins.

1228. Emperor Frederick II in Cyprus. He is recognised as suzerain.

1229. Frederick II returns to West.
Rising of Cypriot barons against his deputies.

1232. Battle of Aghirda; Imperialists defeated.

1233. Imperialist garrison of Kyrenia capitulates.

1249. Henry I takes part in Seventh Crusade.

1253-1267. Hugh II (m. Isabel of Ibelin).
Plaisance of Antioch acts as Regent until 1261.

1260. Orthodox Church in Cyprus subordinated to Latin Church by Papal Bull (Bulla Cypria).

1261. Hugh of Antioch Regent. Becomes King on death of Hugh II.

1267-1284. Hugh III (m. Isabel of Ibelin).

1284-1285. John I.

1285-1324. Henry II (m. Constance of Aragon- Sicily).

1291. Fall of Acre and extinction of Latin rule in Syria.

1306. Henry II's brother Amaury usurps power.

1310. Henry II exiled to Cilicia. Returns after murder of Amaury.

1224-1358. Hugh IV (m. (1) Mary of Ibelin, (2) Alice of Ibelin).

1359-1369. Peter I (m. (1) Eschive of Montfort, (2) Eleanor of Aragon).

1361. Capture of Adalia.

1362-1365. Peter I travels in West to obtain support for new Crusade.

1365. Sack of Alexandria.

1369-1382. Peter II (m. Valentina Visconti).

1372. Rioting between Venetians and Genoese in Famagusta.

1373-1374. War with Genoa. Cyprus agrees to large indemnity and cession of Famagusta.

1382-1398. James I (m. Heloise of Brunswick); prisoner in Genoa at accession.

1385. James I released by Genoese and crowned in Nicosia.

1393. James I assumes additional title of King of Armenia.

1398-1432. Janus (m. (1) Heloise Visconti, (2) Charlotte of Bourbon).

1426. Invasion of Cyprus by Egyptians.
Janus defeated and taken prisoner at battle of Khirokitia.

1427. Janus returns to Cyprus after being ransomed.

1432-1458. John II m. (1) Medea of Montferrat, (2) Helena Palaeologina; (mistress) Marietta of Patras).

1458-1460. Charlotte, Queen of Cyprus; retains title in exile until 1485 (m. (1) John of Coimbra, (2) Louis of Savoy).

1460-1473. James II or James the Bastard, son of Marietta of Patras (m. Caterina Cornaro).

1460. James invades Cyprus with Egyptian support and is proclaimed King as James II.

1464. Surrender of Famagusta to James II by the Genoese.

1464. Surrender of Kyrenia to James II.
End of civil war in Cyprus.

1473. James III, posthumous child of James II and Caterina Cornaro. His mother acts as Regent.

1473. Coup d'état by Catalan party. Andrew Cornaro and Mark Bembo are murdered.

1474. Intervention of Venetian Captain- General of the Sea Peter Mocenigo with the fleet. Collapse of the Catalan regime.
An order banishes all Catalans, Sicilians and Neapolitans from the island and their property is confiscated.

1474. A Venetian provveditore and two councellors are appointed.

1474-1489. Caterina Cornaro Queen of Cyprus after death of James III.

1479. Mark Venier tries to assassinate the Queen.

1487. Charlotte dies in Rome.

1489. Caterina Cornaro cedes Cyprus to the Venetian state and goes to Asolo.

1489-1571
THE VENETIAN PERIOD

1510. Caterina Cornaro dies in Venice, still bearing the title of Queen of Cyprus, Jerusalem and Armenia.

1517. Ottoman Sultan, having conquered Egypt, becomes Suzerain of Cyprus.

1562. Conspiracy of Greek Cypriots against Venetian rule.

1570. Turkish invasion force lands on the island and captures Nicosia.
Siege of Famagusta begins.

1571. Famagusta capitulates to Turkish commander Lala Mustafa.
Breach of capitulation by Turks and annexation of island to Ottoman Empire.

1571-1878
THE TURKISH PERIOD

1572. Expulsion of Latin hierarchy and restoration of Orthodox hierarchy.

1578. Mutinous Turkish troops kill the Governor Arab Ahmed Pasha.

1641. Suppression of Pashaliks of Paphos and Famagusta.

1670. Cyprus downgraded from Pashalik and put under Kapudan Pasha.

1673. Rebellion of Mehmed Agha Boyajioglou.

1680. Boyajioglou executed.

1703. Cyprus transferred to direct jurisdiction of Grand Vizier.

1745. Cyprus removed from Grand Vizier and created an independent Pashalik again.

1746-1748. Abu Bekr Pasha, only well-regarded Governor.

1751. Cyprus returned to direct jurisdiction of Grand Vizier.

1754. Archbishop and Orthodox hierarchy made responsible for collecting taxes.

1764. Chil Osman Agha appointed Governor.
After more than doubling taxes, Chil Osman Agha is killed in revolt.

1765-1766. Revolt of Khalil Agha, Commandant of Kyrenia.

1777-1783. Haji Baki Agha Governor.

1820-1822. Küchük Mehmed Governor.

1821. Execution of Archbishop Kyprianos and three bishops.

1833. Insurrection of Ibrahim of Paphos, known as Giaur Imam.

1849. Cyprus included in Pashalik of Archipelago.

1856. Government takes over collection of taxes from Archbishop.

1861. Cyprus an independent province.

1868-1871. Cyprus put under vilayet of Archipelago.

1878-1960

THE BRITISH PERIOD

1878. Under the Cyprus Convention Britain assumes administration of the island which remains formally part of the Ottoman Empire.
Sir Garnet Wolseley first High Commissioner.

1880. Greek established as medium of education with Turkish in Turkish schools.

1881. Administrative supervision transferred from Foreign Office to Colonial office.

1883. First meeting of elected advisory Council.

1908. Riots in Nicosia over election of Archbishop.

1914. Cyprus annexed by Britain in consequence of outbreak of war with Turkey.

1923. Under Treaty of Lausanne Turkey renounces claim to Cyprus in favour of Britain.

1931. Greek elected members resign from the Legislative Council.
Pro-*enosis* riots in Nicosia.
Government House is burned down.
Constitution suspended.

1941. Prohibition on political parties rescinded.

1947. Lord Winster appointed Governor. His proposals, including an elected legislature, rejected.

1948. Elections for a consultative Assembly are boycotted.

1949. Ethnarchic Council created under Archbishop Makarios II. All Greek Cypriot parties represented on it.

1950. Plebiscite of Greek Cypriots, organised by Archbishop Makarios II shows 96% in favour of *enosis*.
Election as Archbishop of Makarios III.

1954. Further British proposal for a Legislative Council is rejected.
Frustration of first appeal to UN by Greece leads to strikes in Cyprus.

1955. Campaign in favour of *enosis* started by EOKA under Lt-Gen. (later Gen.) George Grivas, code-named 'Dhighenis'.
A state of emergency is declared.
Tripartite conference in London.

1955-1957. Sir John Harding (later Lord Harding of Petherton) Governor.

1956. Archbishop Makarios exiled to the Seychelles.

1957. Radcliffe proposals rejected.
Turkish Cypriots declare for federation or partition.
Makarios released from the Seychelles but banned from Cyprus.

1957-1960. Sir Hugh Foot (later Lord Caradon) Governor.

1958. Zurich Agreement between Greece and Turkey.

1959. London Agreement signed by Britain, Greece, Turkey,

Archbishop Makarios on behalf of the Greek Cypriots and Dr Küchük on behalf of the Turkish Cypriots. Cyprus to be an independent state. Treaty of Alliance and Treaty of Guarantee
Makarios returns to Cyprus.
Makarios elected President, Dr Fazil Küchük Vice-President.

1960–
INDEPENDENT REPUBLIC AND INVASION

1960. Cyprus becomes an independent republic on 16 August.

1961. Agreement on British Sovereign Bases is signed.

1963. Archbishop Makarios submits proposals for amendment of the Constitution.
Outbreak of intercommunal fighting.
'Green Line' dividing communities in Nicosia established.

1964. Turkish officials withdraw from administration.
Turkey threatens invasion.
Security Council resolution in support of Cyprus sovereignty denounces threat or use of force.
Arrival of UNFICYP.
Conscription is introduced.
Grivas returns and assumes command of Cyprus National Guard.
Fighting in Tylliria area.

1965. Señor Galo Plaza, UN mediator, publishes report and proposals which are rejected by Turkish Government.

1966. Joint communiqué signed by the Governments of Cyprus and Greece that any solution excluding *enosis* would be unacceptable.

1967. Military coup in Greece.
Fighting between National Guard under Grivas and Turkish Cypriots in Kophinou area leads to Turkish ultimatum.
Ultimatum accepted by Greek junta which withdraws troops, and Grivas, from Cyprus.
Turkish Cypriots announce formation of 'Provisional Cyprus Turkish Administration'.

1970. Attempt on Makarios' life.

1971. Grivas returns secretly to Cyprus.
Start of renewed campaign for *enosis* by EOKA-B.

1973. Makarios re-elected President.

Start of renewed campaign for *enosis* by EOKA-B.

1974. Death of Grivas.
Makarios demands withdrawal of Greek officers.
Conspiracy against Makarios inspired by Greek Junta.
Presidential Palace destroyed.
Nikos Sampson declared President.
Turkish invasion.
Glafkos Clerides Acting President.
Makarios returns in December.

1975. Start of inter-communal talks place in Vienna.

1977. Meeting between Makarios and Denktash.
Death of Makarios.
Spyros Kyprianou succeeds as President.
Bishop Chrysostomos of Paphos succeeds as Archbishop and Ethnarch.

1978. Spyros Kyprianou returned as President for five-year term.

1979. Kyprianou and Denktash meet in Nicosia under the auspices of UN Secretary-General Dr Kurt Waldheim.

1981. Elections for House of Representatives under new electoral system (reinforced representational).

1983. Kyprianou re-elected President for a second term.
Unilateral declaration of 'Turkish Republic of Northern Cyprus' in the part of Cyprus under occupation by Turkish troops.
Security Council condemns the declaration and calls on member-countries to respect the independence, sovereignty and territorial integrity of theRepublic of Cyprus.

1984. Señor Pérez de Cuéllar, UN Secretary-General, convenes 'proximity talks' between Kyprianou and Dentash.

1985. High-level meeting between Kyprianou and Dentash under the auspices of the UN Secretary-General proves fruitless. Proposals rejected by Kyprianou.

1988. Dr George Vassiliou is elected President.

1990. Renewed talks between Vassiliou and Denktash end in a deadlock when proposals of Secretary-General rejected by Denktash.

1991. Parliamentary elections.
UN Secretary-General rejects demands for sovereign status proposed by Denktash.

1993. Glafkos Clerides elected President.
Commonwealth Heads of Government Meeting in Nicosia and Limassol.

BIBLIOGRAPHY

ALASTOS, D.
Cyprus in History (London, 1976)
BROWN, A and CATLING, H.W.
Ancient Cyprus (Oxford, 1975)
CATLING, H.W.
Cypriot Bronzework in the Mycenaean World (Oxford, 1964)
'Cyprus in the Late Bronze Age', *Cambridge Ancient History* (3rd ed.)
Vol. II part 2 (Cambridge, 1975)
CHRISTODOULOU, D.
'The Evolution of the Rural Land Use Pattern in Cyprus', *World Land Use Survey 2* (London, 1959)
COBHAM, C.B.
Excerpta Cypria (Cambridge, 1908, 1969)
CONSTANTINE PORPHYROGENITOS
De Administrando Imperio; with commentary (London, 1963)
COOK, B.F.
Cypriote Art in the British Museum (ed.) (London, 1979)
CRAWSHAW, N.
The Cyprus Revolt: An Account of the Struggle for Union with Greece (London, 1978)
CROISET, F.
Le conflit de Chypre (Brussels, 1973)
DIKAIOS, P.
A Guide to the Cyprus Museum (3rd ed.) (Nicosia, 1961)
Enkomi Excavations 1948-1958 (Mainz, 1969)
EKDOTIKE ATHENON SA (Publishers)
Istoria tou Ellinikou Ethnous; 16 vols (Athens, 1970- 1976)
ENLART, C.
Gothic Art and the Renaissance in Cyprus; transl. and
ed. by HUNT, Sir David (London, 1988). Original French edition
(Paris, 1899 and Famagusta, 1966)
FOLEY, C.
Island in Revolt (London, 1962)
FOOT, Hugh
A Start in Freedom (London, 1964)
GJERSTAD, E.
Swedish Cyprus Expedition, Vol. IV, Part II (Stockholm 1948)

HACKETT, J.
History of the Orthodox Church in Cyprus (London, 1901)
HARBOTTLE, Michael
The Impartial Soldier (Oxford 1970)
HILL, George
A History of Cyprus; 4 vols (Cambridge, 1940–1952)
HUNT, David and HUNT, Iro
Caterina Cornaro, Queen of Cyprus (ed.) (London, 1989)
JENKINS, R.J.H.
Studies on Byzantine History of the 9th and 10th Centuries (London, 1970)
KARAGEORGHIS, V.
Salamis (London, 1969)
The Civilisation of Prehistoric Cyprus (Athens, 1976)
Kition, Mycenaean and Phoenician Discoveries in Cyprus (London, 1976)
Cyprus, from the Stone Age to the Romans (London, 1982)
KARAGEORGHIS, V. and GAGNIERS, J. des
La Ceramique chypriote de style figuré (Rome, 1974)
KITROMILIDES, P.M. and EVRIVIADES, M.L
Cyprus in *World Bibliographical Series* Vol. 28
(Oxford, 1982)
KOUMOULIDES, J.T.A. *Cyprus in Transition, 1960-1985* (ed.) (London, 1986)
LUKE, Harry
Cyprus Under the Turks, 1571-1878 (London 1921, 1969)
MARITI, G.
Travels in the Island of Cyprus (translated by COBHAM, C.B.) (London 1971)
MAIER, F.G.
Cyprus — from Earliest Times to the Present Day (London, 1968)
MAIER, F.G. and KARAGEORGHIS, V.
Paphos: History and Archaeology (Nicosia, 1984)
MICHAELIDOU-NIKOLAOU, I.
'Prosopography of Ptolemaic Cyprus', *Studies in Mediterranean Archaeology,* Vol. XLIV
(Gothenburg, 1976)
MITFORD, T.B.
'Roman Cyprus' in *Aufstieg und Niedergang der Römischen Welt,* II.7.2 (Berlin, 1980)
MORRIS, D.
The Art of Ancient Cyprus (London, 1985)
MYERS, J.L.
Handbook of the Cesnola Collection, Metropolitan Museum of Art (New York, 1914)
MUSEUM OF FINE ARTS
Boston: Art of Ancient Cyprus (Boston, 1972)
ORR, Capt. C.W.J.
Cyprus Under British Rule (London, 1971)
PELTENBURG, E.J.
'Recent Developments in the Later Prehistory of Cyprus', *Studies in Mediterranean Archaeology*
Pocketbook 16 (Gotenburg, 1982)
Early Society in Cyprus (ed.) (Edinburgh, 1989)
POLYVIOU, P.G.
Cyprus — The Tragedy and the Challenge (London, 1975)
Conflict and Negotiation, 1960-1980 (London, 1980)
PURCELL, H.D.

Cyprus (London, 1969)
ROBERTSON, I.
  Blue Guide to Cyprus (London, 1990)
RUNCIMAN, Steven
  A History of the Crusades (Cambridge, 1951-1954)
  The Great Church in Captivity (Cambridge, 1968)
SAKELLARIOS, A.A.
SIMMONDS, A.H.
  'Extinct Pygmy Hippopotamus and Early Man in Cyprus', *Nature* 333, 1988
  The Geography, History and Language of the Island of Cyprus (Athens, 1891)
SJÖQVIST, E.
  Problems of the Late Cypriote Age (Stockholm, 1940)
STANLEY-PRICE, N.
  'Early Prehistoric Settlement in Cyprus', *British Archaeological Reports International Series 65* (Oxford 1979)
  STEWART, J.R.
  'The Early Cypriote Age', *Swedish Cyprus Expedition* Vol. IV, Part 1A
  Lund, 1962)
  STYLIANOU, A. and STYLIANOU, J.
  The Painted Churches of Cyprus (Nicosia, 1964, extended edition London, 1985)
  History of the Cartography of Cyprus (Nicosia, 1980)
TATTON-BROWN, V.
  'Cyprus B.C. − 7,000 Years of History', *Exhibition Catalogue* (ed.) (London, 1979)
  'Ancient Cyprus', *Exhibition Catalogue* (ed.) (London, 1987)
  Cyprus and the East Mediterranean in the Iron Age (ed.) (London, 1989)
THUBRON, C.
  Journey into Cyprus (London, 1975)
VANEZIS, P.N.
  Makarios: Faith and Power (London, 1971)
  Makarios: Life and Leadership (London, 1979)
VERMEULE, C.
  Greek and Roman Cyprus (Boston, 1976)
VESSBERG, O. and WESTHOLM, A.
  The Swedish Cyprus Expedition, Vol. IV, Part 3 (Stockholm, 1956)
XYDIS, S.A.
  Cyprus, Reluctant Republic (The Hague, 1973)

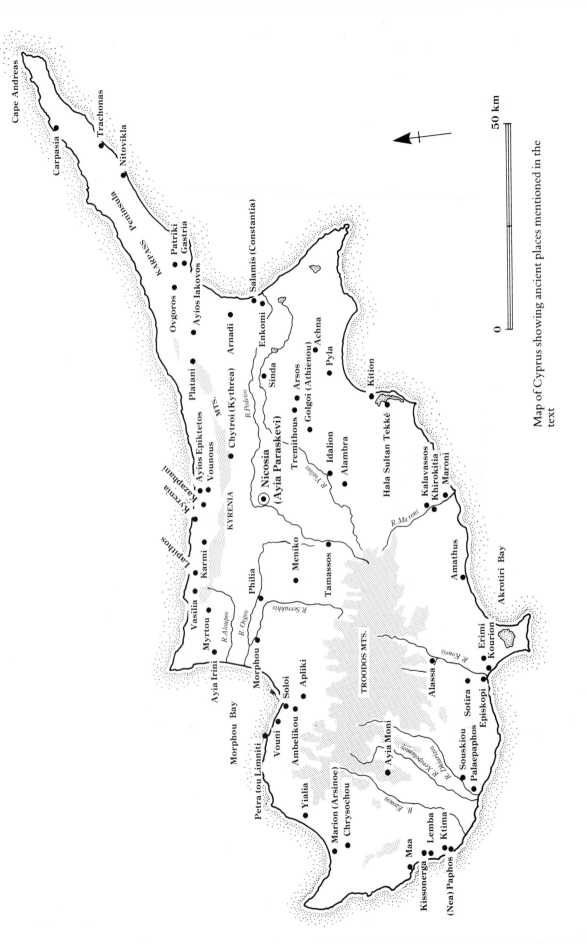

Map of Cyprus showing ancient places mentioned in the text

Cape Andreas

Carpasia

Trachonas

Nitovikla

KARPASS Peninsula

Patriki

Gastria

Ovgoros

Ayios Iakovos

Salamis (Constantia)

Enkomi

Arnadi

Platani

Ayios Epiktetos

KYRENIA MTS.

Chytroi (Kythrea)

Vounous

R. Pedieus

Sinda

Arsos

Achna

Tremithous

Golgoi (Athienou)

Pyla

Kition

Kyrenia

Kazaphani

Lapithos

Nicosia (Ayia Paraskevi)

Idalion

Alambra

Hala Sultan Tekké

Karmi

Philia

Meniko

R. Yialias

Kalavassos

Khirokitia

Maroni

Vasilia

Tamassos

R. Ovgos

R. Serrakhis

R. Maroni

Myrtou

R. Aloupos

Amathus

Ayia Irini

Morphou

TROODOS MTS.

Akrotiri Bay

Morphou Bay

Soloi

Apliki

Alassa

R. Kouris

Erimi

Kourion

Vouni

Ambelikou

Ayia Moni

Sotira

Episkopi

Petra tou Limniti

Souskiou

Yialia

Marion (Arsinoe)

Chrysochou

R. Dhiarizos

R. Xeropotamos

Palaepaphos

R. Ezousa

Lemba

Ktima

Maa

Kissonerga

(Nea) Paphos

0   50 km

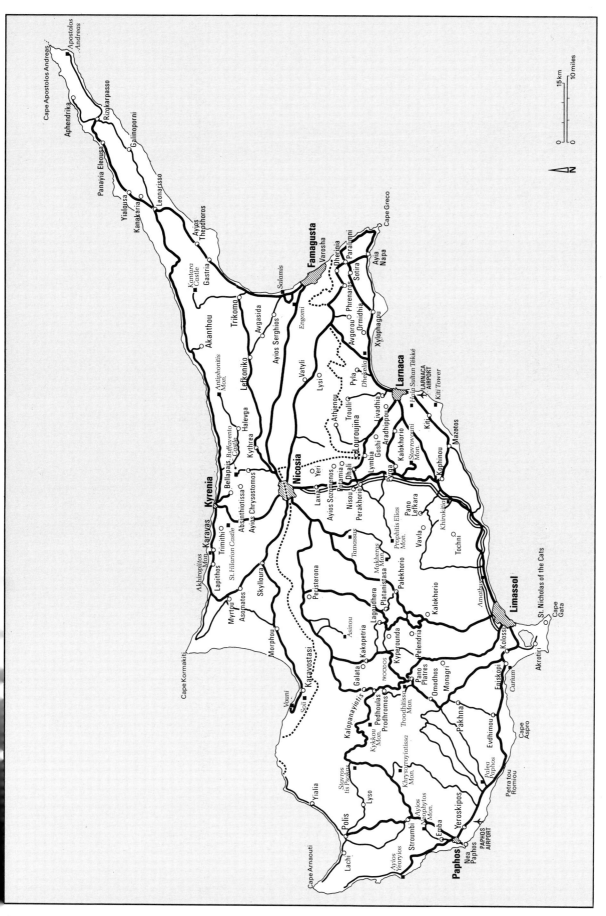

Modern map of Cyprus showing routes to places of interest

A satellite photograph showing the central plain of Mesaoria between the Pentadaktylos range to the north and Troodos to the south

Map showing the pre-1974 distribution of Greek and
Turkish villages over the island

● Greek

○ Turkish

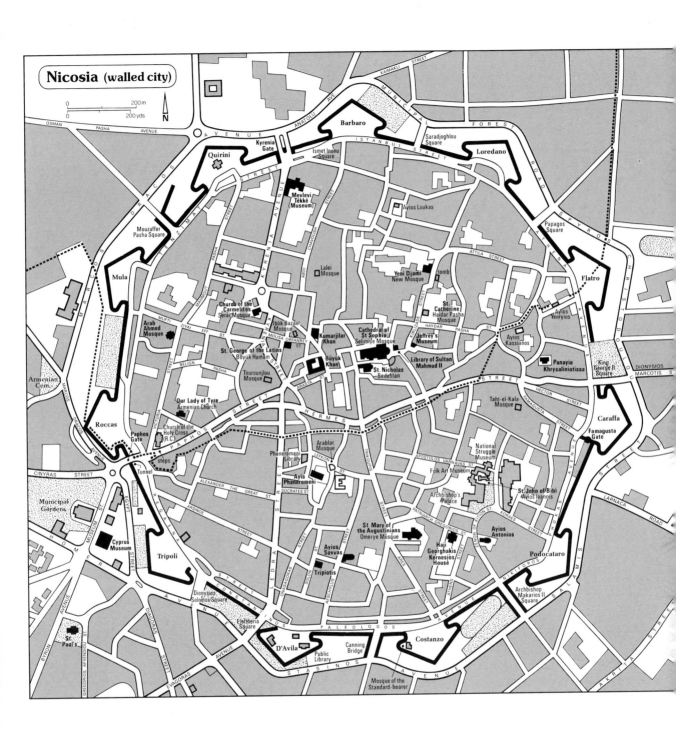

Nicosia (walled city)

0 — 200 m
0 — 200 yds
N

OSMAN   PASHA   AVENUE

Barbaro

Quirini

Kyrenia
Gate

KAIMAKLI STREET

MUNICIPAL

FORES

Saradjoghlou
Square

Loredano

ROAD

Ismet Inonu
Square

ISTANBUL   STREET

ANATOLU   AVE

AVENUE

Mevlevi
Tékké
(Museum)

Ayios Loukas

Papagos
Square

CHRIST

SPYROS

Mouzaffer
Pasha Square

PASHA

KYRENIA   AVENUE

ABDI

CHAKOLOU

Lalei
Mosque

Yeni Djami
New Mosque

tomb

ATTILA   STREET

Flatro

Mula

ZIYAI EFF

MAHMOUT

PASHA

Church of the
Carmelites
Serai Mosque

Iblik Bazaar
Mosque

MOUSA ORFANBEY
ST

St.
Catherine
Haidar Pasha
Mosque

Ayios
Yeoryios

ODOULOU

Arab
Ahmed
Mosque

MUFTI

Kumarjilar
Khan

Cathedral of
St Sophia
Selimiye Mosque

HAYDAR   PASHA   ST

KOSTAZAE

Jeffrey's
Museum

Ayios
Kassianos

St. George of the Latins
Büyük Hamam

BELIGN   PASHA

Büyük
Khan

St. Nicholas
Bedestan

Library of Sultan
Mahmud II

STREET

Panayia
Khrysaliniotissa

King
George II
Square

DIONYSIOS

MARCOTIS S

Armenian
Cem.

MARCOS

Tournjlou
Mosque

ARASTA

HERMES

HECTOR

FAMAGUSTA

Caraffa

Our Lady of Tyre
Armenian Church

Taht-el-Kala
Mosque

STREET

Famagusta
Gate

Roccas

Paphos
Gate

VICTORIA

Church of the
Holy Cross
(R.C.)

PAPHOS

steps

STREET

Arablar
Mosque

LEFKON

TRIKOUPI

National
Struggle
Museum

CINYRAS   STREET

Tunnel

INGRES   AVENUE

EGYPT   ST

Phaneromeni
Library

Ayia
Phaneromeni

APOSTOLOS VARNAVAS ST

Folk Art Museum

St John of Bibi
Ayios Ioannis

LARNACA

ROAD

ALEXANDER THE GREAT   ST

SOCRATES ST

Archbishop's
Palace

MUSEUM ST

Municipal
Gardens

Cyprus
Museum

ARSINOE

STREET

ATHENS   STREET

KORAES   ST

Tripoli

HOMER

KREACRA

CONSTANTINOS STREET

LEDRA   STREET

SOLON

ONASAGORAS ST

ARGYLLUS

ARIS

St Mary of
the Augustinians
Omerye Mosque

Ayios
Savvas

Tripiotis

PATRIARCH GREGORIOS ST

Haji
Georghakis
Kornesios House

Ayios
Antonios

HOKAS AVENUE

Archbishop
Makarios II
Square

NIKIFOROS

ALASIMI

Podocataro

BYRON   AVENUE

GREGORIOS   ST

APENIDOU ST

DIAGORAS   STREET

St.
Paul's

Dionysios
Solomos Square

Eleftheria
Square

EVAGORAS   AVENUE

PALEOLOGOS   STREET

STASINOS   AVENUE

D'Avila

Public
Library

Canning
Bridge

Costanzo

Mosque of the
Standard-bearer

LARNACA   ROAD

AKRITTA   STREET

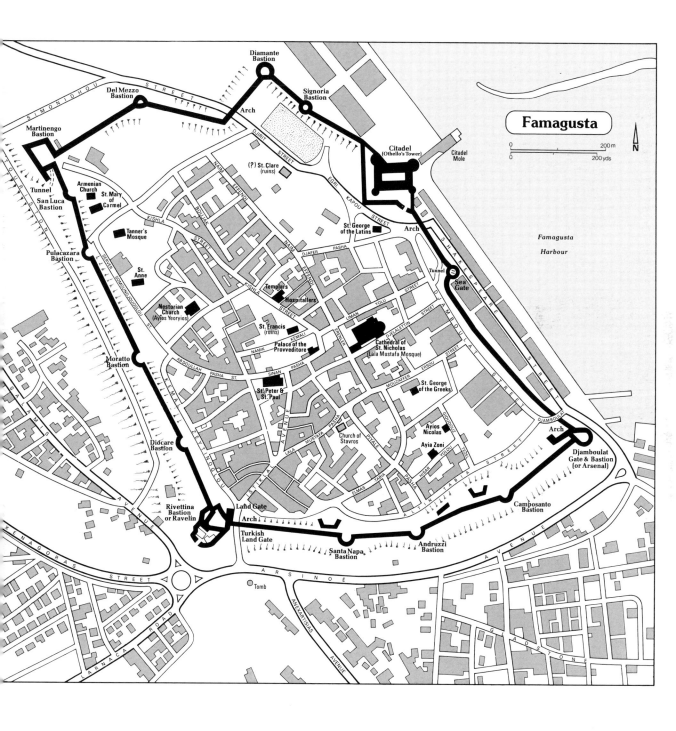

Famagusta

0 _____ 200 m
0 _____ 200 yds

N

Famagusta
Harbour

Diamante
Bastion

Signoria
Bastion

Arch

Citadel
(Othello's Tower)

Citadel
Mole

SIMONIDHOU STREET

Del Mezzo
Bastion

DJIRIT STREET

(?) St. Clare
(ruins)

Martinengo
Bastion

Tunnel

San Luca
Bastion

Armenian
Church

St. Mary
of Carmel

EFENDI

NAIM

BOMJAK STREET

EGRI

KAPOU STREET

St. George
of the Latins

Arch

Tunnel

Sea
Gate

TOURISTON

KISHLA

Tanner's
Mosque

St.
Anne

SILVER SIMONJOU/DJOLOU ST.

KISHLA

STREET

NAIM EFENDI

DJAFER PASHA

Templars

Hospitallers

LIMAN YOLU STREET

KEMALI

D.FLALETTIN

Cathedral of
St. Nicholas
(Lala Mustafa Mosque)

FRENK

ERSOU STREET

DJAMBOULAT STREET

SHAKESPEARE STREET

Pulacazara
Bastion

Nestorian
Church
(Ayios Yeoryios)

St. Francis
(ruins)

Palace of the
Provveditore

NAMIK

KEMAL

Moratto
Bastion

ABDOULLAH PASHA ST.

SINAN PASHA

St. Peter &
St. Paul

LALA MUSTAFA PASHA

PIYALE

MOUZAFFER

St. George
of the Greeks

GOUDOUNLI YOLU

Ayios
Nicolas

Arch

Djamboulat
Gate & Bastion
(or Arsenal)

ZEYNOGLOU STREET

KEMAL

AVENUE

Diocare
Bastion

Church of
Stavros

Ayia Zoni

ALTINTABIA STREET

ISTIKLAL AVENUE

TABIA

ELMAS

MISIR PASHA

Camposanto
Bastion

SALAMIS

XENAGORAS STREET

Rivettina
Bastion
or Ravelin

Land Gate

Arch

Turkish
Land Gate

LARNACA ROAD

ARSINOE STREET

Santa Napa
Bastion

Andruzzi
Bastion

Tomb

ANEXARTISIAS AVENUE

GLADSTONE

AVENUE

CONTRIBUTORS

Prof. Nicolas Coldstream, FBA is Emeritus Professor of Classical Archaeology at University College, London and a Fellow of the British Academy; he has published books on *Greek Geometric Pottery, Kythera, Excavations and Studies* (with G.L. Huxley); *Knossos, the Sanctuary of Demeter*, and *Geometric Greece*.

Sir David Hunt, KCMG, OBE is a former British High Commissioner in Cyprus who before entering the Diplomatic Service was a historian and archaeologist (Fellow of Magdalen College, Oxford); he has written two autobiographical books, *A Don at War* and *On the Spot — an Ambassador Remembers*. His latest publications are a revised edition of Enlart's *Gothic Art and the Renaissance in Cyprus* which he also translated into English and (edited with Iro Hunt) *Caterina Cornaro, Queen of Cyprus*.

Prof. Vassos Karageorghis, is Professor of Archaeology at the University of Cyprus. As Director of Antiquities, Cyprus, from 1963 to 1989, has been in charge of many excavations there and has published numerous books including *Excavations in the Necropolis of Salamis; Kition*, and *Cyprus from the Stone Age to the Romans*. He has been Professor of Classical Archaeology at Aberdeen University and a Fellow of Merton and All Souls Colleges, Oxford. He holds the Order of Merit, First Class, of the Federal Republic of Germany, La Légion d'Honneur of France and is a Member of the Accademia dei Lincei, the Royal Swedish Academy and others.

Dr Demetrios Michaelides is Associate Professor of Archaeology at the University of Cyprus. He has previously been with the Cyprus Department of Antiquities and has served as Archaeological Officer for Paphos. He has excavated in Italy and Libya, and since 1982 has been in charge of many excavations in Paphos District, including that of the House of Orpheus. He has written books and articles on Cypriot archaeology, among them *Cypriot Mosaics* and *Mosaic Floors in Cyprus*.

310

Prof. Edgar Peltenburg is Professor in Near Eastern Archaeology at the University of Edinburgh and has directed excavations at prehistoric sites in Cyprus and the Middle East; among his published books are *Recent Developments in the Later Prehistory of Cyprus; Lemba Archaeological Project Volume I* and (ed.) *Early Society in Cyprus*.

Sir Steven Runciman, CH, FBA is an Honorary Fellow of Trinity College, Cambridge and a Fellow of the British Academy; he has written numerous books on Byzantine history. He is also the greatest living authority on the Crusades, of which he has published a history in three volumes. Among his latest works are *The Byzantine Theocracy* and *Mistra: Byzantine Capital of the Peloponnese*. He holds numerous honorary doctorates from British, Greek and American universities.

Dr Veronica Tatton-Brown is an Assistant Keeper in the Department of Greek and Roman Antiquities at the British Museum; she has excavated in Cyprus, south Italy and Carthage. She edited the catalogue of the British Museum Exhibition *Cyprus BC*; wrote *Ancient Cyprus*, a catalogue of the A.G. Leventis Callery of Cypriot Antiquities at the British Museum and (ed.) *Cyprus and the East Mediterranean in the Iron Age*.

INDEX

Abd al-Malik, Caliph 149
Abdul Hamid II, Sultan 248, 251
Abdul Mejid I, Sultan 248
Abu Bekr Pasha 238
Achaeans 39, 45
Achaemenid Dynasty 84
Achaia, Principality of 176, 293
Achilles 62, 64, 132
Acre 147, 181, 195, 197
Adalia 152, 199-200, 241
Adelphi 117
Aegean 1, 8, 23-4, 32-4, 39-40, 44-5,
   47-8, 50-1, 58-9, 64, 83, 159-160,
   234, 250
Aelianus, P. 122
Africa 256, 269
Afro-Asians 282
Agapenor, King 45, 47
Aghirda Camp 278
Aghirda, battle of 185
Ahab, King of Israel 62
Ahmoses, Pharaoh 24
Aimery, King of Cyprus 180-81,
   184, 194
Aion, House of 131-2
Ajax 48
AKEL 274, 282
Akheiropiitos Monastery 154
Akhelia 166
Akhenaten, Pharaoh 35
Akrotiri 139
Akrotiri Peninsula 1, 4
Alalakh 35
Alambra 16
Alasia (also Alashiya and Asy) 17,
   35-6, 40
Alassa-Pano Mantilaris 27-8
Albania 274, 293
Aleman, Joanna l' 221
Aleppo 237
Alexander II, Czar 257, 259
Alexander the Great 84, 87, 97-8,
   104, 108, 292
Alexander, Patriarch of Antioch 140
Alexandretta 259, 278
Alexandria 99, 105-6, 110-11, 137,
   197, 199-200, 261
Alexius II Angelus, 171
Alexius I Comnenus, Byzantine

Emperor 158, 160-61, 166, 222
Alexius II Comnenus, Byzantine
   Emperor 170
Alice of Champagne, Queen of
   Jerusalem 181-4
al-Malik al-Adil, Sultan of Egypt
   181
al-Malik al-Ashraf, Sultan of Egypt
   197
Al Mina 58
Amathus 53, 59, 65-7, 71, 82, 91,
   101, 106, 116, 129
Amaury, brother of Henry II 197
Amazon 132
Ambelikou 16
Ammianus Marcellinus 122
Ammon 102
Amphitrite 132
Anat 73, 90
Anatolia 1, 11, 13, 35-6, 108, 112,
   125, 152, 159-160, 164, 170, 172,
   227, 234, 236, 259, 261, 272, 292
Anglure, Lord of 205
Anjou 196
Anjou, Charles of, King of
   Jerusalem 196
Ankara 130, 278-9, 285, 287
Antalcidas, Peace of 86
Anthemius, Archbishop 142
Antioch 122, 125, 127-8, 134, 140,
   142-3, 163, 165, 168, 170, 187, 195
Antioch, Hugh of, Regent 195
Antioch, John, Prince of 203
Antiochus IV Epiphanes, King of
   Syria 98, 110-11
Antonine Emperors 122
Aphendrika 167
Aphrodite 41, 43, 47, 59, 73-4, 85,
   90, 93, 101-3, 107, 109, 120, 125,
   129, 134
Aphrodite, temple of 129
Aphrodite-Astarte 72, 76, 89
Apliki 25, 36
Apollo 90, 93, 101, 107, 132
Apollo Alasiotas 40
Apollo Hylates 73, 90, 121, 129
Apollo Keraeatas 40
Apollonios of Kition 122
Arab Ahmed Pasha, Mosque 252

Arabs 145-9, 193
Aragon 201,212
Arcadia 40, 47, 49, 65, 292
Arcadius, Archbishop 146
Archipelago 235, 251, 262
Ardahan 260-61
Argives 47
Argolid 30, 47
Argos 62
Ariadne 133
Aristila 96
Armenia, Kingdom of 205, 212
Armenians 146, 168, 171, 174, 187,
   197, 227
Arnadi 81
Arodaphnousa 221
Arpera 238
Arsinoe Philadelphus 102, 107
Arsinoe IV 112
Arsos 77, 83, 107
Artemion 114
Artemis 90, 101
Artemis Paralia 91
Ashmolean Museum 41
Asia 16-17, 20-21, 60, 86, 196, 228,
   256, 259, 269
Asia Minor see Anatolia
Asine 47
Asinou 161, 167, 222
Asklepieion 124
Asklepios 90, 119, 128
Asolo 213
Assizes of Jerusalem 188
Assyrian Empire 59, 62, 65-6, 68,
   292
Assyrian Civilisation 57, 60, 62, 79,
   81
Astarte 53-4, 56-7, 72-3, 76, 90, 101
Ataturk, Kemal, President of
   Turkey 261
Athena 90, 95, 103
Athens 68, 82-3, 85-6, 91-6, 109,
   269-70, 273, 277-9, 282, 286-8, 293
Athienou 43
Attlee, Clement, Prime Minister 274
Augustus, C. Julius Caesar
   (Octavianus),
   Roman Emperor 99, 112, 119-20,
   122, 125, 292

313

318